Call them irreplaceable

Call them irreplaceable

by John Fisher

drawings by Hirschfeld

𝔰𝔡

STEIN AND DAY/Publishers/NEW YORK

FOR RICHARD DREWETT

Other books by John Fisher:

Funny Way to be a Hero
The Magic of Lewis Carroll
George Formby: The Ukulele Man

Al Hirschfeld drawings from the collection of
The Margo Feiden Galleries, New York City
© Al Hirschfeld 1974

First published in the United States of America, 1976
Copyright © 1976 by John Fisher
All rights reserved
Stein and Day/*Publishers*/Scarborough House,
Briarcliff Manor, N.Y. 10510

Library of Congress Cataloging in Publication Data
Fisher, John, 1945–
    Call them irreplaceable.
    1. Entertainers—Biography. I. Title.
PN1583.A2F5   791'.092'2   [B]   75-37777
ISBN 0-8128-1927-6

Designed by Lawrence Edwards

Printed in Great Britain by
Ebenezer Baylis and Son Ltd
The Trinity Press Worcester and London

Contents

CALL THEM IRREPLACEABLE is intended as a tribute to many qualities—energy and elegance, craftsmanship and cool, intelligence and wit, and always that intuitive flair of the great entertainer for meeting public demand at a hair's breadth moment before the public itself has realised just what it wants. In turn the tribute is motivated by an unashamed blend of hero-worship, wonder and nostalgia. But that last word is misleading. While any entertainer only ever succeeds because he corresponds to a specific moment in time, the subjects of this book are curiously above nostalgia. They are great by virtue of an indestructible quality which gives them an immediacy beyond the period of which they were apt symbols. If it does nothing else, true star quality abolishes the difference between then and now and like a Gershwin melody or a Keaton movie will work for all time.

Here is a clue to one further quality which these performers all share. It is something apart from 'star quality' itself, a civilised attitude laid on top of the god-given gift and as such its perfect complement—namely, 'style'. One means more than mere wishbone elegance, the way to hold a cigarette, to trail a fur. It stems from an utter conviction in one's own self-hood; it is an overriding refusal to compromise, to respond to one's environment on anything but one's own terms. Neither mere self-assurance nor conceit, it combines pride and bearing and a dash of stoicism, a prism through which all aspects of normal behaviour come to be refracted. Without letting go of their lifeline to reality, they were, throughout the period of their initial success, always one perfectly assessed, stylised step away from it, even Crosby in his persona of the 'regular guy'. Merely at this level, they would still be above mere nostalgia, the mechanical recreation *now* of what was commonplace *then*, because they were anything but commonplace at any time.

The entertainers discussed are essentially stage performers, at least as presented here, not because they did not translate to the screen—one of them, Astaire, found his greatest triumphs in what he first suspected to be an alien medium; all of them have made a mark with varying degrees of success on celluloid—but because their facility for exploiting the here and now, the vibrant moment at the core of the best vaudeville tradition is to this writer one of their most appealing. It flourishes most spectacularly in the intimate reality which theatre or cabaret offer, and which the cinema, for all it might claim otherwise, can only pretend to do. With the exception of Astaire and Crosby, these performers have all found in the live, lone spotlight the perfect milieu for displaying their special individualism and the scene of their greatest triumphs as entertainers, for the simple reason that here is the only medium which can honestly assert itself in the present and thus correspond to what they are about. But Fred and Bing, so central to the tradition the others represent, still qualify. Both were nurtured in vaudeville and carried its sap in their veins when they chose to specialise in other media. In the history of popular song Crosby went on to represent the apex of a triangle begun by Jolson and completed by Sinatra; Astaire, bringing a theatrical approach to the screen, elevated the stereotype of the solo song-and-dance man to a position in the choreographic pantheon which the pedestrian buck-and-wing pioneers that preceded him could never have envisaged. And while neither of them courted live audiences after their peak success, there were still the benefits, the television recordings in theatre conditions to testify to a casual artistry capable of producing an excitement of white-heat intensity amongst those fortunate enough to be looking on.

Along such lines of qualification the twelve names featured virtually choose themselves. Moreover, one is dazzled by how appropriate some of those names are, living proof of W. H. Auden's claim that 'like a line of poetry, a proper name is untranslatable'. Note how appropriately Astaire rhymes with 'flair' and 'devil-may-care', Bing with 'sing' and 'zing', even Benny with 'penny'. Likewise, there is the apt stamp of Durante, the élan of Chevalier with its final acute flourish, and a whole grimoire in Sinatra which will need a paragraph to unlock. In the address at the Memorial Service in London after The Master's death, Sir John Betjeman summed up both the dilettante and the pragmatist in Coward: 'Noël, with two dots over the "e", / And the firm decided downward stroke of the "l".' Cocteau saw a similar parallel between the name and nature of Marlene Dietrich: 'Your name at first the sound of a caress, becomes the crack of a whip.' One is reminded that Samuel Butler once said that the true test of imagination was the ability to name a cat; one could reasonably add 'or a totally original entertainer'. In a world where meaning is increasingly eroded by platitudes, plain sloppiness, and technological gobbledygook, these names hold their own with the same justifiable self-confidence their owners show on stage.

Collectively these performers comprise that incomparable streamlined élite which in its universal popularity dominated entertainment in the 'thirties, 'forties and 'fifties, a star-spangled cummerbund around the waist of the century. By themselves they all admit to that watertight individuality summed up by Somerset Maugham when introduced by S. N. Behrman to Eddie Cantor, one of the few other entertainers who conceivably might have made these pages: 'He looks remarkably like himself, doesn't he?' But either way they all share a sense of particular environment which this book as a whole hopes to capture as it defines the specific world each exemplifies while on stage, its relevance to their actual lives, and the germ of their appeal, hopefully without dampening the spark of actual performance. There can be no question that the names discussed will sustain their legendary status for many generations; this book aims to add future flesh to the legends, and in attempting to distil the essence of their ephemeral art, to convey to those generations quite simply what they *did*, at the same time awakening in them the sense of wonder aroused by the particular star in his or her heyday.

Al Jolson

You ain't heard nuthin' yet . . .

THERE HAD BEEN great live entertainers before, but when Al Jolson performed, his impact never failed to obliterate their memory with a sea-over-sand efficiency. When an audience had recovered from his incisive frontal attack in the name of theatre, their once-robust, now anaemic images might return to the public consciousness, but they now paled into insignificance beside the fresh, vibrant memory of the man who in the first quarter of the twentieth century billed himself—and without dispute—as 'The World's Greatest Entertainer'. In this respect, his power could be seen to have uncharitable, if not destructive, overtones amongst his fellow performers. Yet put into a proper perspective, he would come to symbolise a spring of vitality upon which all subsequent entertainers in his part-sentimental, part-razzamatazz tradition would appear to draw for inspiration, versatility, life.

There could be no mistaking the wanton energy of his lean figure, with its face daubed in burnt cork, on edge in the spotlight, as extravagant and unpredictable as the small tinselled ball balanced giddily on a sideshow jet of leaping water; the essential difference was that Jolson's motivating force was a swirling tornado. No entertainer has come nearer to embodying the concept of the performer as a force of nature. When Jolson himself insisted that he changed neither his basic style nor delivery over fifty years, he was unconsciously corroborating what one knew instinctively from watching him, that his total effect derived from within. Rightly or wrongly, once he first found his form he never developed—from the point of view of the live stage he had no need to. But given that form and an audience, this compulsive entertainer could hardly ever wait for his music.

Writing in 1924, Gilbert Seldes, a pioneer writer on the popular arts, equated Jolson's quality with the daemonic of the Great God Pan, in the strictly mediaeval sense of the word, as it implied intensity of action. Once Seldes had stated his possibly misguided surprise that anyone could be so possessed in such an essentially Protestant and business-oriented community, and disregarding the possibility of such possession as a product of frustration, he hurled the performer from the page: 'He flings into a comic song or three-minute impersonation so much energy, violence, so much of the *totality* of one human being, that you feel it would suffice for a hundred others.' Far from apocryphal is the story that on 22 December 1911, when Jolson cut his first recording (the George M. Cohan composition, 'That Haunting

Melody' from *Vera Violetta*, and a nonsense novelty, 'Rum Tum Tiddle'), for the Victor Talking Machine Company in Camden, New Jersey, the engineers had to curb that energy in a strait-jacket in order to keep the all-singing, all-dancing Jolson within controlled distance of the acoustic horn which served in pre-electric days as a microphone.

It was physically impossible for Jolson in performance to keep anything in reserve. His slogan, 'You ain't heard nuthin' yet', was more than a talismanic throwaway, rather a personal avowal of his attitude towards an audience. He first used it in 1906 in San Francisco to acknowledge the reception—a cross between religious mania and mob violence—that greeted one morale-boosting performance on a makeshift stage in a theatre strewn with debris during the immediate aftermath of the famous earthquake. With a winsome jack-in-the-box impudence, he would repeat the claim at almost every public performance in subsequent years, winking outrageously and determinedly hurling his arms across the footlights as if attempting to separate the Red Sea, but never before doing more to justify his presence on stage than one would have expected of Cantor and Cohan and Fanny Brice all together. True to his word, he would then proceed to do twice as much again.

Jolson's impact, however, stemmed only in part from his seemingly effortless exertion of sheer physical energy. Galvanising that energy was the most overpowering ego of any entertainer. Long before Norman Mailer in an appraisal of Muhammad Ali pinned the concept down as 'the great word of the twentieth century', Jolson was himself treading that same tightrope of the psyche which 'gives us authority to declare we are sure of ourselves when we are not', and which places his own performance on a level of significance with those monumental feats and nightmares of human destruction which Mailer sees as the prime function of ego.

As he commanded a stage with the elegant air-cushioned bludgeoning we associate with Ali today, there was nothing to hint at insecurity in the typical Jolson performance. And yet, backstage in the star dressing room of New York's Winter Garden Theatre, which the Shuberts virtually built around him in his honour, if he read of the success of a contemporary playing some small date, or heard that there was just one vacant seat out front, he would take it as a personal affront. The mere idea of competition made him forlorn to a degree rumoured as bordering on the masochistic. When an audience showed what he regarded as undue fondness for a troupe of performing elephants on one of his shows, he fired the elephants. He employed a dresser, one Louis Schreiber (later to become his agent within the William Morris Organisation), whose sartorial rôle proved subsidiary to the diplomatic function which obliged him to orchestrate the dressing-room taps in such a way that the sound of rushing water would always drown the intruding applause accorded the other performers in the show. In Jolson's eyes, they were all would-be pretenders to his throne. Once, when he was recuperating from fatigue at Palm Beach, one of the Shuberts, distraught at having a theatre, Jolson's theatre, vacant, dropped the merest hint that arch rival Eddie Cantor had taken no less than 45,000 dollars in one week on Broadway. Instantly refortified, Jolson scurried back to the Great White Way to top him. Nor was it enough for the public to know how good he was: his fellow performers, often dismissive of him as a struggling tiro, had to be indoctrinated as well. And so he persuaded the Shuberts to inaugurate his now legendary series of solo Sunday concerts. That observance laws forbade his wearing black-face was a small forfeit to pay in order to secure the esteem of one's own profession.

On stage, however, Jolson was safe and secure, his total bearing uninhibited and unafraid, one of almost militant hauteur. So dominant was his ego, so strong his love-affair with the audience, that half-way through a production show it was nothing for him suddenly to jettison the script, saunter towards the footlights and with headline frankness demand of the audience: 'Do you want me—or do you want the show?' He never failed to receive the answer he wanted and, sweeping the rest of the cast under the carpet of his conceit as if he were doing them a good turn by allowing them the rest of the night off, would proceed to extemporise songs until his lungs gave in, the cue for the houselights to be raised and the audience now to sing to him.

Only Jolson could arrive on a stage an hour later than scheduled and proffer as his excuse, amid the tumultuous applause: 'Sorry I'm late, folks, but it was cold and I stopped by for dinner at the little restaurant next door. It was such a good dinner that I just couldn't leave it. But now that I'm here, do you mind if I make up on the stage?' The slick application of the burnt cork, interspersed with Jolson's inconsequential asides, was at once an entertainment of its own and a fit preliminary to his usual instruction to a distraught stage manager: 'Don't bring the horse on yet. I'm gonna sing to the folks by myself tonight.'

It was nothing for him to go on for two hours, allaying the audience's physical hunger with five-pound boxes of candy which he would instruct the ushers to hand around at his own expense, and finally giving in to his own: 'I'm feeling hungry, so I'm going back to that restaurant now. But there's a swell piano in there, and if any of you feel like it, why don't you wait till I've had something to eat and join me? Then I'll sing a couple more songs for you.' He was never short of that early morning audience to do just that.

Such was the performing life-style of the entertainer who, when kidded early in his career that he had never played the Palace, replied, 'I can tell you the exact date I'll play the Palace—the day Eddie Cantor, Groucho Marx and Jack Benny are on the bill. I'm gonna buy out the house, tear up all the tickets but one, and sit there yelling, "Come on, slaves, entertain the King".' His was the most expansive ego of all, and, however unfeeling, vindicated with little strain: not one of his contemporaries, however exalted, ever questioned his eventual superiority.

The Jolson mystique began at birth. The young Asa Yoelson entered the world at Srednig in Russian Lithuania some time between 1880 and 1888 during the Russian Pale of Settlement when no one was disposed to think of formalities like birth certificates. (Later, Jolson himself decided upon 26 May 1886 as his birthday, though at his death life insurance companies disputed the claim, anxious to add six years to his total life span.) The son of an impecunious rabbi who emigrated to America in 1890, Asa joined his father in the New World four years later, the time it took for sufficient money to be mustered to pay not merely his fare, but those of his mother and four other children. Emotionally disoriented by his mother's death the

14

following year and his father's re-marriage twelve months later, he soon found that his first ambition, to be a cantor, had been overtaken by strong yearnings towards a theatrical career.

It was in 1898, hearing the band of the 15th Pennsylvania Volunteers play 'Goodbye, Dolly, I Must Leave You' as they marched the streets of Washington D.C., the family's adopted home, that this aspirant amateur first saw the glimmer of a professional reality. When the bandmaster heard the young minstrel singing to the trudging rhythms he offered him the post of singing mascot. The regiment was en route to Cuba to fight in the Spanish-American War. Jolson got as far as their camp at Florida, where he was declared to be too young to be taken to a battle zone. The escapade at least fired his spirit of adventure, and he would run away from home with increasing regularity to sing in cafés and saloons, at one point even a circus. In fact his potential big break was nearer home than he could ever have expected. On a visit to Washington's Bijou Theatre nothing could restrain his lone soprano from ringing out from the balcony during the otherwise muffled community singing prompted by entertainer Eddie Leonard, as he went about his great speciality, 'Ida, Sweet As Apple Cider'. The young Jolson received an ovation and was invited back again and again by Leonard to boost his own act, declining only when he was offered the opportunity to tour with Leonard on a professional basis.

Soon he would change his name from Yoelson to Joelson, the one constructive result of a traumatic week spent with a group exotically titled 'Rich and Hoppe's Big Company of Fun Makers'. The 'e' was not to disappear until 1903 when his name proved too long for one particular publicity picture and the superfluous vowel was excised on printer's advice. He had already Americanised 'Asa' to 'Al' in a non-theatrical context not long after arriving from Russia.

Later in the same year as the Leonard partnership, 1899, history repeated itself when he sang once more from the audience during the act of a buxom bump-and-grind queen, Aggie Beeler. Her invitation for him to join her Villanova Touring Burlesque Company was accepted, even though he still had no guarantee that he would ever appear in full view on stage, as distinct from being shelved away on a series of anonymous balconies. This engagement led to his being spotted for what is officially recognised as his first professional stage appearance, in a crowd scene in Israel Zangwill's *Children of the Ghetto* at New York's Herald Square Theatre on 16 October 1899. The immediate future saw him touring as a boy soprano in the vaudeville act of Fred. E. Moore, 'Introducers and Promoters of High Class Ballads and Popular Songs', until his voice broke, and also in partnership with his brother Harry as 'The Hebrew and the Cadet', in which Jolson in West Point uniform displayed his whistling prowess in counterpoint to his sibling's song.

Jolson would achieve no indelible mark of success, however, until 1904, when he first adopted black-face. Three years later he was spotted performing solo at Pantages Vaudeville House, Little Rock, Arkansas, by Lew Dockstader, the most important name in minstreldom since E. P. Christie and Stephen Foster. Dockstader was so impressed that Jolson was performing under his aegis by the following year. The minstrel magnate guaranteed

15

him not merely big billing, but the chance to play as a single act within the essentially corporate framework of the minstrel show. Within another year, Jolson had eclipsed Dockstader himself as the lead attraction.

In later years, Al's brother Harry was often accused of blacking up himself to ensure that some of his brother's glory rubbed off on him; ironically, in fact, there is reason to believe that the burnt-cork approach was in part suggested to Al by the initiative of his brother, who was using a black-face routine as early as 1902. Jolson himself would explain how he adopted the technique on the advice of a Negro dresser who told him, 'You'd be much, much funnier, boss, if you blacked your face like mine. People always laugh at the black man.' Innocent when said, such a statement would add an uneasy burden to the weight of criticism Jolson already had to bear in the more cautiously liberal climate towards the end of his career, namely that such a characterisation was an insult to the Negro, relegating him to a substratum of society, a burnished court jester under white man's rule. It could be argued that by the time Jolson had copyrighted the technique the public was so attuned to the unreality of the burnt-cork mask, its whimsical detachment from the real world, that it didn't really matter. The white-as-black Negro counterpart was now accepted by people of both colours not as a figure of inferiority, a painful reminder of days of enforced slavery, but as a traditional comic type. What should be emphasised is that in his portrayal of a minstrel-show habitué Jolson, all but a few songs aside, drew far more readily for inspiration upon less prominent characters like Zip Coon, Jimmy-Crack-corn-but-I-don't-care, and Jim Dandy. These figures—pert, emancipated and frontiers-claiming—were not only far removed from the servility, childishness and lack of ambition so long associated with the archetypal Jim Crow figure of the mid-nineteenth century, but were also only a short stride away from the free-spirited, white-faced Yankee Doodle Dandy, terrestrial archangel of the twentieth-century American Dream.

What is beyond dispute is the effect Jolson's decision to black up had on his performance. What nerves he may have had in the early days of his career disappeared as soon as he found himself protected by that mask of burnt cork and those bulbous white lips, capable of a smile that was as the aurora borealis to cotton plantation and theatre auditorium alike. Perversely, the make-up gave his features, and in turn his personality, a definition they would not otherwise have had, a glinting lustre alongside which his own complexion would in comparison suggest unglazed, less finely turned clay. At the end of his life, when he had long discarded the cork, he was scheduled to perform in a benefit at the Hillcrest Country Club, haunt of the Hollywood vaudeville set. Unsure of himself, he was steered back to confidence by Jack Benny's suggestion that just for once he revert to black-face. As Benny later said, 'Somehow he could lose himself under that make-up'. It also did wonders for making approaching old age appear youthfully indeterminate.

No chocolate veneer, however, could disguise the fact that he was nothing if not a Jewish performer, from the chalk-gloved fingertips of his far-flung arms to the innermost strings of his heart. His piercing black eyes professed that deep sensitivity endemic in the battered immigrant communities overspilling from Eastern Europe at the time. It was Jolson's own membership

16

of a persecuted minority group which almost surely invested him with the authority to make those occasions when he *did* exploit the pathos within the minstrel genre acceptable to the Negro himself. When he sang of 'My Mammy', he was singing of his own strong-armed Yiddish mother rather than of the rotund, apple-pie-serving, apron-strung caricature from the Deep South, the mother whose funeral had first confronted the boy Jolson with the stark reality of a lonely, individual existence. Through harnessing the harmless exuberance which he found in the Negro entertainment tradition to the lilting poignancy of his own plight, he was able to make an audience respond with double-edged certainty.

Jolson's vocal style represented the very marrow of his Jewishness, the legacy of a family that had sung in synagogue for five generations. However much he might attempt the nasally exaggerated, molasses-coated *vibrato*, the white man's parody of the negroid baritone, in an effort to conceal what remained of the Lithuanian-Yiddish enunciation he had brought across the Atlantic (even interpolating authentic 'da dada' scatting in his coon songs), he could not disguise the shaking cry in his throat, the pleading intensity of the Hebrew blues. The stentorian richness and melodic intuition of his voice had been trained in a religious context since childhood when, as soon as his son could articulate, rabbi Moses Yoelson had propped open his mouth with matchsticks to ensure that he came as near as possible to producing the true rabbinical wail. As Michael Freedland explained in his informed biography of the singer, music, inextricably linked as it was with prayer, amounted to a whole new religion aside from the Judaism which had occasioned it. Jolson would not become the great cantor of his father's ambition, but the benefit of this early training, together with natural abundance of emotional power, contributed to a resonance which was reported to make the walls of less sturdy theatres vibrate even without the assistance of a microphone.

Arguments as to how 'good' a singer he actually was are futile. He could not admit to the technical refinement of a Caruso, though he once followed the operatic star on no less than the latter's own home ground, the Metropolitan Opera House, New York. At a special gala to mark the Armistice of 1918, Caruso had barely finished accepting his applause for '*Vesti la giubba*', when Jolson thrust himself into the spotlight with his auspicious cry, 'Folks, you ain't heard nuthin' yet'. The opera critics were appalled, but the audience was energised, not least Caruso who invited this new rival back to his hotel to give an impromptu private performance. Cultural arrogance prevented the critics from seeing what Caruso as a practising performer had grasped intuitively—that when it came to selling a song, there was no one who could match Jolson. He sang the sentimental numbers with a heart-in-the-mouth conviction and marching drive that saved them from the death-kiss of ridicule and enabled all but the most resistant in his audience, if not to believe in his tear-stained mythology of 'Mammy', 'Sonny Boy', and those magnolia-scented plantations, at least to reconcile it with the more personalised need we all share to plumb the depths of the subconscious for nostalgia and self-pity.

In a press interview given to coincide with his 1929 film, *Say It With Songs*, Jolson, uncustomarily on the defensive, admitted: 'As for "Mammies" and "Sonny Boys", of course, they aren't real life. In real life Sonny Boy would generally rather sock you on the jaw than climb upon your knee. Most of the Mammies, instead of having hands all toil-worn and that sort of thing, are stepping out with their boyfriends and having a good time.' He seemed to contradict that statement every time he sang.

He had a way of contorting the pronunciation of a significant word, of drawing out a vowel, of roller-coasting his r's, which to his detractors might recall the first attempts at speech made during a post-dental anaesthetic thaw, but which gave impetus both to meaning and excitement. This unpredictability during the life-span of a lyric is legendary. No verbal phrase was sacrosanct. He could vary the beat of a number to hair-trigger extremes without for one moment being in danger of losing it. In full vocal flight this innate rhythmic *élan* was his most valuable asset. He drove his up-tempo songs along like no one before, to such a frenzied degree that it became a challenge for musicians to keep up with him.

There survives an early 1928 recording of Jolson singing 'Golden Gate', a fast-moving eulogy to California as a substitute for Heaven on Earth which he helped to write. The singer's pressing tickertape urgency is apparent not merely from the way he craftily sneaks in fragments of a 'rat-tat-tat' reprise between words where no lyricist would ever have intended them, but from the abrasive reprimand to the orchestra snarled impatiently out of the side of his mouth at one point during the session: 'Come on! Get hot!' This is Jolson at full pressure, the Jolson who, when he sang as he so often did of destination, whether California, Kentucky, or 'Alabamy Bound', assumed to an audience the whistle-flaunting, full-steam-ahead locomotion of the trains which would transport him there. But more than that, he was the singing equivalent of the mythical illusionist who, asking his audience to look as far as they could see, proved they could see even further. Jolson never accepted horizons as far as his own vocal achievement was concerned. As George Jessel pointed out on his death, the last eight bars would never fail to be as big as *Tosca*: 'He gave majesty to the popular song.'

It was a voice which was inimitable and for that reason would suffer the most attempts at unsuccessful imitation. As he grew older, so it grew deeper, many would say better, and, after a malaria-induced operation to remove part of his left lung towards the end of the Second World War, at least four notes lower than it had been before surgery. And yet from the very first moment of his success there was never a time when his voice could not be instantly identified. As a stylistic influence in the history of popular song it does not claim too wide a niche, so essential to its success was Jolson's unique wrap-around personality. But if Crosby was waiting in the wings, it is as well to remember that he personally had been influenced in no small way by Jolson himself. As a gesture to the changes then rampant in that history, at the end of his last radio show for Chevrolet in 1932, he is said to have taken the microphone off its stand and, with the words 'It's a sad day when Jolie needs a mike to sing into,' hurled it to the floor. Jolson's *spiritual* influence, however, on every entertainer who was ever lured on stage by the heady prospect of a live audience response is another matter entirely.

His songs probably represent the most familiar, most quotable, most widely sung canon of any performer. After his first hit, with 'You Made Me Love You' in 1913, unknown composers were soon attracted to him as a

WARNER BROS. SUPREME TRIUMPH
AL JOLSON
in
"The JAZZ SINGER"

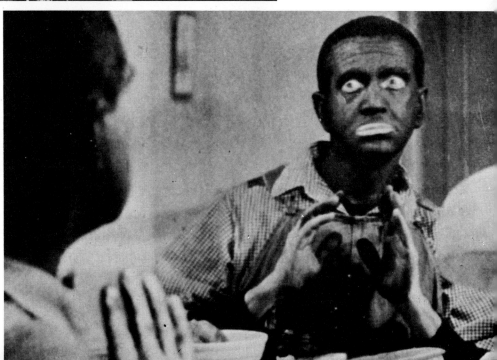

sounding-board for their own hope-heartened wares. As early as 1910, while he was still in the Dockstader line-up, he had been persuaded by Tin Pan Alley to be amongst the first to try out what would prove to be Irving Berlin's initial success, 'Alexander's Ragtime Band'. His name would not be especially associated with that triumph, and so it was with almost poetic justice that he enjoyed the full prestige of trail-blazer when eight years later at a Jolson party a young song-plugger named George Gershwin played what would prove not merely his own first hit, but the biggest money-earner he would ever pen, 'Swanee'. Although it could have been tailored for him, Gershwin had written it with Jolson far from his mind, to be sung by fifty dancing chorus girls boasting electrically-lit fairy lights on their satin slippers, in the Capitol Theatre's *Demitasse Revue*. It failed to make any impact until brought into contact with Jolson's own special electricity. He would be in his forties before he set eyes upon the actual Swanee river, but in performance would wring every last drop of longing from what he saw immediately at that party as quintessential Jolson material. And when it was decided that the authentic dancing Jolson, as distinct from Larry Parks playing him, should be featured in one long-shot scene in the film of his life, it was 'Swanee' which he sang.

Jolson's instinct for choosing the right songs to sing, shared in partnership for forty years from 1910 with Harry Akst, the song-plugger who had first introduced him to 'Alexander's Ragtime Band', would with radar-like accuracy single out tunes like 'There's a Rainbow 'Round My Shoulder', 'I'm Sittin' on Top of the World', 'Toot-Toot-Tootsie', 'April Showers', 'Is It True What They Say About Dixie?', 'For Me and My Gal', and Jolson's own favourite, 'Rock-a-bye Your Baby with a Dixie Melody'. Appropriately it would be left to Irving Berlin, twenty years after their professional paths first crossed, to pen the song that would express Jolson's own singing philosophy, 'Let Me Sing and I'm Happy'. In a way, it was a superfluous addition to his repertoire. No audience needed Jolson actually to tell them of the exultant joy in his heart when he sang of Dixie charms, cotton fields, or Mammy's arms, tackled crazy words, sad refrains, or low-down blues, or provoked a response of laughter, tears or toe-tapping.

Jolson was a far more visual entertainer than the memory of his vocal style and an inventory of song titles can convey. In addition, his act comprised a whole catalogue of mannerisms which stand today as welcome shorthand references to that studied abandon with which he put across a song: the one-sided fall to bended knee as a fulcrum of emotion, first used, Jolson would bizarrely insist, when around 1913 a suitably poignant moment in the song 'Down Where the Tennessee Flows' allowed him to relieve the painful pressure of an ingrowing toenail; the upturned gloved hands clasped at chest level in supplication; the emphatic pat-a-cake beating together of those same hands, now pancake-flat in joy; the trembling of that white nether lip shadowed dramatically by the arrogance of the upper; the outward thrust of those same lips into their own absurd Donald Duck bill; the carefree flittering of his fingers on outstretched arms; the earnest clutching of those same fingers to his heart. Jolson knew that the more detail, the more movement he provided for an audience to pin its attention to, the less likely would that attention be to stray. Early in his career he developed a nimble, on-the-spot dance, as valid an accompaniment to the right song as any orchestra might provide. Even more sensationally, he was the first performer to adopt the runway, a platform bridge running from stage apron to the back of the stalls and hitherto used only in burlesque, for use in the legitimate theatre. He was never happier than when he was careering up and down this indulgent link with his audience with that distinctive half-skipping, half-jumping strut which doubled as a dance and a frantic attempt to make everyone feel welcome. Seldes described Jolson singing 'Row, Row, Row', for which he would turn plank into appropriately nautical prop: 'He would bounce upon the runway, propel himself by imaginary oars over the heads of the audience, draw equally imaginary slivers from the seat of his trousers and infuse into the song something wild, roaring and insanely funny.' In full swing his total physical presence might suggest roller-skate delirium, but there was about his every movement, every gesture, a slender lizard-like grace, alert and free of dross. He would make you believe that the sweat streaming unsurprisingly down his face was a shower of diamonds.

When Jolson was not singing or dancing, he was talking. He was the first performer to talk through the second verse and chorus of his songs, switching from singing to conversation or vice versa as the mood took him. He was the first performer to preface those songs with excursions into autobiography. One of his introductions went something like:

> I was nothing. Just a poor little kid on the streets of Washington D.C., shining shoes, selling papers or anything. I can remember the first job I ever got singing. I was passing the stage door of the theatre on 29th Street in New York City. The great Fay Templeton was rehearsing a new song. I stood there and listened and listened until I was singing along with her. Finally I remembered I was hungry. Ah ha—you get awful hungry when you are eleven years old. So I started walking down towards the Bowery. And I kept hearing the piano-player playing that tune and I kept getting hungrier too. I didn't have any money so I went to a joint named McGirk's or something like that and I asked the guy if he'd give me a cup of coffee if I sang a song. He said, 'Okay', and the song was . . .

His hold on an audience was so secure that only then did he begin to sing, 'Rosie, you are my posy, *you* are my heart's bouquet'.

On other occasions he would be more concise, and come closer to recalling his early billing as 'Al Jolson, comedian': 'Here's one thing you won't believe—this song was dedicated to me!' He would then launch into 'Baby Face', kidding his way through the lyric to the point of self-caricature, the song still the show-stopper of old but now irresistibly funny at the same time. He was not above raising his voice to outrageously absurd *fortissimi* for astringent comic effect on those occasions when he found himself weighed down by the overt sentimentality of a number: 'It isn't raining rain, you know, it's raining *vi-o-lets*.' And then, for all his vanity, he would sit modestly dangling his feet over the edge of the runway, joking and gossiping in casual tête-à-tête with the audience, confiding in them the amount he had invested in the show or the well-being of the wife or sweetheart of the moment. When an actual gag surfaced, it was in true Jewish tradition, often rooted in truth:

> I bought my dad a coat last week. It cost 200 dollars. A lovely coat. But I knew what my dad would say about that, so I persuaded the clerk to change the label for one that had a twelve-dollar price tag. Yesterday, I asked him how he liked the coat. 'Fine,' he said, 'It was a wonderful coat for twelve dollars. So wonderful that I sold it to Uncle Moshe for twenty dollars. You didn't know your father was a businessman, did you?'

Jolson would plead on stage that it really was a true story.

Jack Benny in tribute to Jolson's comic achievement once said that he 'could make you laugh for two hours at a stretch'. It is hard to believe, however, that this ability sprang from a defined comic attitude, an intrinsic comic personality, so much as from his sheer magnetic pull on an audience, which made it behave as he wanted it to. He once confided to George Jessel in his dressing room before a show: 'Gee, they're a pipe! Never had audiences like 'em. They laugh when they buy their tickets! Show you what I'm gonna do tonight . . .' He then went on stage and deliberately gave his jokes the wrong pay-off lines. Still the audience laughed. It all came down to that high-voltage atmosphere that crackled around him the moment—head held imperially high—he seized the limelight, together with a shrewd understanding of what makes an audience tick. In 1925, Robert Benchley wrote of his performance in *Big Boy*: 'The word "personality" isn't strong enough for the thing that Jolson has. Unimpressive as the comparison may be to Mr Jolson, we should say that John the Baptist was the last man to have such a power.'

Jolson spun a web of reciprocity with his audience, never missing those chances to talk about his humble beginnings and so make himself one with the total public. He knew, as all demagogues know, that only by first descending below the level of the people would they ever allow him mastery above them. He had also grasped as vividly as any solo entertainer before or since the true nature of his own genre, the one dramatic form where the performer's line of vision continually extends beyond the footlights. There is a line from one of his lesser known but most vibrant songs, 'Bright Eyes', where he tells an imaginary girl that her 'eyes are traitors—they give you away'. He once confided to the young Ralph Reader, a juvenile in *Big Boy*, 'Remember that your eyes are searchlights'. Certainly Jolson's were—that is the one thing his films do prove. At the Winter Garden Theatre he would nightly instruct the electrician to turn up the houselights so that he could see, so the cliché goes, the whites of the audience's eyes. Such a gesture, like the runway, was an affirmation of his own love affair with that audience, an opportunity to brace himself the more happily in the ozone of their approval. But when the lights were down, no entertainer made the convention which placed him in the spotlight and his audience in darkness seem less like a statutory game of hide-and-seek.

Although the top vaudeville performer of his generation, Jolson's peak as a 'live' entertainer coincided with a series of 'book' shows at the Winter Garden Theatre, spanning a ten-year period from 1911 to 1920. He had his début at that theatre in its opening production, *La Belle Paree*, complete with score by a young songwriter called Jerome Kern. There followed in regular succession *Vera Violetta*, *The Whirl of Society*, *Honeymoon Express*, *Dancing Around*, *Robinson Crusoe Junior* and *Sinbad*, in which he first sang the hat-trick of 'Swanee', 'My Mammy' and 'Rock-a-bye Your Baby with a Dixie Melody'. In 1921, he changed theatres to score a personal triumph in *Bombo* with a new hit hat-trick in 'April Showers', 'Toot-Toot-Tootsie' and 'California, Here I Come'. Appropriately, the new venue bore his name: Jolson's 59th Street Theatre. Four years later he scored a further success in *Big Boy*. In fact he never had a flop, but not necessarily as a result of any quality inherent in the material that loosely justified the titles. As one could expect, often the shows did not come alive until Jolson threw aside the shackles they imposed upon such a freewheeling talent as his own, and dismissing the rest of the cast launched into what the audience had come to see: a demonstration of the true nature of the vaudeville art, where pure self holds sway, where the performer *is* rather than *acts*. Merely for the record, it is worth mentioning that up until that point in most of the shows he played a variation on a stock black-face character called 'Gus', described by Seldes as a 'scalawag servant with his surface dullness and hidden cleverness, a creation as real as Sganarelle'.

Until Jolson had his Winter Garden début, black-face had never been featured on Broadway in a 'legitimate' show. Now, in retrospect, it is extraordinary to see how much his career came to pioneer new trends and developments, to set new records in this way. The runway and the Sunday concerts have already received mention. He was also the first performer since the era of the great actor-managers to hold a financial interest in one of his productions; to take a Broadway show on a tour of small provincial towns; to earn more than 10,000 dollars a week from personal appearances (and that before the First World War); and the first star of his magnitude to entertain American troops during that war. Nowhere, however, was his influence as a trailblazer more searingly felt than in the history of the cinema.

Jolson first became interested in the prospect of permanence on celluloid in 1923, when D. W. Griffith persuaded him to make a silent movie entitled *Mammy's Boy*. The singer, however, was so appalled at seeing the first rushes of himself in a non-singing rôle that he immediately absconded to Europe, leaving the film unfinished. Jolson had no signed contract, but this did not prevent Griffith suing him for breach in a New York court three years later. Jolson was unable to prove to the jury that he was a 'rotten actor'—the excuse he had given—and Griffith won a verdict of 2,627 dollars against the star. However, in the same year he ventured to try his hand with the burgeoning medium again, when a new system invented by one Dr Lee de Forest showed itself capable of capturing his voice as well as his image. When de Forest sold his invention to Warner Brothers, Jolson was summoned to make a short entitled *April Showers*, featuring the title number, 'Rock-a-bye' and 'When the Red, Red Robin Comes Bob-Bob-Bobbin' Along'.

Amazingly, when it was shown at New York's Colony Theatre, neither audience nor studio took its fluttering synchronisation very seriously. It would require Warner Brothers to fall on impossibly hard financial times before, in desperation rather than faith, they would risk all on a sound feature. They selected the George Jessel Broadway hit, *The Jazz Singer*, as their vehicle. There was an almost prophetic irony in its subject matter, a Jewish boy's resistance to his parents' ambition that he become a cantor in the ultimate cause of the vaudeville stage. Jessel himself lost the part by insisting on more money; Cantor turned it down, partly out of sympathy with his colleague, and partly out of conviction that it would be impossible to follow him in the rôle. It was then offered to Jolson who asked for 75,000 dollars, almost double Jessel's earlier demand, and, since he shrewdly agreed to accept payment in Warner shares in lieu of salary, won the day. He even won a crucial change in the Jessel story. In the stage play the prodigal did return to become a cantor; in the film, having soothed his father on his death-bed with a rendering of 'Kol Nidre', Jolson, as had to be, went on to see his mother cheer him from the auditorium as he sang, inevitably, 'My Mammy'.

Before shooting, there was no intention that the film should be anything but a silent picture but for the interpolation of Jolson's songs and relevant background music. Jack Warner would later attribute its qualification as the first 'talking picture' to a 'freak accident', but to anyone conversant with the total Jolson personality, there was nothing freakish about the un-inhibited 'Wait a minute . . . wait a minute. You ain't heard nuthin' yet' ad-libbed with cameras and sound still running as he basked in the applause for his song, 'Dirty Hands, Dirty Face'. Jolson was only worried about his next song, 'Toot-Toot-Tootsie', but there could have been no more apt introduction lingering in any entertainer's subconscious for such a revolutionary development as the coming of speech to the cinema. As soon as Warners' saw the rushes, they realised the breakthrough staring the industry in its face and had an actual monologue specially scripted for Jolson to deliver to his mother between choruses of 'Blue Skies' later in the film.

When the picture opened in New York on 6 October 1927, its success lived up to the most bizarre expectations. The talkies had arrived, and within time Jolson's own shares in Warner Brothers would in consequence be worth no less than four million dollars. The following year he repeated his triumph with another part-talkie, *The Singing Fool*, in which he introduced the song 'Sonny Boy', destined when recorded to become the first popular disc to sell first one, then two, and eventually three million copies. *Singing Fool*, a sob-inducing tale of parents in combat over the custody of a child, would proceed to gross five and a half million dollars, two million more than *The Jazz Singer*, a record not broken until *Gone with the Wind* eclipsed it ten years later.

Sadly, in spite of his pioneering contribution to the story of the cinema, Jolson did not sustain a personal success in the movies. For all the cutting abandon with which he had been able to tear through layer after layer of sentimentality in those first two features, with successive films that same sentimentality would cloy. As people became more and more attuned to the dimensions of the new medium, the Jolson personality would prove over-large for the screen. The nature of film, with its rigid machinery of definitive positions, changing lenses, editor's scissors, cut right across that uncontrived spontaneity which on stage represented his trump card. As the cinema progressed, he found neither the director who would prove sympathetic to this cause nor the one to reconcile his talents to the technical advances made. And something else was missing. He once described the effect which continual exposure to the cinematic treadmill had upon him; it made him feel 'like one of those dolls whose strings are pulled to the right for a smile and to the left for a sad expression. I couldn't wait until evening came, when friends would be gathered around who would ask me to sing . . . I hungered for the sound of actual people.' And all the while the talking picture was taking its toll of vaudeville, the entertainment form which Jolson handled best.

In an attempt to arrest the inexorable slide upon which his career now became set, he turned to radio, but that medium also was to advance from its embryonic stage of bombastic vaudeville stereotype to the more original suave, relaxed subtlety provided by Allen, Benny, and Crosby. By the late 'thirties, the name Jolson spelt 'has-been' in neon-lit capitals. He had made a polite gesture of 'semi-retirement' in 1933, but nothing could keep such a compulsive performer away, even if it meant in 1939 being reduced to third billing in the film *Rose of Washington Square*. There was never any question, however, that the original incandescence of his talent had burnt itself out.

The proof came with America's entry into the Second World War. One afternoon the entertainer, morose and melancholy at the thought of being passé, was sitting in a New York hotel suite, with his accompanist (the songwriter Harry Akst) when, in eerie parody of that influential day in 1898 when he had been swayed by the stirring fife and drum of the Pennsylvania Volunteers, there came into earshot the strains of a military band marching along Fifth Avenue. His reaction was numb. Jolson loved a parade, but, in his own words, 'not when it passes me by'. He watched it file past without a smile, and then immediately telephoned the Pentagon. He was revivified when he put the receiver down to inform Akst, 'We're going overseas, Harry, to entertain those boys'. Within weeks he had rediscovered his favourite audience, was back on his own parade. At the same time, he gained a new respect within his profession.

After the war, Hollywood, in acknowledgement of the new lease of life Jolson had bestowed on the film industry almost twenty years previously, returned him the compliment of loosely basing a film on his switchback ride of a life. When Jimmy Durante joked in a radio programme, 'And you notice, Mr Jolson, I don't need Larry Parks to play the black keys', he was almost certainly touching a raw nerve as far as Al was concerned. But if Jolson did not get to play himself on screen, being confined to singing the songs on the soundtrack for Parks to mime and appearing in that one long-shot of 'Swanee', when the movie offers *did* then come in, Jolson, a millionaire throughout his career, could turn them down. He had found an even wider personal audience back at the radio microphone, and it was a measure of the success of this 'in person' comeback as much as of *The Jolson Story* that the film was followed by a sequel, *Jolson Sings Again*, which proved almost as popular.

Where *The Jolson Story* scored over other 'biopics' was in the accuracy with which it presented, amid the overwhelming patchwork of backstage clichés, the driving psychology of its entertainer, a man only happy when he was singing or bowing at the shore of tumultuous applause. Eddie Cantor put it in a nutshell when he said of his rival and friend (who gave him his own signature song, 'If You Knew Susie', because he thought it didn't suit himself): 'What amazed me was that this great personality had never learned how to live. He couldn't; there was something chemically wrong. The minute the curtain rang down, he died.' George Burns is fond of mocking with equal accuracy: 'It was easy enough to make Al Jolson happy. You just had to cheer him for breakfast, applaud wildly for lunch, and give him a standing ovation for dinner.' He married four times, but marriage always took a back seat to his audience. He gave a banquet for his fourth bride, of twenty-one years, 'only because it'll give me a chance to show her how I work with an audience. She's too young to have seen me.'

Jolson was predictably dismissive of the comeback the film brought him: 'That was no comeback. I just couldn't get a job.' Reinstated as 'The World's Greatest Entertainer', as if he had never been away, he was voted in 1947 the most popular male singer in America, ahead of both Crosby and Sinatra. Around this time he was beseeched to follow the successful American trail made by contemporaries like Benny, Hope, and Kaye to appear at the London Palladium. His reply had a staccato impact: 'Everyone's a sensation there. I like to set records.' He could claim few friends within his profession, but no contemporary would ever dispute his supremacy. Little had changed since he had had the gall to take an advertisement in *Variety* at the end of 1911, soon after the opening of *La Belle Paree*, which read: 'Everybody likes me. Those who don't are jealous. Anyhow, here's wishing those that do and those that don't, a Merry Christmas and a Happy New Year.'

With that boomeranging irony that seemed to be over-active throughout his career, the activity which finally put him back in the limelight was responsible for his death. When war broke out in Korea, Jolson, at his own expense and against doctor's advice, was the first entertainer to be active at the front-line. Within two weeks of his return, he collapsed exhausted in a San Francisco hotel prior to making a guest appearance on Bing Crosby's radio show. But he never let down that instinct which qualified his as the supreme ego amongst entertainers. As he lay dying he told the doctors to 'pull up a chair and hear a story or two'. Then he delivered the line which in his own still starstruck eyes made it all worthwhile: 'Hell, Truman had only one hour with MacArthur. I had two.' Within minutes he was dead.

Jolson once described himself as 'the greatest master of hokum in the business'. Certainly no one before him had ever shown a more certain instinct, a more unremitting sense of alertness for exploiting, whether on or off stage, every single moment available for audience effect. He kept it up right to the end and then for a while his reputation maintained the momentum. On that night of 23 October 1950, the lights of Broadway, to which he had long ago referred proudly as 'my street', were turned off in his memory. Traffic was brought to a standstill in Times Square. At the Friars Club in Los Angeles, no less than Harry Cohn, the ruthless, granite-willed dictator of Columbia Pictures who had made *The Jolson Story* a reality, burst into tears. When crowds of more than 25,000 thronged to the Temple Israel in Hollywood for his funeral, Jessel summed it up for him: 'Jolson's turned them away again.'

Maurice Chevalier

Every leetle breeze . . .

JEAN COCTEAU ONCE observed that Paris had two monuments, 'the Eiffel Tower and Maurice Chevalier', an impression reinforced by the almost quirky coincidence that saw the minstrel born only a few months before his architectural counterpart was completed, a fact of which he never tired of boasting. The mature performer was as French as the Tricolour, but at the same time one could claim with even greater accuracy that he was as universal as the colours red, white and blue. Chevalier himself insisted that the cardinal influence on him when young was the Anglo-American music hall. Watching the crazy tempo of the Tiller Girls in Paris dancing to the strains of 'Yankee Doodle Dandy', he was cast under the mysterious spell of a rhythm which he would himself in later life be able to convey with a mere flick of the shoulders and which he soon learnt could stir audiences as potently as any other form of entertainment: 'What I did was to mix the American novelty and old French humour so that even to the French I was something new.'

The Stars and Stripes proved to be of even greater significance when upon reaching Hollywood his flair for the risqué became intensified beneath the arc-light of the old American folk myth that Europeans, the French in particular, are sexually superior to lesser civilisations. He encouraged this as a permanent facet of his characterisation, anxious no doubt to smother the less than romantic image implied by his notorious reply at a Hollywood dinner party to the suggestion of no less than Garbo that they should on the spur of the moment partake of a midnight dip: '*Mais, le Pacifique est glacial.*' It is said that Garbo never spoke to Chevalier again. Meanwhile the Union Jack had also fluttered to effect, and not merely in the influence of English music hall artists like George Robey, Little Tich and Wilkie Bard. The insignia of straw boater and tuxedo, which became a symbol for a special type of Parisian roué were ironically based upon a typically English gentleman spotted by Chevalier sauntering along London's Piccadilly wearing the odd combination just after the First World War; from that moment until late in life he purchased his famous trademark six at a time from a firm in Luton, Bedfordshire, makers of boaters 'by appointment to Harrow School'. In this way his portrayal of what he described as 'The Universal Frenchman' was pieced together, to be sustained by his own appreciation of the whole string of jokes it embodied. It was to nobody's surprise that in the Paris concert at the end of his seventy-fifth birthday tour the English songs should almost outnumber the French. And if surprise was to be registered at all during the seemingly endless parade of farewell performances given by this spry entertainer, it was in recognition of a birthday as far back as 12 September 1888, of a career that saw its professional début as early as 1900, and yet of a performer who was into his forties before 'Louise', the song which consolidated his international reputation, was written.

Chevalier was a product of Ménilmontant, a down-at-heel quartier to the north-east of Paris. The ninth child of Victor Charles, by his son's admission a house-painter and a drunk, and Sophie Josephine, a braidtrimmer and lacemaker, he weathered the storm of their marriage for eight years before his father left home, three years before his death. Of their ten children, only three would survive into adolescence. The grinding poverty of his early life bears a haunting parallel with that of Chaplin. Like Charlot, Chevalier would spend an extensive period in an institution before taking his first employment at the age of ten. The apprentice engraver, however, fired by visits to local music halls, soon found his attention distracted by aspirations shared with his brother Paul to become a professional acrobat. The sandpiles along the Rue Sorbier provided a perfect setting for their amateur stunts and within a year he had secured a trial, without salary, as the human apogee of a trio employed by the Cirque Medrano. From his position balanced on the head of another, he had to leap into the air and perform a somersault, while the middle one jumped to the floor to allow Maurice to land on the shoulders of the anchor man. One day during practice his foot slipped, he broke his nose and a temporary veil was drawn upon his theatrical career. Later in life, however, Maurice would express his debt to the disaster: 'It all helped my sense of timing and directed my path of destiny.'

The immediate destination of that path embodied a succession of diverse employments as an electrician, a painter of dolls, a clerk, and a maker of thumbtacks. Luckily each job professed an even greater degree of monotony than its predecessor, and in an attempt to retain his sanity the twelve-year-old personification of 'Titi Parisien', or the Parisian Urchin, began to sing for spare centimes in the Café des Trois Lions at Ménilmontant. This establishment was typical of the *café-concert* entertainment of the time and analogous to the less sophisticated working men's clubs in the north of England today. The difficulty he then found in singing in any way other than three keys higher than his accompaniment did not prevent him passing an audition at the smarter Casino des Tourelles for a regular engagement at twelve francs a week. His career as an entertainer was now officially launched, and none was more overwhelmed than the youth at the centre of it all: 'I was rather like a puppy suddenly abandoned on the boulevard.' In actual fact, resilience was second nature to him. Booed off the stage as he may have been in those early years, by audiences shocked at a small boy presenting dubious adult material, he persisted until in 1904 he achieved the impressive double of winning a contract for the Parisiana, the leading music hall of the boulevards, and winning over the thorny audience at Marseilles, on a par, in terms of notoriety, with that of Glasgow for the English music hall comedian or his native Philadelphia for W. C. Fields.

'*La grande occasion*', however, would not occur until 1909 when he was invited by Mistinguett, the pert flower-seller from Les Halles, destined to become Chevalier's feminine counterpart in Parisian legend and already at the height of her career, to participate in her act in a new plumes-and-jewels production at the Folies Bergère. The climax to their routine of comedy dialogue involved a slap-happy quarrel, rapid reconciliation, and an acrobatic dance of literally careless rapture in which, clasped in each other's arms, they toppled over a sofa, on to a rug, and rolled themselves up in the latter. Eventually they unwound and, still waltzing, disappeared suddenly through a window. One evening, so the story goes, unrolling took longer than usual and dancing partners emerged as lovers. At the end of his life he still regarded her as his greatest romantic love. They sustained their liaison throughout Chevalier's military service in the First World War and a period of imprisonment by the Germans during which he learnt English from a Durham miner P.O.W., whose Geordie vowels doubtless played their own part in shaping the most respected pidgin English accent of all time. After the Armistice, however, the lovers increasingly became rivals. His individual success now threatened to dwarf that of Mistinguett herself and, as Chevalier explained: 'We were serving the same kind of drinks, you understand? . . . Two dogs in front of the same bone, with our fangs well bared. And since Mistinguett had the prettiest teeth in the world . . .'

Long before he fell prey to her charms, Chevalier had acquired a spirit of independence which now prevented him, as the dancing partner whom she had chosen to throw her own talent into relief, from merging modestly with the background. Significantly, in his various autobiographical writings, the concept of 'independence' recurs through all his descriptions of ending relationships with women, and always not far away is the rejoinder to the effect: 'If she had only understood how I felt, I don't think we'd have ever grown apart.'

No sooner had they split than Chevalier found himself acting out the shrewd intimation of an earlier attachment. In 1908, while they were both playing Lyons, he had met Colette, who based the character Cavaillon in her book *The Vagabond* on Maurice. She described him then as 'this tall young man who walks like a human snake, as if he had no bones, and whose anxious, wandering pale blue gaze tells of acute neurasthenia'. That very neurasthenia now became so acute that he toppled over into a nervous breakdown and very nearly committed suicide. Nursed back to health by the dancer who would become his only wife, Yvonne Vallée, he made a comeback with the show *White Birds* in London in 1927, seven years before the marriage ended in divorce. The greater part of those seven years were spent in Hollywood.

Irving Thalberg of M-G-M had originally provided Chevalier with a screen test in Paris, but it was Jesse Lasky of Paramount who showed interest in what Thalberg had subsequently dismissed. Lasky signed him to his first Hollywood contract, under which his initial film, *Innocents of Paris*, in 1929, proved a general embarrassment; his second, *The Love Parade*, in the same year, was a spontaneous success. In Ernst Lubitsch Chevalier had almost instantly found a director with pinprick sensitivity to his own style coupled with a more general flair for Continental sophistication, rare at first hand in Hollywood itself. Lubitsch put the aspect of his star which he most valued in a nutshell when he said that Chevalier could 'make even the most scabrous situation acceptable'. A D'Artagnan of the boudoir, he could suggest sexual bravado with a wink, a glance, without ever becoming distasteful. So firmly was his tongue kept in his cheek, that a verbal approach could never be relied upon anyway. After seven years at the top in Hollywood, he left America on a matter of principle over billing, adamant that he would rather be top of the bill at the Montparnasse Casino for a hundred francs a day than second at New York's Palace at a thousand dollars daily.

Thalberg, who had long ago rescinded his judgment on that early screen test, and now wanted to put Grace Moore's name above his, vouched that he knew Chevalier would be back, 'and by the big door'. But Thalberg would never have guessed how. He may have had a shrewd premonition that by about 1951 a cinema mind as enterprising as Billy Wilder's would want to film the life story of an already legendary entertainer with Chevalier playing himself. Unfortunately plans which seemed to be sturdier than concrete capsized. Chevalier, accused of Communist tendencies after a camera crew had persuaded him to sign, both in innocence and out of humanity, the Moscow-inspired Stockholm Peace Petition against the use of thermo-nuclear weapons, was refused a visa back into the United States. It is less likely, however, that even Thalberg would have visualised Chevalier making a triumphant comeback in Hollywood itself as late as 1958, with an honest projection of his now elderly self in the film *Gigi*, the first of a series of appearances as a dapper but ageing roué, his twinkle undimmed and scene-stealing prowess intact. One must be thankful that no 'biopic' did unheedingly close the curtain too soon.

By this stage of his career Chevalier had proved that there had never been a French entertainer more elegant, more streamlined than himself. But while Hollywood may be seen to have served as an obvious finishing school, it is hard at first glance to reconcile the quietly confident, urbane *boulevardier* with the precocious teenage jester billed '*Le Petit Jésus*' (translated 'Wonder Boy') whose comic technique, floundering between lack of advice and no sound judgment of his own, was as crudely Aristophanic as inserting his hands in his pockets and thrusting out his trousers to the monologue:

> *Iron willed*
> *I only know*
> *When one is a man*
> *It must show!*

Clad in check suit with padded shoulders and capped by his extra-large young head, his twiggy, gawky presence, together with a seeming innocence, tickled the collective funny bone of his audiences. For another song he wore over-stressed rouge make-up and a toy képi on his head; using the barrel of a toy rifle for a trumpet as he stomped ungainly around the stage, he confided:

> *There goes another pane of glass*
> *And I see the glazier pass,*
> > *Chasseur, Chasseur.*
> *In your tail you have a pain,*
> > *Chasseur, Chasseur.*

Do you want the hand of sister
To rub it for you, Mister?
There goes another pane of glass;
Here comes the glazier past.

It was all far removed from the later image of subtlety and refinement of the entertainer who became a universal symbol for an elegant, sophisticated, if naïve, love ideal, the love that misguidedly thinks it does know reason.

It is tempting to go scurrying to his autobiography in search of that one moment in the hour-glass of his life when the early crudity finally tapered off to emerge as the polished suavity for which he became renowned. There was the advice from P. L. Flers, the producer of the Folies Bergère, to 'try to be more proper on stage. Relax. Don't strain too hard for comic effects', advice that played its part in Chevalier's conscious development from putting across a song with mechanical obscene gestures to relying upon the natural mesmeric resources of his own personality. There can be little doubt that Mistinguett herself did more than most to encourage the cultivation of his overall urbane image. But it is misleading to be so specific. In the last analysis the germ of his celebrated assurance and expertise, if not yet his taste, was discernible from the very first night he earned his supper singing; derived from his assiduous observation and subsequent attempts at impersonation of the leading exponents of French and later British music hall. Amongst his idols were the irrepressibly fastidious Mayol with his teasing voice and pompadour ever poised to prance off his head jaguar-style; the pathetic clown Dranem, with his pointed, sand-castle hat, check misfits, and tragi-comic pretence at naïveté; the diminutive Little Tich who in his big boots, in fact wooden slats as long as he was tall, presented an act of eccentric dancing that only animated cartoon could emulate; the lesser-known dancer Norman French who introduced the 'step dance' novelty to Paris and whose sartorial elegance and lazy manner may well have made the greatest individual impression on the young Maurice. Boucot, Serjius, Dorville and Claudius were other names from the French stage which Chevalier would not wish their posthumous audience to forget. By watching them all he gradually assimilated the studied precision and strong inventive authority that played a far more crucial part in the finished Chevalier 'style' than the relatively superficial idea of romance which it went on to champion. The proof of this is that in his solo concerts he could resort sparingly to earlier red-nosed panache without any hint of incongruity.

With such a wealthy accumulation of technique, it is not surprising that in time his forte proved to be the world of the one-man show, not merely presenting a single act on a variety bill, but sustaining a full dramatic span of two-and-a-half hours on the strength of personality alone. This he would do on the most cavernous of stages, in an atmosphere which but for his presence teetered on the antiseptic. He allowed no orchestra, no acrobatic or dancing *hors d'oeuvre*, no scenery except stock beige drapes, and, in so far as he would often keep the houselights up throughout a performance (taking a leaf out of Jolson's book), no theatrical lighting as such. The only concessions he did make to artifice were a pianist and a Pandora's box of properties that included a pigtail, a kimono, an old coat, the odd hat or two.

He once described this type of performance as 'the most difficult and honest thing we do in our profession'. But even with due allowance for the challenge involved, it is bewildering to think that the man who as much as any other gave his individual stamp to this form of theatre did not cross his personal Rubicon until the late 'forties, when he was in his sixties. Inspired by the one-woman show of Ruth Draper which he had seen a decade before, and in spite of warning advice from friends like Marlene Dietrich and Charles Boyer, he had come to terms with an aspect of his character which he did not reveal at length to his public until he published the memoir, *I Remember It Well*, within months of his death:

> I am a simple type, the man of my one-man shows. Anything that does not go along with this side of my character makes me profoundly uneasy. When I go to noisy parties and galas, I feel like a peasant at a palace reception—that is to say, nervous and tight around the collar. The only places I really feel comfortable are at home, *chez moi*, with the people I trust, and all alone on stage. There I can be myself with a theatre-full of people who have come to see me, just me, my white hair, my past, my present.

Mistinguett needed only four words to describe the bond of almost domestic intimacy Chevalier could achieve with an audience: '*Il a le fluide*.' When asked to define her meaning, she could do no more than shrug her puzzled shoulders, but Colette, the nearest Mistinguett could ever admit to a literary counterpart, knew instinctively what was implied when she herself wrote of Chevalier: 'Happy the favourite who has built between himself and the public that mysterious invisible bridge of atoms.'

With footlights and orchestra pit reduced to formless matter, he was able all the more readily to strike up the mysterious rapport that not only gives individual definition to the dark hazy blur of a myriad faces, but leaves no member of the audience in doubt that this is the case. Max Bygraves, the nearest Britain has produced since Harry Lauder to a solo entertainer combining Chevalier's popularity and approach, once knowingly compared an audience to a group of people in danger, frightened and anxious for someone responsible to take charge. In this context, the sheer authority of the performer is of paramount importance; the entertainer becomes the leader. When James Agate said of Chevalier that he had 'the one quality which transcends all others—the quality of being a success', he came as close as anyone to defining this basic presence in the French minstrel. He omitted, however, two points. For all his complete self-assurance, Maurice, like Max, never allowed it to stand in the way of the common touch which made him irresistibly likable to his mass audience. It should also be stated that Chevalier's authority was nothing if not a playful one. At the risk of reducing his audience to their second childhood, he stood for the Santa Claus figure whom they have seen enter not down the chimney, but through the bedroom door, and who with an adroit wink and an air of don't-let's-tell-anyone has secured their innocent complicity in a game where he skilfully holds the upper hand.

The Chevalier presence made itself felt with the first thrust of that lower lip silhouetted in the wings. Once likened to that of a cheeky orang-outang, the lip endured as his most consistent trademark because his most personal, providing its own bridge to the audience in whom he was about to confide about love and life and hope. It was, however, only one detail on a heraldic shield which would also depict that haloesque straw boater tilted at almost blasphemous angle over the bountiful, peasant face with its diamanté eyes, apple cheeks, and crinkly flashing teeth; the saucy, wide-open smile, quizzical at times, but never a *masque fixé*; and the single-button, moonlight blue tuxedo that was in fact a hybrid between tuxedo and lounge suit in a conscious effort to eschew 'false elegance'. This mass of detail was brought before the audience with a springy measured stride. In spite of this, he deliberately exaggerated the shortness of his legs by the length of his jacket so that with his slightly protuberant derrière and toes turned niftily in, one could instantly accept the validity of his comment to Lubitsch when the latter first offered him the rôle of a prince in Hollywood: 'With my swinging walk, I can only play commoners.' Not a little of his success as a stage performer was due to the elasticity of his legs, the suppleness and physical precision acquired during younger years as an acrobat and a *boxe-boy* in music hall standing him in expressive stead not merely during brief thumbnail character sketches, but also in his seemingly endless minstrel's promenade. Merely in the fact that he found it difficult to remain totally still on stage, he lived up to his delightful assessment of himself when young as 'a travelling salesman of amusement'. Few performers have been more exuberant—without being frenzied—before an audience. It was, though, an articulate exuberance, his jack-knife extension of a leg a sheer affirmation of that determined *joie de vivre* which he hallmarked as his own.

Chevalier was a firm believer in life's rosy side who attributed his artistic longevity to his being 'sort of a sunshine person'; but one would be doing this optimist amongst entertainers an injustice if one were to infer from the above that he had no pathos, that he was not capable of being grievously hurt, that his act didn't imply shadows away from the sun. There were the self-mocking yet touching references to his own age: 'Growing old isn't so bad—when you consider the alternative.' It is doubtful if in later life he was ever able to sing his little song about the ageing fox-terrier despised by his canine cronies as 'too old even to cock his ears' without thinking either of his own advanced years or of his young self back on the boulevards, a puppy again. Spanning the years between was his own genial celebration of love, but while this struck his audience as gay and inspiring, for the man renowned world-wide as an expert practitioner of *l'amour*, the thoughts he articulated on his eightieth birthday could never have been far away: 'I suppose I have made a success of everything in my life except the most precious thing, which is love. I should have taken it more seriously than I did.' He resented the 'shabby little romances' of his youth and regretted that those earlier years had not instilled a 'more poetic attitude toward love'. When Cocteau named him '*Le Grand Sympathique*' he was describing the natural complement between a deeply sensitive, doubt-ridden, private sadness and the cheery cock-a-hoop vitality that was its public manifestation.

The chief language of this philosopher on stage was naturally that of his 'sawngs'. Many, including himself, would emphasise that he did not possess a good singing voice, to the point where he would make comic capital out of

it. The line 'My voice is very bad; I have the 'flu—but don't worry because, after all, when I have no 'flu, my voice is not very good either!' remained in his act long after the day in 1930 when it was prompted by the truth. And yet he was an accomplished *diseur* with a delivery as evocative as any in the annals of song, best described in portmanteau fashion as churgle or guckle, irresistible in its buoyant handling of rhythm and the almost sly earnestness that made sure you heard every last Gallic syllable. The vocal technique that amounted to half speech, half song, suited admirably a performer who in English-speaking countries became as popular for the hesitant English explanations with which he preceded his French items as for the songs themselves.

Naturally his programme remained flexible, each night 'to be selected from the following repertoire'. His faithful followers would have been crestfallen, however, if it had not encompassed a stroll along some of those Parisian streets of which he proved the most affectionate topographer. There was the proud, defiant '*Sur l'Avenue Foch*'; '*Quai de Bercy*', evocative of wine barrels piled on high, Chevalier with hands sunk into trouser pockets, jacket collar upturned, and eyes downcast, typifying every outcast who ever looked out ruefully from beneath his brows on a waterfront; '*La Marche de Ménilmontant*', with its self-portrait of earnest vigour beneath devil-may-care exterior. Most meaningful of all was '*Place Pigalle*', which gave full scope to his talent for characterisation as he deftly etched in the *types* to be met on those shady *trottoirs* at which Paris winked her other eye. The drug addict, the pickpocket, the leering, effeminate spiv, the tout for the *cinéma bleu*, the lecherous octogenarian up from the country and gloating over the buttocks of the Folies girls for the first time, all sprung graphically to life as he acted them in song, a parade which he described as the greatest show on earth since the heyday of P. T. Barnum. The detail with which he could invest the presentation of a single song had the cosy definition of a Brueghel painting, and nowhere more vividly than along the Place Pigalle.

Moving abroad from Paris, Chevalier presented '*A Barcelone*' as an illustration of the way a song evolved. When he was appearing in the French provinces he met, so he would confide, 'two leetle Spanish sisters, vairee good lookeeng girls; one was the singer and the othair deed the danceeng'. (He raises his arm, clicks his fingers, and stamps his feet in nostalgic celebration of their friendship.) He liked them so much he asked his pianist to write a song in their honour. Self-effacingly at first, the pianist begins to play for Chevalier, who could be hearing the music for the first time. Eventually after word-building and many changes and additions, 'the song was feeneeshed . . . The tall girl can sing eet and the leetle girl could dance eet'. And then in time he developed a parody, this his own cue to disappear into the wings to don a toreador's shining black hat, attach castanets to his fingers, and generally appear ridiculous. What followed turned his jauntiest song into one of his funniest routines as, still every inch a Frenchman, he strutted with wedge steps around the stage, hand on hip, glaring at the audience in mock rebuke, clicking his digits—'Not bad, eh?'—with abandon before launching into the dance proper. He would lean over the apron and read the audience's mind— 'I surprise you, h'mm?'—but the funniest verbal gambit came not from this nor from the song itself, but from the 'Holés' which he kept sneaking gratuitously into the lyric. And then, catastrophe! His castanets will click no longer, try as he will and does, until finally he gets his nose caught between them.

'*Mandarinade*' was another bizarre diversion, 'a vairee trageek Chinese love sawng' in which, sporting an outlandish pigtail and slanting his eyes with his fingers, he portrayed an ancient Chinese mandarin, indicating the slanting tears that he imagined to be the natural effluent of Chinese eyes. This mandarin was bent on committing hara-kiri because his saucy young wife had left him. His intended fate was not so incongruous as it might sound; throwing inscrutability to the trade winds, Chevalier was anxious to explain: 'I know they nevair commeet hara-kiri in China, but, you know, I had to have a strawng endeeng for the sawng.'

More than mere guides to Paris and gazetteers of faraway places, Chevalier's performances were also breezy homilies on 'thees lurf beeznees'. In fact, the love between man and woman was the most persistent motif in his entire repertoire. Even in his tribute to '*La Seine*', the river winding around the Isle de la Cité was interpreted as the embracing arms of a woman. The song '*La Leçon de Piano*' set a courtship to music in ingenious fashion, the pedestrian 'la, sol, fa' notes of the girl at her practice conveying volumes of amorous 'I, love, you' intent to her lover, to the extent that when they do marry 'he ees so used to flirteeng een between the notes, you understan', that when it comes to the beeg moment that naht, he can't help theenkeeng een between the notes. You know what I mean . . .'

His sheer presence on a stage encompassed the seven ages of *l'amour* from 'ze crush' through 'you've brought a new kind of lurf' to the final consolation of the Indian-summer 'tendairness' that he found 'deepair, an' more lahsteeng, an' not so tireeng'. He carried his banner for Eros into his eighties without a suggestion of lechery. Not for nothing did he refuse to appear in the film of Nabokov's *Lolita*. Even at that age he would skittishly explain on stage how he looked forward to his hundredth birthday, when he would be praying to God for 'a leetle more time—I've jurst fallen in lurf'. Not that, if those twinkling eyes were an indication, he didn't derive immense, even if vicarious, satisfaction from recalling in song his nostalgic reunion with an old flame in 'I Remember It Well'. He closed the concerts of his farewell tour with the simple assertion that his career had been a 'long, long lurf affair' with the public and the wish that 'now I'd like to kees everybody'. It is a measure of his skill that he could toss such pebbles of sentiment into the pool of the auditorium without causing a ripple of embarrassment.

By way of encore there were always those sprightly, *faux-naïf* little songs which first established his reputation. To accompany the spiralling defiant ecstasy of '*Ma Pomme*', his rollicking old tramp would seemingly abandon equilibrium, flinging his arms forward while leaning backwards with the stance of a man about to sink to his knees, not in supplication, but in intoxicated pleasure. '*Valentine*' contained 'a veree yumann story' of a little girl, so cute and sweet, whose minute features he sketched dextrously in little airy circles on his chest. In time she is separated by fate from her first love, and many leaves of the calendar fall before this Juliet is reunited with her Romeo; but now, alas, he finds her past recognition, no longer *petite* and delicate, and with double chins into the bargain. Or he might have closed with 'Louise', that wistful wisp of a signature tune bequeathed to him by

Innocents of Paris, his first Hollywood film. Of such simple little songs he could make small dramas of remarkable vividness. By the time his success had enabled them to achieve their own status as folklore, it was almost as if a British troubadour were successfully mining 'Sing a Song of Sixpence' and 'Little Miss Muffet' for hidden emotional depth.

As the years progressed, so the Chevalier act made concessions, both satirical and sentimental, to the times. He would satirise rock and roll trends, the sinuous body that Colette discerned here coming into its own. He would conclude a *rondeau populaire* on the Ages of Man, which highlighted the chief landmarks in his life at ten-yearly intervals, with the lilting nostalgia of 'I'm Glad I'm Not Young Any More', but not before his introduction to the song '*Vingt ans*' had made its opening concession to youth: 'When I say twantee years old, I can't help lookeeng at the ceiling because that ees exactly 'ow old I would lahk to be . . . Eet says een the song, you een the audience, who are luckee enoff to be twantee, don't waste one minute.' He would fix them with a fairy godmother's eye: 'lurf, lurf, lurf.' At whatever age, however, the close of his act was almost predictable: gushing white horses of applause; bows as ineffective as Canute in stemming their tide; a wave of the straw hat; maybe—as most often—an admission: 'I get such a keek tonaht that eet hurts!'; an arm thrown out in final exultation, its upturned thumb pointing to a thirsting mouth, symbolic invitation for the whole world to come and share his champagne; final curtain.

If one facet of his performance cries out for recognition, it must be his capacity, so consistently Gallic and yet in his case so neglected, for make-believe, his skill in creating so much out of so little, a flair that would reach its zenith in the more stylised art of Marcel Marceau. One must not overlook the fact that these powers as a mimic, if not as a mime, while enhancing virtually every song he ever performed, were sufficient to sustain several displays of virtuosity in which music remained an outsider. There was his solo parade of sometime spectators, that included a clergyman, a Las Vegas drunk, and an obstreperous reveller on a Saturday spree. There were '*Accents Mélodiques*', a bewildering quicksilver demonstration of what half a dozen languages would sound like to a listener who did not understand them. At the core of his performance was a faultless instinct for the truth, a truth all the more remarkable in that it was ever droll, never obscured by a patina of sentimentality which remained only one short, perilous, but always carefully assessed step away from much of his material.

His mimetic ability was as flesh to the bone of an impeccable sense of craftsmanship, which amounted to far more than mere surface charm. No gesture was ever out of place, ever without meaning. It was as if chance had been polished out of existence. The merest shrug of the shoulders, the most casual twirl of the straw hat had been rehearsed to the last atom-splitting detail. He knew that only so would he ever be able to achieve an illusion of spontaneity and in so doing make that illusion real. It is well known that while he was a house guest of Mary Pickford in Hollywood he would, according to his hostess, go out on the lawn every day complete with boater and rehearse his entire act.

But one must not give the impression that he took himself so seriously for fun to be eroded. There were times when he had the irresistible cheek to embrace chance herself with open arms. And so he could serenade the Queen Mother at the 1961 Royal Variety Performance in London with 'You must 'ave been a beautiful baby—'cause Majestee, look at you now'; get the venerable Charles de Gaulle, no less, to join him at a charity gala in a refrain of '*Ma Pomme*'. The older he grew, so the cheek became more and more enshrouded in a schoolboy's mock-innocence. And where the schoolboy is galvanised into action by his fellow pupils, so Chevalier seemed to derive his essential energy from the audience. In the later years he boasted of containing 'a kind of flame of youth'. He had known for most of his performing life that 'one must learn to bow out five minutes before the audience stops clapping'. Happily, and in spite of those apparently endless farewell concert tours, he took his own last bow a respectable five minutes before the flame burnt out.

He once detailed to Peter Daubeny, the impresario, what must amount to the most concise—for such a vast career—theatrical autobigraphy of all: 'My career consists of low comedian with red nose; low comedian without red nose; going elegant with straw hat and jacket; music-hall comedies; Hollywood; return with straw hat and jacket to Paris; one-man show; return to America and dramatic actor.' It is a career all the more remarkable in that from the time he first hit his early Parisian stride, while he may have suffered what might have appeared setbacks, he never took a serious dip in popularity, was always ensured of an ecstatic following in whatever country he made his performing arena at any one time. There was only one occasion when he suffered the threat of serious decline, when tainted with the stigma of Nazi-collaboration for supposedly singing to German troops during the Occupation. Contemporary press reports waver between his insistence that he sang neither for the Germans nor in Germany, only before German-held French prisoners, and an account that claimed he did cross the Rhine to perform, his price for the release of ten prisoners who were actually freed as a result. Whatever the true version, he survived plans by the Resistance to sentence him to death, even rumours that he had been killed, and by the close of 1944 was cleared after due investigation of the allegations made against him. When he returned to the Paris stage it was as if nothing had happened. The audience was probably shrewd enough to realise that the basic adrenalin that pumps into an entertainer the urge to perform, the will never to disappoint, whether his audience be cosseted in theatre seats or standing impromptu, in evening dress or in uniform, was at the root of his dilemma.

The only charge that could be labelled against him is that of a now legendary—though inconsistent—meanness, the tenacity with which he clung to his wealth in later years. While donations were given unstintingly to actors' charities, the extent of the hospitality accorded a sweltering English production crew filming in the grounds of his house was a jug of plain tap water served through a trade entrance. Here was the inescapable outcome of a philosophy inculcated since childhood. Only an individual who had witnessed the kneegrazing drudgery of the mother he affectionately called La Louque (after her habit of pronouncing words with the Flemish suffix 'ouk'), who had subsisted on a diet of baked potatoes and herb tea, who had found himself supporting his family at the age of fourteen, could possibly ever know the

42

true value of money. Ironically, the estate, named after his mother, where Chevalier ended his rags-to-riches story at the age of eighty-three, once belonged to the English philanthropist, Sir Richard Wallace; it was Wallace who many years before had donated hundreds of drinking fountains to the streets of Paris, the fountains on which the urchin Maurice had once depended for his own drinking water.

The great entertainers always happen to be those who are either quite impervious to (Keaton and Hope, for example) or absurdly provocative of impersonation. It does not need saying that Chevalier belonged to the latter category. His reputation at the peak of his early Hollywood period was such that in their film *Monkey Business* the four stowaway Marx Brothers all found themselves simultaneously impersonating the great Maurice in an attempt to double-cross their way past the passport counter at the end of an ocean voyage. Even the straw-hatted Harpo managed to slur through a version of 'If a Nightingale Could Sing Like You'—and far more accurately than his brothers, strapped as he was to the phonograph on his back. In 1931, when that film was made, no one in any country where French or English was spoken could have failed to recognise the object of the Marxes' parody. It is a measure of Chevalier's continuing stature that, until his death, at no moment was the extent of that recognition seriously undermined.

Jimmy Durante

Goodnight Mrs Calabash,
wherever you are

I T WAS AS if the heckler who imagined he could do better than the fellow on stage, could wait no longer and, taking theatrical convention by the scruff of the neck, had cock-snooked his way into the spotlight. The rasping, tearaway force of Jimmy Durante was born of a dauntless impudence perfectly attuned to the hooligan decade of the 'twenties which saw his first success. While the audience rapport to be achieved by Jack Benny would prove as snug and compact as cricket ball in padded glove, that of Durante resembled the weighted googly ball of Meadowlark Lemmon homing in zig-zag fashion on the net, none the less sure for all its wobbling independence. In addition, he is as cosily American as L'il Abner, as extravagantly so as Barnum and Bailey. One critic saw in him more than a mere substitute for the latter: 'Looking at Durante is like watching all three rings of a circus at once.' There is nothing subtle about him. If distinguished critics could see Mickey Mouse in Fred Astaire, it is then surprising that no one could discern Donald Duck in Durante, a common language in their joky obstreperousness. His rough-house energy, his intensity of action, and his Calibanesque appearance are all natural elements of the violent Utopia of the animated cartoon.

No comedian ever revelled more playfully in his own ugliness: 'I know dere's a million good-lookin' guys, but I'm a novelty!' The receding chin, beady ferret eyes, and the bald head scratchily clinging to a last few wisps of hair, all play their part, but are still overshadowed by the most famous nose in show business. Cole Porter, seeing it possessed a hidden quality worth preserving in the aspic of his own talent, catalogued 'the nose of the great Durante' between Inferno's Dante and a Waldorf Salad, in his 'You're the Top' inventory of good taste. Durante himself, however, was probably aghast that his tomahawk of a nose should be provided with so distinguished a stepping stone to respectability. The title of one of his nasal-oriented songs, 'It's My Nose's Birthday Today', pinpoints the extent to which he allowed the Schnozzle to dominate his entire personality. As he emphasised in the accompanying patter to the song: 'It was de foist time in history dat a noise outweighed de child.' Far more relevant, however, is his other 'first': never before had a comedian gone to such lengths to delegate one aspect of his total physical make-up to the rôle of stooge. The 'schnozz' is Durante's most consistent fall-guy, out on a limb—or should it be feature?—living a life of its own. Its real-life inseparability from its owner only intensifies his rough-diamond attitude towards it. Where Cole Porter spotted an unexpected elegance, no one was ever more disparaging than Durante himself.

He first made fun of the nose in 1923 at his Club Durant, where he would begin his act by stabbing an exclamatory finger at the prize exhibit: 'Here it is, folks. Yes, it's real. It ain't gonna bite you, and it ain't gonna fall off. Any famous people in de audience can autograph it.' In later years, however, it had achieved more than curiosity value, the excuse for a welcome surrealism to enter his patter:

> You know sump'n?—the schnozz felt kind of bad dis morning. You know, Jules Bodell invited me up to his farm—you know he raises bees—and when we got up dere he took me straight to de beehive. Then he said, 'Jimmy, stick yer noise inside—see how dey work.' Well, I stuck my noise inside de beehive and what happened? One of de bees looked up and shouted, 'Run for de hills, boys—they're comin' for de honey with a steam shovel!'

The joking belied the distress earlier experienced by the young Durante, when as a sensitive, hollow-chested weakling in the hoodlum-infested 'Five Points' slum area of Manhattan, he was continually humiliated with cries of 'Naso', 'Hooknose', and 'Lookit, the big-nose kid!' On one occasion a brawl ensued, but even Jimmy's piston-packed legs couldn't spirit him away fast enough to prevent his nose being broken. The torn cartilage dating from that occasion never mended and the swelling that made an already prominent feature even more worthy of attention never subsided. Durante subsequently revealed the instinctive flair, shared by all great comedians, for turning his shortcoming to comic advantage. Now he has only to spot competition in the audience or amongst the band to bellow: 'Git de schnozz on dat guy. My job's in jeopardy. Either he goes—or I go.' But beneath all the razzamatazz which saw the nose insured with Lloyds for one million dollars as well as imprinted in cement outside Grauman's Chinese Theatre in Hollywood, it would be hard not to discern an undertone of sadness. Sometimes deep emotion will overtake the comedy in his act. He can be so moved by it that a tear will drop from his eye down the nose itself; but he is never subdued for long: 'An' it's a brave tear dat starts dat journey!' Off stage he has been a little more forthcoming. In the early 'fifties he confided to his biographer, Gene Fowler: 'All through life, even when I am makin' a fortune on account of the big beak, and while I am out there on the stage laughin' and kiddin' about the nose, at no time was I ever happy about it. It was a catastra-stroke!'

Although the nose set the seal on his physical appearance, Durante was not content to rely merely on nature. The ubiquitous battered grey felt hat which assumes the rôle of the original slapstick when his anger is roused and the offending party has to be buffeted accordingly; the shapeless, shabby, single-breasted suit which is more a comment on his own demeanour than on his tailor's skill: 'I wear a new suit an' de next day it's old'; the damp exploded firework passing for a cigar, the moist end of which he is forever snipping with minuscule scissors; all enhance his overall stance, that of a distraught penguin given to excesses of arm-flapping and flustered strutting.

Durante was born on 10 February 1893, on Manhattan's lower East Side, a mere hundred yards to the south of Chinatown and only two blocks to the north-west of the East River. Along with contemporary Joe E. Brown and few others since, he was destined automatically to become one of that distinct breed of ethnological clowns indeterminately Jewish, Italian or East European. In actual fact his mother, from whom Jimmy inherited his nose, was a Neapolitan, his father a French-Italian barber, one time of Salerno. The youngest of a family of three boys and a girl, he was christened James Francis. The tag 'Schnozzola' was first volunteered by Jack Duffy of the vaudeville team of Bernard and Duffy, when Jimmy was playing the Club Alamo in Harlem at the beginning of his professional career. Between these names he became known affectionately to friends and family alike as 'Rag-time Jimmy', having landed his first professional job at seventeen as a pianist in Diamond Tony's saloon on Coney Island. By 1916, he had gathered around him a five-piece Dixieland band for the Alamo. 'Jimmy Durante's Original Jazz Novelty Band' was an early billing and within a year he was revealing a gift for comedy that had so far been dormant. The idea was that Jimmy should stand at the piano as he played with one hand for the shimmy dances popular at the time, all the while 'insulting' the drummer, Johnny Stein, with his one-liners. During his Coney Island days his friend Eddie Cantor had already suggested this technique, but then Durante had replied: 'Gee, I wouldn't do that, I'd be afraid people would laugh at me.' Gradually, however, the comedy became essential, if only to compensate for Jimmy's own admission that when they played, say, a fox trot, they had to display a sign which said 'fox trot' for the customers to know how to respond.

The locale most readily associated today with Durante's early career is the now infamous speakeasy, the Club Durant. Having found himself earning no less than a hundred dollars a week at the Club Nightingale during the immediate post-war boom, Jimmy was eventually convinced by waiter and confidant, Frank Nolan, that with a place of his own he could graduate to the proverbial million. In retrospect the mis-spelling of the venture seems appropriately symbolic of his own disregard for spelling, but at the time that missing neon 'e' itself spelt out the hundred dollars which Durante and his partners just didn't have. After furnishing the loft of a used-car saleroom on West 58th Street in makeshift club-deco fashion, the only capital remaining at Durante's disposal during that Autumn of 1923 was talent, but not merely his own.

At the Alamo, he had already sown the seeds of a friendship with baritone Eddie Jackson, a sometime singing waiter of sentimental songs. Jackson, three years younger than Jimmy and of Brooklyn-Jewish origin, had lasted only one night at the earlier club. His only claim to fame prior to meeting Durante had been a spell working in a bookbindery under a young Italian foreman named Al Capone. He had recently formed another song-and-dance team with Harry Harris, and it was with Harris that he now entered the new venture, both putting up 750 dollars, along with Nolan and Durante, each partner maintaining a 25 per cent interest. The early days were shaky, but one of the few regular customers was Lou Clayton, born Lou Finklestein in East Brooklyn in 1887 and a celebrated soft-shoe dancer. Sensing the potential of the venture and possibly the springboard such an environment could provide for the still unmined comic talent of the young Durante, Clayton insisted on becoming a partner and eventually bought out Harris's share. Gradually the legendary team of Clayton, Jackson and Durante evolved, the names in that order because of Clayton's already established reputation and because they sounded right that way. Their trinity of loyalty would endure throughout the years, long after they had ceased to perform together. They sang what many thought to be their swansong in the 1931 Broadway musical *The New Yorkers*. But Clayton remained at Durante's side as his chief confidant, manager and guardian angel until his death in 1950, while Jackson would return to add his own charm to the Durante stage act after Jimmy's not entirely successful sojourn in Hollywood. Phil Silvers once said of Clayton and Durante that their loyalty was that of a father and son. It is ironical that Jimmy's actual father, never enthusiastic about his son's aspirations for the stage, should wait until his eighty-second year before seeing Durante perform on stage. The production was *The New Yorkers* and when, after the show, Jimmy asked him, 'Well, pop, howd'ya like my work?' the barber from Salerno replied, 'Lissen, Son, les not get in an argument.' The nearest Clayton ever had to a contract with Durante was a signed picture of Schnozzola: 'To my dear pal and partner, Lou, until death do we part.'

Meanwhile, back at the Club Durant, Jimmy had initially restricted his performing duties to piano-playing. Clayton, with extra push from Sime Silverman, the founder-editor of *Variety* who would christen the trio 'The Three Sawdust Bums', and was arguably the most powerful man behind the scenes on Broadway, now catapulted him into the arena as a comedian. Starting from scratch, their shenanigans relied heavily on the impromptu, scoring off the unique environment the trio had created for themselves. To savour the full bloom of that humour, one must appreciate the pure Runyonesque density of its typical audience. When Durante looked out over the crowd and with mock jealousy exclaimed, '*Every*body's tryin' to get into de act', he was reporting the simple truth. The paying guests on a not untypical evening would include Slapsy Maxie Rosenbloom and Walter Winchell, Ed Sullivan and Vincent Youmans, Walter Chrysler and Otto Kahn, Al Jolson and George Jessel, even criminals like Legs Diamond and Waxey Gordon. Runyon himself based several of his racing stories on incidents from Clayton's life as well as stating in print that he doubted 'if a greater café combination ever lived'. For 'café' one should, of course, read 'speakeasy', bearing in mind that Durante, with his brusque, knowing ad-libs imparted a new, though no more innocent, connotation to the word. With the exception of Jolson there has never been an entertainer to match the sheer high-voltage thrust of his personality. The finest testimony to his talent is that so many super-charged egos, including Jolson himself, should have paid money to place themselves in a position to be enthralled by this frantic little jumping-jack of an entertainer. It may have been psychological masochism. It certainly wasn't just the liquor, even if his own effect on an audience was like that of neat vodka. As Sammy Cahn has indicated, what set Durante apart from other comics is that 'he came on like everyone else went off'.

The comedy proved as catch-as-catch-can as the crowd, beginning the moment guests entered the room. If a customer was a personal friend, Jimmy would start singing:

49

Here comes a friend of mine,
Sit him down at table nine,
See dat he don't buy no wine,
Because he is a friend of mine.
Skeet, skat, skat, skeet, skat, skoo.

The friend was then invited to strike a pose which would be given spot-lighted attention. Some overplayed it. On one occasion, Paul Whiteman's trousers fell to his ankles. If the friend came in with a girl, Jimmy would take his arm, Clayton hers, and absent-mindedly they would lead them to separate tables. Jimmy would then express his own illogical surprise: 'What happened? I came in with a girl.' Eventually they would be reunited, amid the pouring of much wine and even greater laughter. Another speciality of the house was the echo song. Jackson and Durante would commence the floor show proper with Eddie in the kitchen and Jimmy at the far end of the main room. Both using small Rudy Vallee-style megaphones, Eddie would sing 'I love', and Jimmy, as if at the other end of an invisible line, would repeat the words in tempo: 'I love . . . I love . . . The birds . . . The birds . . . The bees . . . The bees . . . The trees . . . The trees . . .'. Eddie by now had appeared in the room and Clayton had slid his way between the two. Nor was the nose overlooked. Jimmy would assume centre position, with Clayton to his left, Jackson to the right. Both would feel so threatened by the ant-eater appendage that nothing could restrain their fury as they set about thwacking it with their hats. When this failed, they had nothing to lose by making a grab for it:

Durante: Whadd'ya think will happen to my noise if youse guys don't quit hangin' onta it?
Jackson: By the end of the year it will grow into a banana.
Durante: What'll we do with it den?
Clayton: We'll have bananas and cream.

At other times one of them would grasp the Schnozzle and yell out that he had struck oil. The other would ask, 'Where?' The answer was a foregone conclusion.

The extraordinary gusto of their comic business, as it bounced from one to the other with Jimmy storming backwards and forth, always the centre of attention, set a standard for improvised cabaret humour that has never been surpassed. It would be inaccurate to say that they pulled out all the stops, but only for the simple reason that in their crazy world the stops were inexhaustible. Clayton once imagined himself in the shoes of a customer:

You'd come in at eleven o'clock and leave at seven o'clock the next morning. You wouldn't know where the night flew by, because at no time was there a lull in the place, and that's how we got sayings like 'There's a lull in the place', 'What happened?', 'The piano must be busted'. And those things were cues, and we'd start doing something.

One customer was the immortal George M. Cohan, of Yankee Doodle fame. On his initial visit he had never been to a speakeasy before and his first dumbstruck comment was to query: 'Don't those guys ever sit down?' By the end he was so exhilarated that on his way out, his debts already discharged, he put down an extra hundred dollar bill by way of appreciation. Later in his career Cohan attempted to analyse his own special attraction: 'I am not a comedian and I can't get laughs. So I try for enthusiasm.' No wonder he was impressed by Durante. Never had a true comedian gone about the business of raising laughs so enthusiastically. After eighteen months, the Club Durant was due almost inevitably for its own Great Sleigh Ride. Federal agents, admitted to the Club by the naïve Durante when they assured him: 'You remember us, don't you, Jimmy?', slapped padlocks on its doors no less than a week after their host had benevolently plied them with free liquor. But it no longer mattered. The atmosphere of the establishment, seedy and disreputable as it may have been, had served its purpose as the whetstone for a unique comic talent. The sheer uninhibitedness of his technique could have known no better *alma mater*.

Over the next six years the trio would jitterbug their way around the nightclub circuit with successful forays into Broadway, until Hollywood, in the voice of Irving Thalberg, beckoned. The M–G–M invitation, however, was extended to Durante alone. The possibilities for him as a solo artist were unlimited, and with Sime Silverman on hand to settle what had appeared an equally unlimited personal dilemma he took them. Sadly, though, in a film climate which was scared of allowing such an idiosyncratic comic talent romantic involvement and hence leading man status, Durante was restricted mainly to supporting comedy-relief. Also at the mercy of atrocious material, his career floundered. A triumphant personal tour of Europe in 1936 would allow him some breathing-space, but from 1938 to 1943 his career dived traumatically to what he described as its 'lowest pernt'. Going solo had paradoxically meant an erosion of his essential individualism. He must have long realised that the split-second spontaneity of his unique style could never be translated to celluloid with complete satisfaction. His already low spirits at this time were lowered by the deaths of first his father, then his wife. His depression, however, never spilled over into self-pity and with Clayton at hand as manager to prize him out of the doldrums he bravely took the only possible cure—a live audience. To Durante himself his opening night at the Copacabana in 1943 must have been like a second baptism. Back in the old routine, his own producer again in the truest vaudeville tradition, he need have had no fears. In his own words, his success was 'colossial'. Then, as in subsequent years, he was never anything less than a sell-out at the Copa. On that first comeback engagement tables were at such a premium that he could joke, and make it sound excruciatingly funny into the bargain, that he had dropped a collar button one night, whereupon 'a waiter t'rew a table cloth over it and seated five people before I could recover it.'

Gene Fowler labelled Jimmy 'half-hooligan; half-saint'. The polarity hints at another, far more intriguing ambivalence in the Durante appeal. Few comedians have ever enjoyed a warmer intimacy with their public, an intimacy that encourages security and relaxation in the live audience quite as much as the principal goal of laughter. And yet Jimmy has also succeeded in generating a delicious sense of danger through his total performance. It is not entirely divorced from that mysterious quality of unpredictability all great artists have, but in this special instance is enhanced by the sheer savagery of his comic attack—which led one critic to describe the feelings of his audience as being like those of spectators at a small Balkan war.

In the desecrated tumbledown shrine of the comedy of destruction Durante must hold a special niche. He has come as close as any comedy performer to translating to live performance the ethos of the animated comic-strip, where anything is possible and physical pain becomes anaesthet-ised. A natural development for a clown whose technique was nurtured in the violent, cut-throat dives of the Capone era, the trend reached an apotheosis in his celebrated 'Wood' number from *The New Yorkers*, if not in the casual mayhem each of the trio accorded the others by way of carefree social acknowledgment. The routine was prompted by a magazine advertisement sponsored by the National Lumber Manufacturers Association which read:

> Almost everyone has been induced to believe that this country is con-fronted by an acute shortage of timber. This is not true . . . Wood built America. Without wood there could have been no America . . . Wood built the homes . . . churches . . . stockades . . . corncribs . . . Wood endures . . . Wood is friendly, wood is economical.

On stage Jackson began by informing Jimmy that he was a blockhead, whereupon Durante, with that sudden twirling on one heel with which he would in an instant bring himself face to face—'Surrounded by assassins!'—with his accusers, real or imaginary, retaliated: 'When you say my head is made of wood, you pays me a compliment.' He then proceeded to declaim an expanded version of the text of the advertisement to the tempo of Kipling's poem 'Boots', while Clayton and Jackson, won over to his cause, hurried back and forth on stage amassing with mounting speed a carpenter's night-mare of wooden objects from pencils and toothpicks through rolling pins and pogo sticks to a rickshaw, a tree stump, even a long birch-bark canoe. And still Jimmy went on chanting, oblivious to the pile around him: '. . . without wood there wouldn't be no America! Our forefathers crossed the prairies in covered wagons made of wood . . .' This was the cue for a donkey to make its way on stage, trot up to Jimmy, lower itself beneath his legs, and hoist him —still eulogising—up and away off stage. It was a great exit, but the point all along was the violent accumulation of the wood itself and the gradual illusion conveyed that they were tearing the place apart in the process. Violins snatched from the orchestra, utensils from the kitchen, furniture, doors, a toilet-seat, even an outhouse were all grist to the mill. A subsequent Broadway show, *Strike Me Pink*, with Durante now performing solo, re-quired a climax to a bicycle-race sequence. Inspiration was at an all-time low until Jimmy, forced to tackle a first-night audience with unfinished material, took the bull by the horns regardless and letting the audience in on his dilemma hurled the bicycle into the orchestra pit. Whereupon the musicians demanded a promise in writing that their working area would henceforth remain impervious to his personal comic maelstrom, straight, as it was, out of a Tom and Jerry cartoon.

Durante's standard cabaret routine is motivated throughout by a basic streak of destructive resentment against life in all its aspects. He has it in for

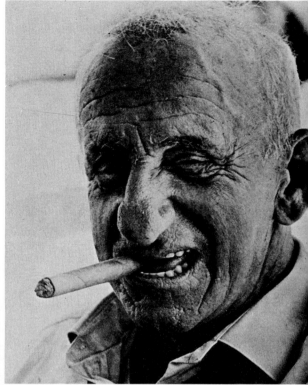

Durante's Jazz & Novelty Band
A. J. Baquet, Clarinet

the musicians, none of whom, least of all his drummer, is safe from the ballistic range of an arsenal comprising old hats, sheet music, glass of water, music stand, telephone, piano stool, piano lid. The impact of each deterrent keeps pace with Durante's mounting irritation at each successive refusal by the band to correct their musical sins: 'Where *is* dat blip-blip in de music? I don't see blip-blip in de music. It's a conspiracy, dat's what it is. Dey're ruinin' de act. I'll give you fifty bucks, you show me blip-blip in de music.' He has it in for latecomers, however discreet their arrival; but if their distraction spells competition he can always play the trump: 'All right, let's everybody start walkin' around', this the cue for the band to leave their seats and, feigning disregard for the audience, start milling around in a Carrollian caucus-race until ordered to return to their booths. Alternatively, a customer may decide to leave early: 'Remember, mistah, I never fergits a back!' He has it in for the management: 'Twelve-fifty for a load of ice with t'ree olives! Dem bosses are t'eves. Twelve-fifty fer t'ree olives and two hunska salary. Well, *somebody's* gotta pay for da fancy new cocktail lounge upstairs!' He has it in for the waiters: 'Dose waiters! Assassins! If you don't tip 'em five dollars more de Union calls 'em out on strike! Let 'em touch dis nose! I'll sue de jernt and turn it into a bowlin' alley.' He has it in for unions generally, and so he waits distraught for a small white piano to be moved centre-stage for one of his arias: 'I can't move it. He's da only one who can touch it. Anybody else touches de pianner—de union closes de whole jernt.' In anger his whole being becomes a tantrum possessed, pupils frozen, head askance, body tense, arms dangling, as he propels his undisciplined way around the floor. There are even times when his own vanity becomes the victim of his playful ferocity; but the personal shortcomings which he enacts always have a triumphant sting in their tail. His toupee may deliberately come off in the general mêlée, but Jimmy is at immediate pains to point out: 'Dere's not much hair, but every strand has a muscle.' In his quest for the Lost Chord, no sooner has the guy who found it lost it again than stage and audience have to be turned upside down in a renewed search, the chaos a token of his own inefficiency, before he finds it a second time by inadvertently sitting on the piano keys.

Durante's solo act managed to retain intact the revolutionary quality which the original trio, with Jimmy as catalyst, first brought to comedy. Such a combination of speed and upheaval and hilarity had not existed in living memory on a live stage. Jimmy proved a one-man whirlwind and left many pondering how the globe beneath him could ever keep up with those sturdy legs, exercised assiduously at the beginning of each day in the knowledge that when Grimaldi's legs failed, that great clown had been forced to hang up his cap and bells. And unlike the subsequent corporate frenzy of *Hellzapoppin* and the Marxes as captured on celluloid, the Durante delirium never at any time became depersonalised. Durante's secret was that for all the high-powered stomping, the abandon of his piano-rending, the hurly-burly of a hundred hats flying, his style symbolised with uncanny accuracy a rhythm of life which he loved and to which the bulk of his mass audience were both resigned and attuned, a metaphor for the tempo, the tensions of the big city. Durante himself explained to Fowler his affinity for New York, and the rhythm of his own performance beneath the surface is unmistakable:

My heart is in New York. I love the tumult of New York. I love the crowd. It's really somethin' that no other city in the world has. . . . In New York you're on your toes. You're up against a kind of storm of thinkin' and doin', and you're on the go all the time. You're not lookin' to get out in the sun because there ain't no sun. It's like a big band playin' all the time. Like a big band. That's the way I'd describe New York. And you want to get out and get in it.

It's like openin' a show. The crowds are comin' in and you're ready. You're out there walkin' up and down behind the curtain. Then you're in the wings. You walk up and down the wings. Then you go in the dressin' room. You go from the make-up table to the coat-hangers and chew on a cigar. You're doin' nothin', but you're ready to go on, and you're fidgety, and you're ready. Like a horse race. And the overture plays. And now you're keyed up, and you throw away your cigar, and go on. And that's the way you always are, and that's the way New York is. It's like the band is playin' all the time.

The Schnozzola provided a fantasy projection of the chaos and anxiety born of an age gaining constant momentum. The frantic pace and the outrageous joy of his end-product was as satisfying emotionally as any conscious orchestral rendering or dramatic allegory of the same theme.

And if he spoke for the frayed nerves of a hectic age, he had the voice to match. Fred Allen referred to Jimmy as 'The Riff-Raff's Caruso', with a voice evocative of 'a dull rasp calling its mate, or an air-raid signal blasting through two layers of gravel'. If the truth were known, his unique sandpaper-and-decibels vocal quality might be traced to the efforts of a sensitive youth to detract attention from an outsize nose. If nature endowed Durante with a raucous voice, there can be no doubt that its owner has spent a lifetime intent on further amplification. But however frayed the tonsils from which it booms, it is a voice resonant with sincerity, benevolence, and reassurance, not least to those countless members of different ethnic backgrounds whose appreciation of his verbal gaffes and misunderstandings was in the America of the 'twenties and 'thirties all the more immediate because that much closer to their own lives. However much he might mispronounce words or misplace the emphasis upon lesser words in a sentence, he is never himself in doubt that the long words he tackles *are* difficult, while, incredibly, never leaving others in the slightest doubt as to the exact meaning of what he says. If a man 'makes a complete haddock of things', we instinctively expect the worst of him. 'All de red corpsuckles is gone from my veins! I'm just a hollow shelf!' needs no annotation to tell us that Jimmy is physically drained. Jackie Barnett, one of his writers, once emphasised how natural this jabberwocky-by-way-of-the-Bowery is to him: 'I had the word "nostalgic" in one of the scripts. I knew it was a big word for Jimmy and wanted him to say it as "neuralgic". I was sure it would bring a laugh, so I wrote "neuralgic" in the script. But when he came to it, he pronounced it "nostalgic".' It is not a pose, at least not the first time round. It is an integral part of his total ethos. No comedian enjoys words more than Durante, no comedian ever arrived at a sub-lingo more in character with the physical climate of his act. When a colleague gave Jimmy the definition of a split infinitive, he could justify his previous ignorance with the same relish with which he would set about dismantling a piano: 'I don't split 'em. When I go to work on an infinitive, I break it up in little pieces.'

Language, possessions, reputations, all exist in Durante's eyes to be shattered, but one feature of the routine does remain comparatively exempt from his insults and, at least in public view, his destructive impulses, namely his 'goils'. Individuals may come and go, but a short string of chorus dancers has been part of his act for ages. The delight of this self-styled 'chaiographer' as he shepherds them about the stage is a cross between that of proud father and satyr on the prowl for illicit sex: 'Positions, goils, positions—get your positions the way we rehearsed and everything will be all right.' (Then, to the audience): 'I just want you to know I produced and directed this number myself.' Any linguistic hurdles to be surmounted are now by courtesy of another language altogether:

> *Girl:* Jimmy, I'd like you to meet our new French girl, Marie.
> *Jimmy:* Come here, Marie. I want to talk to you. How about going out with me tonight?
> *Marie:* Oui, oui.
> *Jimmy:* How about going over to your house with de lights down low?
> *Marie:* Oui, oui.
> *Jimmy:* How about a little huggin' and a kissin'?
> *Marie:* Oui, oui.
> *Jimmy:* Boy, if I can only find out what dat word means—I'm in business!

But Jimmy is far from being a slave to *their* charms. He has the highest opinion of his own virility and can dictate his own terms: 'You know, boys, last week I sang for de Sultan of Pasha, and the Sultan offered me his harem of five hundred beautiful wives. But I turned 'em down—becos when I get up every morning, who wants to find a t'ousand stockings hanging in de bathroom? Not Durante!' He knows there are hundreds who would come running, with no question of not taking their patient place in the queue:

> *Girl:* Make love to me, bewitch me.
> *Jimmy:* I'm doing sump'n. I'll be witcha in a minute.

He has long known that women find a special fascination in ugly men and consequently remains one comedian in full control of his sexual destiny.

It is the songs, however, that provide amid all the mayhem the prime cohesive factor of a Durante performance. In an article for the *New York Times* dated 8 November 1936, following the opening of his Broadway show, *Red, Hot and Blue*, in which Durante was featured alongside Ethel Merman and the emergent Bob Hope, Cole Porter explained the pitfalls of writing a number for Jimmy. It was, he wrote, not a matter of vocal range, as in the case of most artists, but the challenge of capturing the elusive quality of the Durante personality in words and music. No wonder then that most of the songs which became trademarks for his personality bear either in whole or in part his own creative imprint, while the number Porter especially tailored for the Schnozzola, 'A Little Skipper From Heaven Above', is seldom remembered today. But the distinctive jumping style of his absurdist celebration of everything from a love-hate relationship with the Great White Way in 'I Know Darn Well I Can Do Without Broadway (But Can Broadway Do Without Me?)', through his sartorial disregard on frequent Clear Lake, California vacations in 'I'm Jimmy, That Well-Dressed Man', to personal mascot by way of Italian folklore in 'Umbriago', will linger in the mind of an affectionate public as long as the man himself. These, together with 'Who Will Be With You When I'm Far Away, Out In Far Rockway?', 'Did You Ever Have a Feelin' That You Wanted to Go, and Still Have a Feelin' That You Wanted to Stay?', 'So I Ups to Him—and He Ups to Me', 'A Dissa and a Datta', and his signature tune, 'Start Off Each Day With a Song', are a few of the many he has copyrighted over the years, the majority dating back to the uninhibited creative environment of the early nightclub days. Most assured of immortality is the number which began as an exit song at the Club Durant. Jimmy would advise the crowd that they could say it with flowers or sweets, even artichokes or treats, but never with ink, the cue into the nonsense chorus, echoed by all three partners, 'Ink-a-dink-a-doo, Ka-dinka-dee-, Ka-dinka-doo . . .'. He has been acting against his own instructions ever since.

It has long been a joke in entertainment circles that the Durante songwriting business cannot exactly flourish, its sole clientele consisting of Schnozzola imitators and the great original. As Durante says: 'When I sing a song I roo-in it for anybody else. It is the kiss of debt.' And yet, for all his ribbing of his own vocal prowess—'I'm glad dat note came out—on de last X-ray my doctor took, it showed up as a safety-pin'—few have ever been able to project a song with the attack and authority of a Durante. He sings as if his life depended on it. Scorning the subtle effect and with a tempo cunningly set neither too fast nor too slow he gets straight to the sinew of a number, a veritable muscle-man of song, the total effect reinforced by the brash energy of his physical presence. If he has courted subtlety at all, it is in his original innovation of the interrupted song technique of lyric, pause, joke and band crashing in on top of the punch line to resume the song again. Durante has explained: 'There's no comedy song that's strong enough by itself because you keep going on and the audience loses the lines,' And again: 'I avoid the monogamy of just tellin' straight jokes.' He assures his audience he has 'a million of 'em'—jokes that is—and it is in mid-song that most of them get shown to best advantage. Sometimes they have a connection with the music; as 'I hope you don't t'ink dat dis suit is all I own. It's ridiculous —why, I spend 3,000 dollars a year on mottballs alone!' in his Well-Dressed Man number; but more often their position is purely arbitrary. 'I goes inta de Automat and I puts in a lead nickel. What d'ya t'ink comes out? De manager!' frequently pops up amid 'Inka-dinka-doo' for no discernible semantic reason. One can, though, always be certain that joke will be perfectly synchronised with music, his recovery of the lyric in exact counterpoint to the music being played.

When he is not using his songs as a launching pad for his jokes, they provide the perfect excuse for him to show off his brilliant skill at the piano. 'Ragtime Jimmy', as he is affectionately called, may kid that he 'never took a lesson in my life', but Rudi Blesh, distinguished jazz critic and co-author of the definitive *They All Played Ragtime*, has rated Durante in his prime as the best white ragtime pianist who ever played. Even now, to listen to Jimmy playing is an *aficionado's* ticket back through time to the 1910 heyday of ragtime as an art. No white man ever came near him in conveying the authentic Negro drive at the keys. His callous-forming, carpet-wearing knack of pounding the basic beat with the left hand while syncopating the melody in a subtly different rhythm with the right was not only in classic style but entirely spontaneous. When he was a child, his parents paid little heed to his aspirations to become a ragtime pianist; they had their own ambitions for him in classical circles. But Jimmy was adamant from the beginning: 'My perfesser tried to make me play "Poet and Peasant". I played "Maple Leaf", "Popularity", and "Wild Cherries". I couldn't do nuttin' else den, and I can't do nuttin' else today.' In the words of one catch phrase, 'Dat's da conditions dat pervail!', and luckily he kept to them. His parents would feel little pride in the aftermath of their son's guest appearance on the Paul Whiteman radio show: having introduced the number 'Toscanini, Tchaikovsky and Me' with the self-dialogue, 'Can Toscanini play piano? No. Can Durante play piano? I'll show yah,' he found himself by a freak coincidence at the scathing end of Toscanini's tongue in the lift of the Hotel Astor after the show: 'Mr Durante, I just heard your programme; and I want to tell you something: I *do* play piano.' And yet they would have derived consolation from the fact that no less than Jimmy at the keys once accompanied Einstein, who was well known as an amateur fiddle-scraper, at the scientist's request, if not from Jimmy's immediate reaction to the invitation: 'Sure thing. But who's de Perfesser? A concert player?'

Stories of this kind hint at what many will have surmised by now, namely that Durante belongs to that coterie of great comedians who warrant the accolade, if only because they possess a depth of personality which extends beyond the boundaries of public performance. Far from the mere enactment of a part on stage, Jimmy's achievement is at once total and personal; he is his own *rara avis* with Schnozzle for beak. He possesses a spontaneous geiger instinct for detecting the laughter possible in any given situation, coupled with an unselfconscious flair for balancing idiosyncracy upon idiosyncracy like pennies in a pile without toppling. It was Jimmy who at the height of his career supposedly existed on a six-times-a-day diet of raw eggs and cornflakes, the surrogate spinach for his own Popeye. He even forfeited his before-dinner drink because whisky and cereal didn't mix, not that he necessarily noticed the incestuous irony attached. And when the benefit of his energy-food had worn off, this inveterate gambler had recourse to vicarious, less vitamin-dependent thrills. As he reasoned: 'I know I can't win, even if one of my horses comes in, but I like action, lotsa action!'

The size of his personal entourage is legendary, as is his generosity. It is said that when he buys clothes, he always purchases in sextuplicate, and then gives the other five away. And while mere hangers-on usually invite public suspicion and contempt, one is instead grateful to every member of the Durante circus, from musicians to masseur, from manager to cigar-lighter, without whom three-quarters of the stories that contribute to his legend would have been lost to his public. Once on a fishing expedition with

Clayton, he was aroused begrudgingly at 5.30 to ensure an early start to the day. One step behind the rest of the party, he kept bashing each tree he passed with a stick. When asked why, he snapped: 'When Durante's awake, no boid's gonna sleep.' There was the occasion in the Club Durant days when Jimmy and Eddie were surveying the treasure-trove of Cartier's window along Fifth Avenue. One silver cream and sugar set especially took their fancy. Then Jackson saw the price, as much as 850 dollars. 'Yeah,' replied Schnozzola, 'let's wait here till de store opens. Somebody else might beat us to it if we go away.'

Durante stands for an attitude to life important not least for the paradox it contains. At one moment there is Jimmy the defiant, carrying the world and his own resentment on those near-to-strapping shoulders, clapping hands against thighs in ranting exasperation. At another there is the lasting impression he leaves with an audience of a man, for all his fury, incapable of hate. In this way he has adroitly balanced brashness with timidity, an ambiguity reconciled in his nervous anxiety to set the world straight at all costs. In one of his best sermons, Reinhold Niebuhr attempted to define laughter as a no-man's-land between faith and despair. Without realising it Durante was exactly treading this precarious ground. It is also doubtful if he has even seen himself as a satirist, although the savagery of his approach qualifies him for the title in a way which the more placid, however tormented, side of his character would never have allowed on its own. But in breaking down all pretence, and lampooning not only high society but also those aspects of his own proletarian background he most despised, he would wholeheartedly have agreed with the celebrated cynic H. L. Mencken. With the inevitable malapropism on the last word of the first sentence to accommodate his constant satire on the formality of the English language, it is not difficult to imagine Durante himself asserting: 'One horse-laugh is worth 10,000 syllogisms. It is not only more effective; it is also vastly more intelligent.'

When in the early 'fifties Durante transferred his talents from stage to television, his famous 'Hot-cha-cha', hat-shaking, eye-rolling exit of countless live performances was replaced by the poignant, subdued 'And goodnight, Mrs Calabash, wherever you are'. As he walked slowly away into ever diminishing pools of light, he would pause and deliver the line, inviting obvious speculation as to the identity of the lady with the strange name. Although Durante insisted on keeping his secret to himself for a long time, it was subsequently revealed that Mrs Calabash's alter ego was almost inevitably that of his first wife, Jeanne. He had met her in his days at the Club Alamo, and her premature death in 1943 after twenty-two years of marriage was as big a setback as his career ever suffered. Over the years she had had to bear the greater strain of the tug-of-war that exists between an entertainer's public and private lives. Her resentment towards their prolonged separations and the thicker-than-blood masculine camaraderie that existed between Jimmy, Clayton and Jackson, together with her husband's refusal to encourage her own ability as a fellow performer not only led her to drink but, as far as Jimmy's conscience was concerned, hastened her end. Now he would close each broadcast with the exit line that atoned for his own guilt. Here was one comedian who shunned out-and-out pathos, rejected all sentiment, or so his audience thought. In fact, never had pathos been projected at a more personal, more subtle level. Like all the best clues in crime fiction, it was so obvious that no one noticed. He was happy to set the mood, but he never wanted pity. Unlike W. C. Fields, who again never asked openly for sympathy, Durante was lucky in that he had it both ways.

Over the years the enthusiasm of his public has become transformed into irresistible devotion. The knockabout and razzamatazz that exactly suited the age that brought him initial fame have mellowed to encompass warmth and simplicity, together with an affection for the entire human condition, without losing any of their essential edge. When he jokes of his jokes, 'I've got a million of 'em', he could be referring to his friends. He once summed up his own philosophy: 'I figger there are more good people in the world than bad ones. I don't mind if a gent scratches a match on my furniture, so long as he's careful to go with the grain.' Or he could perhaps be referring to his imitators. Like Jolson, like Chevalier, few have had more attention paid them by professional impersonators. It is a further measure of his greatness that they all fall flat, and will continue to do so as long as the great original is prepared to get out on that cabaret floor and unlock his breast in joke and song. In his own words: 'I'm indastructable. Yer know the name "Durante" means "during" in Italian? Maybe I ought to change it to "N. Durante" for "en-during". Whadd'ya t'ink 'bout dat?'

Noël Coward

A talent to amuse

I T IS DOUBTFUL if the range of Coward's enthusiasm for and accomplishment in the theatre will be paralleled this century. He was nothing if not self-deprecating about his many gifts, maybe with an echo of the remark Marie Tempest once directed at him still ringing in his ears: 'I do not think he will ever quite fulfil his great promise, if he does not curb his versatility.' When asked why he was called The Master, he would reply glibly, 'Oh, you know, Jack of all trades, Master of none.' He was far more honest about his achievement when he admitted to the things he couldn't do, like 'performing on the trapeze and sawing women in half'. But even this could not have been for lack of fantasy. His many talents were as diverse as the pebbles in a kaleidoscope; rotate the toy and the pattern shifts, striking again its own gaudy balance between expectation and surprise. In the face of Coward's achievement, the analogy with the nursery toy may appear trivial, and yet its own juvenile theatricality is in comfortable accord with the early part of his career, which straddled that disconcerting borderline between the false security of childhood make-believe and the stark reality of theatre as bread-winner.

His was a childhood animated by toy theatre first nights and weekly pilgrimages to see Gertie Millar in *The Quaker Girl*; soothed by the thought of flowers which she once tossed his way at the Adelphi stage door to be pressed later between bound back-numbers of *Chums*; threatened by the devout silence or, as he saw it, inexplicable lack of applause that would infallibly greet his choral solo of 'O for the Wings of a Dove', at Southwark Cathedral and elsewhere. One comes closer to the more down-to-earth world of the boy professional on learning that the man who would subsequently become the leading playwright of his generation never saw a straight play—as distinct from musical comedy—until he himself had been on the stage for a year. Twelve months previously, at the age of eleven, he had made his début as Prince Mussel the Jester in *The Goldfish*, a production acted by juveniles for juveniles, at the Little Theatre. This was the result of an audition for its author, Lila Field, during which, unaccompanied and Eton-suited, he sang 'Liza Ann'. (He had appeared in answer to a classified advertisement in the *Daily Mirror* for a 'talented boy with attractive appearance'.) The first line he ever delivered for hard cash—one and a half guineas a week, no less—exclaimed, 'Crumbs, how exciting!'; the second, seconds later, 'Oh really, Dolly, good gracious! If you start like that when anybody comes up behind you at your age, you'll have electric wires sticking out all over you when you grow up'. Even then, Coward's delivery had that clipped decisiveness which added its own stamp to his image in later years. There is no need, however, to read his distinctive intonation into that last line to see that its special barbed impatience could have been the work of Coward the author of twenty years later. Significantly, when asked to quote the first lines he ever spoke on stage in a television interview on the occasion of his seventieth birthday, he amended that speech to the appropriately fashionable, but less endearing, 'Hello, Dolly', as if he had foreshadowed the Broadway musical of that name by fifty years. His unerring sense of showmanship is the only licence for an error which pinpoints the unabashed theatricality of his whole ethos.

Coward came to epitomise that tension the theatre provides between sentimental artificiality and hard, devoted grind, between the cosy public façade and savage backstage bitchery, between the escapist magic of the greasepaint and the anxieties of insecurity. No man of the theatre ever allowed his sheer love of theatre to shine more radiantly through his work. The great irony is that *he* should have written 'Don't Put Your Daughter on the Stage, Mrs Worthington', for no one understood with greater sensitivity just why that young lady might want to tread the boards. His own love affair was strong enough to transcend the clichés and ersatz sentiment, even if it did reach a blind alley as far as the new school of actors and playwrights characterised by Method and New Wave was concerned. For the television show 'Together with Music' in 1955, he articulated in song his experience thirty-five years previously of acting in a performance of *The Knight of the Burning Pestle* with a temperature of 103 degrees, giving sixteen members of the company mumps, and ultimately closing the show. He had no qualms now in asking, albeit theoretically, 'Why must the show go on?', with the leading player floundering in an abyss of pain or grief. If in his later years he was illogically intolerant of new dramatic blood on the grounds that 'Political and social propaganda in the theatre as a general rule is a cracking bore', he could, more engagingly, dismiss what he saw as the dull tedium of much contemporary work with that special wit that seemed to gain an extra edge in a theatrical context. Unimpressed by both *mise en scène* and the display of naked flesh in David Storey's rugby play *The Changing Room* he dismissed the two: 'Fifteen acorns are hardly worth the price of admission.' The degree to which his life, spiritually and physically, revolved around the theatre can be seen from the frequency with which his celebrated *mots* had the theatrical background as a sounding-board. Leaving the theatre after seeing one actress play Queen Victoria, he told his companion, 'That is the first time Victoria made me feel that Albert married beneath his station.' His attitude to discipline amongst actors was captured in the rebuke prompted by the listless performances of two actors in one of his own shows, 'a triumph of never-mind over doesn't-matter'. There was that now legendary occasion when Dame Edith Evans as Judith Bliss, during rehearsals for the National Theatre revival of *Hay Fever*, would persist in upsetting the rhythm of Coward's line, 'On a clear day you can see Marlow' by wrongly interpolating 'very' before 'clear'; Coward's frustration as director/author eventually reached its own fever pitch: 'Edith, the line is "On a clear day you can see Marlow"'! On a *very* clear day, you can see Marlowe *and* Beaumont *and* Fletcher!'

His repartee, brazen in its verbal one-upmanship, stoical in its repression of true feeling, has singled out Coward as the brahmin of 'cool'. The image was, however, only one side of a coin which glowed obversely with the sheer white-heat of a fanatical creative energy, resulting in an output of over three hundred songs, fifty plays, around twelve revues, one novel, one volume of verse, two volumes of autobiography, and five books of short stories as only part of a lifetime's achievement. His cool never stood in the way of his dedication and professionalism; where it may have appeared otherwise it was only to reveal a pragmatism fully consistent with a man who would be sitting erect at his typewriter by seven o'clock each morning. And so when a young actor asked his advice regarding the precise motivation behind his rôle in *Nude with Violin*, Coward retorted: 'My dear boy, forget about the motivation. Just say the lines and don't trip over the furniture.' He was as grittily down-to-earth when it came to money matters. With his reputation as a playwright secure, he was bewildered by the magpie tendencies of critics and academics forever searching his work for the chance phrase which they could use as the coathanger for their quite irrelevant theories and fantasies. He recognised the difference between the critical mind and the creative, but it puzzled him: 'It seems to me that a professional writer should be animated by no other motive than the desire to write, and, by doing so, to earn his living.' When in 1921 the editor of *Metropolitan* offered him the sum of 500 dollars if he would turn an early play, *I'll Leave It to You*, into a short story, Coward replied, 'For 500 dollars I would gladly consider turning *War and Peace* into a music hall sketch.'

He was never that desperate. What he did succeed in doing, however, and it bears an eerie parallel, was to play the most influential rôle in turning the hectic, disenchanted mood of the 'twenties—with their crass unemployment, acute housing shortage, uneasy prominence of 'surplus' women—into a wild escapist dream, in which a heady, if often vicarious, mixture of jazz and jive, absinth and animal exuberance made living for the present a mass preoccupation, and superficially endowed the most mundane aspects of life with their own 'mad jazz pattern' or 'slow blues tempo'—for those who wanted either.

His influence, however, as the first of the Bright Young Things was partly accidental. John Osborne put his finger on the pulse of Coward's true status when he wrote that 'Noël Coward, like Miss Dietrich, is his own invention and contribution to this century'. And yet, not entirely 'his own'. Coward was in fact one of the earliest examples of the image, as presented by the media, supplanting the reality. The ambitious Coward knew better than to argue with Fleet Street. As long as the press, their imagination fired by his portrayal of Nicky Lancaster in *The Vortex*, wanted to project him as a casually cynical dilettante, the occasional profligate redeemed by his own talent, Coward was more than happy to comply. He even went out of his way to compound the illusion, flaunting his personality with flair, allowing himself to be photographed taking breakfast in silken pyjamas on a sensuously upholstered bed wearing the cryptic squinting grin—partly the result of blinking at the flashlights—of what he described somewhat regretfully later in his career as 'an advanced Chinese decadent in the last phases of dope'. The invention, of course, gained in maturity acquiring a layer of respectability, a core of indestructibility to the point where a stage direction in Cole Porter's 1935 *Jubilee* could read: 'If no one had ever seen Noël Coward, Eric Dare is exactly what you would expect Noël Coward to look like.'

In the 'fifties and early 'sixties he would turn down three offers to play respectively the part of Professor Higgins in a musical based on Shaw's *Pygmalion*, that of an English officer in a film to be called *The Bridge on the River Kwai*, and the rôle of Humbert Humbert in the screen version of Nabokov's *Lolita*. Subsequently, Rex Harrison, Alec Guinness, and James Mason would themselves become inseparable from the three rôles, rôles which added flesh to the reputations of three highly celebrated performers. With Coward, however, such identification would have intruded upon his own special legend, and perhaps eroded that special magic Kenneth Tynan implied when he said that 'even the youngest of us will know in fifty years' time what we mean by "a very Noël Coward sort of person".'

Maturity both refined and defined his style, a blend of laconic wit, casual charm and elegant ostentation, epitomised visually by the photograph of his tuxedoed figure fastidiously sipping tea in the desert, his own mad dog in the midday Las Vegas sun. For something as unstylish as an advertisement for a new Gillette razor blade he was in 1966 paid thousands for an inventory of those things in which he could still discern 'style'. It read as follows:

    1 A candy-striped jeep
    2 Jane Austen
    3 Cassius Clay
    4 *The Times* before it changed
    5 Danny La Rue
    6 Charleston, South Carolina
    7 'Monsieur' de Givenchy
    8 A zebra (but *not* a zebra crossing)
    9 Evading boredom
  10 Gertrude Lawrence
  11 The Paris Opera House
  12 White
  13 A seagull
  14 A Brixham trawler
  15 Margot Fonteyn
  16 Any Cole Porter song
  17 English pageantry
  18 Marlene's voice
  19 Lingfield has a tiny bit

The inclusion of a Cole Porter song was fortuitious, underlining the approximation of the list itself to an anglicised code for fuller appreciation of 'You're the Top'. Superficially, the most puzzling omission from Porter's own inventory of sixty-three lyric-inspiring delights is Coward himself. But if there

67   was no place for him alongside 'Whistler's mama' and 'Garbo's sal'ry', not even Porter could dispute the massive influence of Coward's style on a whole generation for at least ten years before 'You're the Top' was first performed in 1934.

Coward, who conveniently came of age in the last month of 1920, had far more than a knack for echoing the mores of his generation; rather, as with the Beatles forty years later, he was the prime force in actually founding the identity of his era. His own word from 'The Stately Homes of England' is appropriate: 'r-r-r-rip-representative', with its connotation of drive and initiative. Halfway through the decade he had four shows playing the West End simultaneously: *The Vortex, Hay Fever, Fallen Angels*, and the revue *On with the Dance*. Unknown, or at least infra-dig, was the party where if he was not in attendance, his spirit—beneath archways of cigarette holders, a-swim in a sea of champagne—was not at least felt. He set the then shocking trend of using 'darling' as a common greeting, regardless of whether he was in love with the person or not. He could say in defence of Lady Sibyl Colefax, society hostess of more than usual extravagance, 'I think it's quite marvellous that Sibyl fills her house with artists rather than stuffing it with dull dukes and duchesses', glossing over the fact that all the dukes and duchesses now descended upon his own dressing room. Fêted by the Prince of Wales and Virginia Woolf, Coward bridged the gap between show business and the social aristocracy. He epitomised the social humming-bird of the time, flitting with winsome grace from country-house weekend to Fifty-Fifty Club to the cocktail party attended by those conjured up by Dorothy Parker in her definition of 'sophisticate': 'one who dwells in a tower made of a DuPont substitute for ivory and holds a glass of flat champagne in one hand and an album of dirty postcards in the other.'

As the 'twenties turned into the 'thirties, so social conscience sharpened, a sense of futility and discontent drove nearer home, but not before, in *Private Lives* in 1930, Coward had set down a blueprint for an aristocracy which was pleasure-hungry, bored, even lost:

> *Elyot:* . . . Let's be superficial and pity the poor Philosophers. Let's blow trumpets and speakers, and enjoy the party as much as we can, like very small, quite idiotic schoolchildren. Let's savour the delight of the moment. Come and kiss me, darling, before your body rots, and worms pop in and out of your eye sockets.

However much Coward delighted in the inherent snobbery of his social whirl, he was not above the boredom it would inevitably bring. His own involvement was redeemed by such irony as manifest in the above. Fifty years later he would parody the whole scene in the song 'I've Been to a Marvellous Party' from the revue *Set to Music*, but the evidence suggests he had always been torn between the face-value gaiety and a more cynical view. In the words he gave the character of Leo, in his success of the early 'thirties, *Design For Living* 'It's inevitable that the more successful I become, the more people will run after me. I don't believe in friendship, and I don't take them seriously, but I enjoy them . . . They'll drop me, all right, when they're tired of me; but maybe I shall get tired first.' Here is an attitude more consistent with the incongruously lower-middle-class suburban background which encased Noël's roots. It is in the milieu of genteel poverty rife in the Teddington of his birth (on 16 December 1899), that one sees the source of that tenderness, that concern for the underdog which is as essentially Coward, and as integral a part of his dramatic achievement, as his more publicised aura of sophistication.

One further aspect of his relationship with his age is his romantic attitude to traditional English values. If the social helter-skelter of the fast set provided one outlet for his innate theatricality, the Empire with its grandeur and tradition provided another. Here again he was true to the class into which he was born. It is typical that those songs with an imperial theme— 'Mad Dogs and Englishmen', 'I Wonder What Happened to Him', even the notorious 'Don't Let's Be Beastly to the Germans'—should all appear to ridicule the Imperial cause. In fact, his more studied humour, like his glancing wit, was its own stiff-upper-lip in dealing with emotion. Only late in life did he make his true feelings known. When a colleague detected the strands of Imperial influence running through the retrospective revue *Cowardy Custard*, he acknowledged the observation as music to his ears, 'an accurate perception of (I won't say my philosophy) my outlook on life'. It is good for once to have the words from Coward's own lips, if one hadn't already guessed from Frank Gibbon's closing speech in *This Happy Breed*. It is hard not to believe that in his innermost soul the people of that play meant more to him than the dazzling puppets—albeit puppets capable of a genuine emotion—of *Private Lives*.

Just such ordinary people never lost a sneaking affection for the unique, mother-of-pearl aspect of his personality which in all its superficial brilliance was essentially alien to their humdrum lives. The public was never deterred by the neon-lit vanity of his public image. Here was a charade he would never stop playing, while they, at a safe, media-provided distance could sit back and lap up the legend-making process like a cat its cream. By the time of his initial success he could arrive late and tuxedo-less at a fashionable literary party in Bloomsbury, summon silence, and declare 'Now, I don't want anyone to feel embarrassed'. On the occasion of the Redgraves' silver wedding he sent as a present a silver-framed photograph of himself, looking at a bust of himself, signed simply 'Noël Coward'. Earlier, when a juvenile rehearsing *Hannele* for Basil Dean, Coward, standing in the spotlight of his own precocity, had in retaliation chastised his fraught director: 'If you ever speak to me again in that tone of voice, I shall go straight to my mother.' It was Mrs Violet Agnes Coward who had first drummed into her son the conviction that he was a genius and to whom he would remain bound through life with 'an umbilical cord of piano wire'. At his first press conference, to mark the 1920 opening of his play *I'll Leave It to You*, angry at being introduced as the nephew of the famous organist, James Coward, he forgot her for the one time in his life: 'I am related to no one except myself.'

On his own admission, the best parts in his plays were always those which he wrote for himself, while the description in the script of his cameo rôle in the film *Around the World in Eighty Days* as 'superior and ineffably smug' amused him as 'clearly type-casting'. His self-importance, however, was always saved from teetering over into the distasteful by an inverted sense of understatement. So he could write in his first volume of autobiography: 'My sense of my own importance to the world is relatively small. On the other hand, my sense of my own importance to myself is tremendous.' And again: 'I am bursting with pride, which is why I have absolutely no vanity.' The ambivalence was subtly caught in the presentation of *Cowardy Custard*. While those low-key lines from *Bitter-Sweet*:

> *But I believe*
> *That since my life began,*
> *The most I've had is just*
> *A talent to amuse . . .*

were used to bookend the revue at opening and close, the stage itself was dominated by a larger-than-life photograph of Coward sitting complacently in front of—in fact, to all appearances, actually sprouting—the victorious span of carved feathers with their Winged Victory overtones that hung above the mantelpiece of his drawing room at Les Avants in Switzerland.

No one insisted more vociferously upon his own modesty, his lack of conceit as distinct from pride; no one talked or thought more constantly about himself and his achievements. And yet his confidence in his own ability couldn't hide the fact that his career was not entirely the smooth, silver-spoon-fed ride it tends now to seem. He had to become used to being taken down a peg in full public view. Failure and disappointment appeared in the guise of first night booing and nervous collapse from sheer occupational fatigue, financial disaster and exile voluntarily enforced to recoup security for later years. But, true to form, in the field of comeuppance it took a king to humiliate Coward fully. Having gone out of his way to find tickets for *Tonight at 8.30* for Edward VIII and his party at impossibly short notice, Coward was perturbed when backstage afterwards the attentions of the royal party were all lavished on Gertrude Lawrence, to the total exclusion of the author-producer-co-star of the show. Aggravated, Coward sent word to the Palace: 'He may be the King of England, but I'm the King of the Theatre and I expect him to respect me as such.' Back came the reply: 'Tell Noël Coward to go and fuck himself.'

A soupçon of vulnerability was a considerable asset in sustaining the tolerance and warmth of the public, but nothing compared in this regard to his sense of humour. By his own valuation, his wit and Novello's profile were the first and second wonders of the modern world. His panache for making the surprising sound inevitable and the inevitable sound surprising was valid compensation to all etymologists who complained that his wanton use of 'dear' and 'darling' had debased the language of affection. His impertinent but bitter-sweet retorts, the fruit of a needle-sharp perception and intellectual zest, set up a dragnet from which no one was safe, whether on grounds of sex, status, or nationality. There were three groups, however, which came more than most to bear the brunt of his whiplash tongue: reporters, actresses and critics. When asked in Southern Rhodesia by a persistent girl reporter if he had anything to say to the *Star*, he glared: 'Twinkle.' A similarly vacuous request to 'say something funny' in Australia yielded the equally take-it-or-leave-it 'Kangaroo!' The less than word perfect Claudette Colbert, being

rehearsed by Coward for an American television version of *Blithe Spirit* must have for ever regretted her apology: 'I'm sorry; I knew these lines backwards last night.' The reply sprung to Coward's lips before he could even have thought of it: 'And that's just the way you're saying them this morning.' Sometimes the revenge had longer to ferment. On the London opening of S. N. Behrman's *The Second Man* he was visited backstage by the flamboyant critic Hannen Swaffer, who had earlier figured prominently in the vanguard of attack against his first success *The Vortex*, describing it as 'not the sort of play you would like intelligent Indians to see'. By way of making back-handed amends, he now complimented Coward on his performance in someone else's play: 'I have always said that you act much better than you write.' Coward came back with all his rattlesnake charm: 'How odd; I'm always saying the same thing about you.'

And then there was his sheer mischievousness, devoid of any malice whatsoever: creeping up behind the actor Keir Dullea to whisper: 'Keir Dullea, Gone Tomorrow'; poking gentle fun by letter at the diffident shyness of 338171 Aircraftsman Shaw, alias T. E. Lawrence of Arabia: 'Dear 338171, or may I call you 338?'; and shrugging off an enquiry as to the identity of the minuscule attaché carriaged next to the beaming Queen Salote of Tonga in the Coronation Procession of 1953: 'Her lunch.' One is not far removed here from the world of his plays and observations like 'Very flat, Norfolk'; the similarity in taste between bad sherry and brown paper; and 'You should wash, darling—really it's so bad for your skin to leave things lying about on it.'

More than with any dramatist since Wilde, his stage dialogue was coloured by his own personal idiom. Significantly this extended beyond the two-dimensional impact of the given word. A character in his *Shadow Play* touched the nerve: 'Small talk, a lot of small talk, with other thoughts going on behind.' The page cannot convey the nuances that added substance to meaning, but it instantly telegraphs how he shunned the superfluous with a weight-watcher's diligence. Only so elliptical a style could convey with full impact the knack he had, in life as in his plays, of being able to say one thing while meaning its polar opposite. This is epitomised by the hotel balcony scene between the divorced couple in *Private Lives*, a subtle balance between personal emotional trait and skilful dramatic technique. But, however much of the quintessential Coward permeated his dramatic work, it was not until he ventured into cabaret that audiences were able to appreciate The Master in all his glory.

As we have seen, in the world of the solo entertainer no less than the assertion of pure self holds sway; when Coward entertained, it wore its crown. He was no stranger to the idea of theatrical illegitimacy and in middle age took to the idea of minstrel to café society by something close to royal appointment like Mae West took to sex. As a child he had contemplated treading the boards in a variety act of impersonations of famous stars accompanied by his Aunt Kitty at the piano. It came to nothing. Although S. N. Behrman would later rhapsodise over his party-piece impersonation of Florrie Forde, most corpulent of chorus singers, Coward had to admit of his earlier mimicry: 'It was quite impossible for the acutest perception to distinguish one imitation from the others.' At the same time another aunt, Hilda, enjoyed an exotic reputation as 'The Twickenham Nightingale': 'she sang very high', but not with the verve of great music hall names like Nellie Wallace and George Robey. Glimpses of stars such as these would leave a more than flickering impression upon the eleven-year-old Coward as he toured the Coliseum and other halls under Sir Charles Hawtrey's banner in a sketch entitled 'A Little Fowl Play'. In *Tonight at 8.30*, more than twenty years later, he would portray with vivid affection the seedy, frayed milieu of talent on the decline amid broken-down suburban halls. As a solo entertainer in his own right, however, Coward would have far more illustrious ideas regarding where to play. But first would come the grind.

It is doubtful whether anyone seriously intimated such a diversion in his successful course as actor, playwright and composer until, at the beginning of the Second World War, Winston Churchill offered Coward the advice: 'Go and sing to them when the guns are firing—that's your job.' At first Coward would ignore Churchill's advice, thinking that his talents as a writer had more to offer the war effort in the field of propaganda. To his distress, however, it would be increasingly difficult for the public to reconcile his popular image with a serious position in the Information Service and not too many months elapsed before, true to Churchill's instinct, he found himself in Australia giving the first of an endless campaign of troop concerts that would keep him occupied, together with excursions back into theatre and films, for four years until the end of the war. Amid the uncomfortable setting of mudcaked duck-boards and sombre war hospitals, masquerading as a desert rat with a Bond Street finish, he would possibly for the first time sense his ability to capture and hold single-handed the attention of an audience for an hour at a time, and an audience for the most part far removed from his devoted and conventional West End crowd. After the war Coward would sound out on these audiences: 'In the danger zones they can be wonderful, but transit camps are sheer hell. Either they're waiting to go on leave, in which case they're impatient, or they've just been, in which case they're depressed.' What he could not then have realised was the extent to which that experience would stand him in good stead in the mid-'fifties when enticed by a weekly salary of 40,000 dollars he again deserted the cosy familiarity of London café society, this time for the impersonal brashness of the Desert Inn, Las Vegas. He later described this new audience as 'Nescafé society', but added, 'for that kind of money they can throw bottles at me if they so choose'. *Variety* headlined his success with its own staccato enthusiasm: 'Las Vegas, Flipping, Shouts "More!" As Noël Coward Wows 'Em in Café Turn.'

This second victory of personality over environment marked the summit of his career as a solo entertainer, but did nothing to disprove the fact that his forte as minstrel still remained in the more intimate, nonchalant splendour of London's Café de Paris. He first suede-footed his way down that legendary staircase to the Cinderella strains of 'I'll See You Again' on 29 October 1951, and within minutes had succeeded in asserting outside of a dramatic plot that special quality Dame Sybil Thorndike called to mind in a television tribute on his death: '. . . in spite of his sympathy and his lovingness and his adorableness you felt that slight jab that Noël always had, and which was so exciting always.'

In the spotlight, amused and amusing, his enigmatic personality conveyed at once the archbishop's benign correctness, the general's agitated command, the whimsicality of a Pantaloon, and, with deference to his self-avowed Oriental looks, the inscrutability of a Chinese illusionist. But there was no mystery about the offhand precision with which he dashed off vocally a selection of his songs, songs which his audience had sung in its youth and were later recalled by John Whiting as those 'we sang to our girls driving back in the red M.G. from the Thames pub on a summer night in 1936'. Of his cabaret performance Tynan wrote: 'If it is possible to romp fastidiously, that is what Coward does.' The omnipresent red carnation, the superior, quizzical grin on the weathered turtle face, the modulated interplay of the semaphoric hands, the abrupt beckoning of left index finger should attention chance to stray, all played their part in an exhibition that summed up a lifetime's philosophy of the theatre. After the 'nth' rehearsal for his 1955 television special 'Together with Music' he wasn't satisfied: 'We're still doing it on our nerves—I want it done on technique.' To imply that Coward had no qualms before any performance would be inaccurate and unfair, but the memory of his solo act still stands as a monument not only to his own technique, but to the total concept of the word itself in theatrical terms.

In spite of the frequent jibes about his singing voice—a vocal confidence trick, critics teased, perpetrated by sheer strength of personality—it is an inescapable fact that, alongside the Beatles and, one has it on authority, Cole Porter, no one sang his own songs more effectively than their creator. If his brittle, precise delivery suited well the irony of his speech, set to music and wedded to near-perfect breath control it conveyed without strain either on his part or his audience's what remains the most important aspect of his work to any lyricist, namely its meaning. One fragment of Coward folklore says that if you play any of his recordings at half or double speed, you will not miss one single syllable. It is ninety per cent true. His own assessment of his singing voice varied from 'a bullmoose moo' to 'considerable range, no tone, little music, but lots of meaning'. Most critics favoured a dove terminology, but he did more than just coo. It is tempting to suggest that his voice played its own part in influencing the songs that he wrote, but then to consider the range of his creativity as a songwriter is to think again. And yet the voice was as admirably suited to the cautionary deftness of 'Poor Little Rich Girl' or the tongue-in-cheek drollery of 'Mad Dogs and Englishmen', as to the stouthearted grace of 'London Pride', the haunting nostalgia of 'Some Day I'll Find You', or the casual *ennui* of 'World Weary'.

To survey his full achievement as a songwriter is to see his muse weave its own jazz pattern between satire and sentiment. While his tender handling of the latter quality may not quite reach the inspired humanity of a Lorenz Hart, his exposure of the foibles of that cross-section of our 'sceptred race', the decent British folk scattered around the globe who can regard P. G. Wodehouse as some sort of patron saint, places him firmly beneath the impressive mantle of W. S. Gilbert. Yet his rhyming intricacy and rhythmic inventiveness far transcend those of Gilbert, while, as Beverley Nichols has indicated, for all Coward's allegiance to Sullivan, particularly in his concerted numbers, at the end of the day there is only one tune that does not carry The Master's own melodic 'signature'—namely, 'Dance, Little Lady' —and even that is debatable.

The obsession to make rhymes ensnared Coward at an early age, the jig-saw challenge to an imagination first fired by the 'Pat-a-Cake, Pat-a-Cake' of the Baker's Man of the nursery rhyme. In spite of his father's occupation as piano-tuner, the hold of music was less secure, although a natural ear meant that from the age of seven the young Noël could play blindfold any tune he had already heard on the piano. Until the end of his life, however, he found difficulty in reading music and an even greater difficulty in writing it down, the not surprising aftermath of having had—apart from maternal promptings—only two music lessons in his seventy-three years. Having enrolled with Fred Astaire at the Guildhall School of Music, he was told adamantly by his instructor that he could not use consecutive fifths. Coward retaliated that what was good enough for Debussy and Ravel was good enough for him and promptly left, depriving himself, as he had to admit, of much valuable knowledge that he never deeply regretted for a moment. His decision then 'to try to become a good writer and actor, and to compose tune and harmonies whenever the urge to do so became too powerful to resist' didn't prevent him becoming the one Englishman of his generation to stand on his own in the American-dominated coterie of Gershwin and Rodgers, Porter and Kern. And if on his own admission he could not appreciate 'good' music and Mozart, no one did more to secure its proper status for *good light* music.

The songs summoned so many memories for so many people, and not least for their creator. 'Mad Dogs and Englishmen' was composed without pencil, paper, or keyboard, during a week's drive from Hanoi to Saigon in February 1930, and was first performed, unaccompanied, to Noël's travelling companion, Jeffery Amherst, on the verandah of a small jungle guest house: 'Not only Jeffery, but the lizards and the tree frogs gave every vocal indication of enthusiasm.' The inspiration for 'Parisian Pierrot' came from his sympathy and fascination for the limp rag doll used as a silent partner in the provocative act of a slatternly chanteuse in a tawdry Berlin nightclub in 1922. 'A Room with a View' might recall its own gestation during a period of convalescence from an undiagnosed fever on a Honolulu beach in 1927 or more probably the occasion the Prince of Wales requested the orchestra to play it nine times at the Ascot Cabaret Ball the following year. 'I'll See You Again' was written in a taxi during a traffic jam and 'Dear Little Café', from *Bitter-Sweet*, while The Master was recovering from 'a malady of an intimate nature'. 'Marvellous Party' was a souvenir of the occasion when he took just too literally Elsa Maxwell's invitation to come 'just as you are' to an informal Riviera beach party in 1938. This produced the reverse of the more likely situation: Noël still stood out from the crowd, but this time all the others wore evening dress—'I couldn't have liked it more'.

The sources of his inspiration spanned the globe and in so doing created by courtesy of that razor-sharp comic imagination a universal mythology that embraced Señorita Nina, from Argentina, compulsive wallflower in her country's cause; tough Burmese bandits and small Malay rabbits; the re-lapsed missionary, Uncle Harry; that makeshift Debrett clinging to their stately homes; and the matronly Mrs Wentworth-Brewster to whom life called at the eleventh hour in that notorious bar on the Piccola Marina.

One searches in vain for those songs which cried out to be written as a result of the seemingly endless chain of exotic escapades that befell Coward's own travels, like the occasion when, Jacques Tati-fashion, he caught his heel on a tiger's head and fell flat on his back in departing from a private audience with the King of Siam; or even the song in celebration of the root cause of his clipped speech, developed for the benefit of a mother who, early in life, partially lost her hearing on falling out of a porthole in Madeira. But if these songs never reached the keyboard, there were those by others which were an integral feature of his live appearances and acquired his own special identity in the process. The still-water lyrics of 'Loch Lomond' were ruffled by the fillip of his own upbeat treatment; 'The Surrey with the Fringe on Top' was a title volunteered by Coward in another context when the Actor's Orphanage of which he was President was offered the services of a Surrey Cricket Eleven for its Annual Garden Party, together with the assurance that it would be an All-Star Side, no humdrum county turn-out. And there was the sly, apple-sauce parody of Cole Porter's 'Let's Do It', transforming what now appears as one of the most sophisticated of all pleas for conservation into the successful memoirs of the most cosmopolitan of voyeurs, vicariously providing his audience with its own key into the intimate lives of everyone from the Aly Khan and Marlene, via Davy Crockett 'in that dreadful cap', to Ernest Hemingway who 'could *just* do it'.

Porter was the only contemporary who came near to matching Coward's achievement as composer and lyricist, and his American counterpart in disguising the hard sweat of the creative process beneath a cool, casual veneer. But Porter had no claim to the additional talents of actor, author, dramatist, entertainer. Friends as they were in their socialite way, 'Let's Do It'—Coward's way—was a subtle way for 'Heureux Noël' to gain a sweet revenge upon the 'Young King Cole' who in 1938 had been requested by George S. Kaufman and Moss Hart to provide a 'Noël Coward-type song' for the caricature of Coward, Beverly Carlton, in their impending Broadway hit, *The Man Who Came to Dinner*. The song's title queried on The Master's behalf, 'What am I to do?'. And there was *still* that omission from 'You're the Top'.

The mock-romanticism of Porter's own parody probably cut closer to Coward's emotional quick than any attempt to recreate the droll cynicism of his comedy numbers. He was above all a romantic, a sentimentalist, and just before his death he would look back over a long career and select *Bitter-Sweet*, the work that most characterised this vein, as his all-time favourite. He had earlier written that, aside from the fact that the show combined his talents as he saw them in almost perfect balance, the 'particular mood of semi-nostalgic sentiment, when well done, invariably affects me very pleasantly. In *Bitter-Sweet* it did seem to be well done, and I felt accordingly very happy about it.' The point is that Coward's reaction to his own favourite work parallels his public's reaction to his total achievement. All his talents are inescapably there, though now in a combination that only chance could have ordained; but, even more so, it is a mood of nostalgic sentiment that now, after his death, spells Coward to so many people. No longer the specific feel of a single play vividly coloured by its flashback to the Vienna of the 1880s, this is an escapist twentieth-century mood peopled by svelte women with pastel complexions and foxglove fashions, their tuxedoed cavaliers, and a paper moon.

77

His legend now is answerable only in part to his creative and performing skills. His sheer existence had a flair from the moment early on when he declared his determination 'to travel through life first class'. His smooth way of sipping a cigarette was the tell-tale sign of an unashamed hedonist to whom exercise was anathema: he joked of 'a lot of aspirin and *marrons glacés*' as a secret substitute. Behind the public façade, however, resided an indefatigable energy, but an energy that never defeated its own purpose by preventing the talent it fired from taking stock of itself at the most crucial milestones of its career. There was the streak of cruelty that could surface during nerve-frayed rehearsals and found legendary victims in Dame Edith Evans, Dame Gladys Cooper and Dame Cicely Courtneidge, a cruelty which Hermione Gingold insists found its own sting when Coward, maybe mindful of her wayward performance in *Fallen Angels*, secreted a wasp in the bouquet he sent her on *her* opening night at the Café de Paris. This facet belied the simple description Sir Harold Nicolson wrote in his diary after their first brief meeting: 'A nice, nice man.' Nor was Nicolson contradicted by the unswerving sense of duty to family and friends, country and ideals that prompted Dame Rebecca West to remark on his death: 'I never have been told that he failed to honour an obligation, and if I were I should not believe it'; nor by the charity that was often its only outward sign; not least by his sheer self-respect. And there was courage, inherent in the dignity and reticence with which he conducted his emotional life, a courage tested most nobly by his touching portrayal, at the age of sixty-six, of the ageing author, Hugo Latymer, in *A Song at Twilight*, from *Suite in Three Keys*, his final work for the stage. Latymer had gone to great lengths to disguise his own homosexuality at the cost of severely undermining his talent. Coward's only camouflage was that shrug of polite 'grin and rise above it' indifference with which he was known to suppress emotion of any kind. Tynan has suggested that Coward's whole knack of cool understatement may have had emotional roots in this aspect of his private life. Certainly, in so far as the play itself is an understatement, conveying only indirectly the emotional torture of the conflict between natural instinct and 'the game according to the rules', Coward could be said to have remained cool—and yet still courageous—to the end.

Three years before his death from a heart attack in March 1973, on the occasion of his seventieth birthday, Coward enjoyed the greatest acclaim ever paid a theatrical figure in his lifetime. The culmination of what he described as his 'Holy Week' of Savoy banquet, television tributes, film festival, midnight gala, had been the most overdue knighthood of an honours system as inconsistent as it is archaic. However, it is not merely because the due accolades came in time for him to enjoy them that one feels he would have been little worried by the prospect of death. A well-known Coward story had conjectured his arrival at the Pearly Gates. He is granted entry. The heavens are hushed so as not to miss his first celestial words. He scans the massed rows of angels and archangels and then with tongue-tip precision addresses his query, 'Which . . . which . . . is God?' Not that the most backward angel could have failed to recognise The Master, resplendent with red carnation. One recalls the line he spoke in the film *The Scoundrel*: 'That's the proper place for life—in one's buttonhole.' He must always have known that life, like the flower, was as disposable as it could be fragrant.

Jack Benny

Love in bloom

No COMEDIAN HAS ever achieved a greater effect with such a seeming minimum of effort. On stage Jack Benny just stood there, a paragon of understatement and apparent inaction, that incredulous panoramic stare meeting his audience's gaze with the eye-probing decisiveness of an oculist's torch. His friend and professional rival, the brilliant raconteur George Burns, once said that Benny stared at an audience for so long that dread set in to the point where they were afraid not to laugh. But there was more to Benny than an instinctive understanding of the psychology of inertia. He would know exactly what Virginia Woolf meant when she said, 'One of the virtues of having a system of values is that you know exactly what to laugh at'. Few comedians more assiduously educated the public to their behaviour pattern. Over the years he shrewdly compiled a personal case history of traits and trademarks, so ingeniously inter-knit that a glance, a shrug, a 'H'mm', a 'But—' would act as a signpost to the total identity, leaving the audience in no doubt of what was happening behind, under, and around what he was saying or hinting.

Although it might seem that Benny had displayed uncharacteristic vigour and diligence in amassing his personal montage of conceit, thrift and self-disparagement, all sustained to an almost pathological degree, he always insisted that each individual trait was in embryo the product of chance, rather than of skilled forethought. Ironically, however, his pernickety pretence at miserliness, first suggested by the disproportionate success of a couple of stingy jokes on a passing radio show, was totally consistent with his economy of movement and style as intimated in the opening line of a monologue he delivered at the Los Angeles Orpheum Theatre as early as 1927: 'Ladies and gentlemen, on my way to the theatre this evening— nothing happened', and then, after a monumental pause, 'Goodnight'. He soon discovered that stinginess was the easiest facet of human nature with which to get laughs, and taking over where Harry Lauder left off, succeeded single-handed in appropriating a comic tradition hitherto associated with a complete nation. Significantly, Lauder was the most successful of all performers from the authentic British music hall to tour the United States, maybe because audiences found that the archetypal stingy Scot which he came to represent had something relevant to say about the dream of success that was as adrenalin to the emergent business classes of the New World. But if Scottish tradition had been the first to articulate within a vaudeville context the realisation of the masses that such a dream could be eroded by seedy, anxious greed, both material and spiritual, it was not until the emergence of Benny, a product of lower middle-class America himself, that full identification was possible. And with the advent of radio, the same comment was conveyed to the widest possible audience.

There was, however, a simpler level on which Benny's penny-pinching could be appreciated, that of the exaggerated truth of the best caricature. In the film *The Fifth Chair*, it was not enough for Benny to sell a fan his necktie; he also had to barter the paper for it to be wrapped up in as well. And because of his immaculate pre-conditioning of the audience, the same motif could be made to rebound upon him when thoughts of actual finance were far from his mind. When Benny ran out of sugar in a radio show it was funnier than if any other comedian had done so. The shortage, however, was only by way of setting the scene. Taking a cup he departed for the house of his neighbour, Ronald Colman. The crunch of footsteps grazed the air as he walked along the sidewalk. Then a pause, the metallic clink of coin against porcelain, and Benny's mousy, surprised expression of gratitude, 'Thank you'. The same sidewalk witnessed arguably the most extreme of these exercises in thrift. Walking back home with the Oscar Ronald Colman had lent him to show his valet, Rochester, Benny was halted by a hold-up man: 'Don't make a move. Your money or your life?' For fourteen seconds there endured what with another comedian would have been a yawn-inducing hush, before Benny snapped his reply, 'I'm thinking it over'. But in this instance the laugh not only came as soon as the bandit delivered his demand, but was sustained with increasing momentum for the entire pause. This sequence has been quoted more than any other in description of Benny's work. Surprisingly, however, everyone omits one crucial detail, namely that on this occasion Benny went on to top even himself. It transpired that the bandit was in desperate need of money for his wife and children, at which Benny surpassed his legendary best: 'Well, you didn't have to pull a gun on me. If you wanted money, all you had to do was ask!' The lingering drawl on that final syllable pointed perfectly the ingrained consternation with which Benny weathered the insults of a world readier to trample him than all others.

Hand in glove with his miserliness was the tenacity with which he clung to his youth, so much so that he could obtain equal comic mileage from reversing the legend. The aptness of the number 'thirty-nine' proved itself when Benny, having already leapfrogged his way in slow motion through extended spells at thirty-six, thirty-seven and thirty-eight years, announced his fortieth birthday. But forty failed to strike the same comic chord which its predecessor had done, fans rebelled, and in spite of a television special blatantly labelled 'Jack Benny Turns Forty' and an extensive article in *Collier's Magazine* on his self-willed change of life, Benny reverted to the age which trial and error had proved to be symbolically correct. As he later admitted, forty was not a funny number, but he could not explain why. By his last years he had reached the age when he could derive laughter from self-mockery of his actual advanced years. So in his stage act he reasoned that Sinatra was not the only star with his own rat pack: 'I have a gang too. Only in *my* gang we have Edward Everett Horton, Spring Byington, Walter

Brennan. We call our gang "Ovaltine a Go-Go". We sing and play Lawrence Welk records. Sometimes we get high and speed them up a little.' And yet the 'thirty-nine' joke, far from being undermined by this actual admission of years, co-existed successfully with it. The success of both jokes depended not only upon the audience knowing that he was older than thirty-nine, but upon the fact that he still looked far younger than his correct age, the looks of a man whose attitude to retirement was clear and precise: 'What would I do? I don't do it now. Why do it later?' On any other basis both jokes would not merely be unfunny, they would also be sad. As it was, they were neither.

That he lied so readily about his age was only one strand of a fabric of vanity and conceit that swathed the figure of this maverick manqué from head to toe, from fictional toupee to preening stance. Anything that threatened the sublimity of that stance was anathema to him. And so, the complete poseur, he constantly tried to behave above his age, looks, social position, not to mention talent. The contrast between the hauteur of his entrance as Hamlet in the play-within-a-play in the film *To Be Or Not To Be* and his need to be prompted on the opening line of the speech from which the film takes its name, only strengthened public opinion that no ham was ever so desperate, nor so intoxicated by the prospect of applause which would never come. These many layers to his characterisation were more than mere patches sewn onto a jester's motley; each informed the other to the point where jokes could be appreciated on several wave-lengths, among which miserliness was predominant. In this way the line which constituted his television début, 'I'd give a *million* dollars to know how I look', became more than a comment on vanity. Similarly, the relish with which he announced each foray into live performance towards the end of his life, 'It may mean nothing to *you* . . . but the Prudential is *thrilled*. I won't tell you just how much insurance I have . . . but when *I* go . . . *they* go', was more than a humorous gloss on age.

Benny was, in fact, born on St Valentine's Day, 1894, the son of Orthodox Jewish immigrants and dry-goods merchants, his real name Benjamin Kubelsky. His mother had insisted on moving temporarily to Chicago for his birth, so that he would later be able to claim what was, in her estimation, a more illustrious place of origin than that of Waukegan, Illinois, the family home where he subsequently grew up. When he was only six, his father stretched the domestic budget to buy a violin for a hundred dollars, whereupon the young Benny had to be disciplined into taking the lessons required to justify its cost. His parents' ambition that he should one day take his place among the élite of the concert world became hamstrung when nine years later he secured a job as fiddler at eight dollars a week in the pit of the local Barrison Theatre. The truancy occasioned by afternoon matinées led in turn to his expulsion from Waukegan High School, separation from his family, and at seventeen his partnership with Miss Cora Salisbury, the leader of the Barrison pit band, as a touring vaudeville act under the title, 'Salisbury and Benny—from Grand Opera to Ragtime', in which he provided a serious violin accompaniment to Miss Salisbury at the keys. Within two years he had formed his own combination with Chicago pianist Lyman Woods, 'Benny and Woods'. If, as he scraped his way from the 'Poet and Peasant' overture, through 'The Rosary' to 'Everybody's Doing It', he was still a long way from delivering a funny line on stage, humorous touches were gradually simmering to the surface, in the way, for example, his expression would light-heartedly register effort during the harder passages, his raised little finger nonchalance during the carefree ones.

He finally broke into comedy for its own sake in 1918 when, enlisting in the United States Navy, Benny found himself assigned to the Great Lakes Naval Training Station. Having declared his profession as 'musician', he was given band duties; unfortunately, in those robust surroundings his fiddle-playing was as welcome as a cat screeching. When a disillusioned Benny volunteered his talents at a sailors' concert, he found his playing jeered until, following the advice of fellow rating and later fellow actor, Pat O'Brien, he put down the violin and ad-libbed in desperation: 'I was having an argument with Pat O'Brien about the Irish navy this morning.' In the hubbub of the moment, he continued to ad-lib, interspersing his comments with snatches of playing, the first clear token of the comedy format on which he would in later years stamp his own distinctive hallmark, even though comedy band-leader Ben Bernie had been doing a similar routine for several years. When, later, the Great Lakes Revue was staged for Naval Relief, Benny, on the strength of his flat-as-a-pancake delivery, found himself playing the comedy lead of 'Izzy There, The Admiral's Disorderly'. And then, with hostilities over, he launched out as a solo performer on the vaudeville circuits with the tag 'Ben K. Benny: Fiddle Funology', all the while clinging to the violin, both for mascot security and, as experience would tell him, to make his jokes appear that much more impromptu. Audiences were kept poised on the brink of expectation that he was about to play, even though in fact he used it only at the close of his act to provide a jazzy exit.

Within two years, to avoid confusion with Bernie, he had changed his name yet again, at last to Jack Benny, sub-styled 'Aristocrat of Humour', thereby identifying himself with Paul Muni, born Muni Weisenfreund, who had also adopted his first name as his last. The touring mill imparted a polish to his style which led one critic on the *New York Times* to describe his act as 'the most civilised in Vaudeville', and that long before he scored as a headliner at New York's Palace Theatre in 1924. His appearance the following year in the Shubert revue, *The Great Temptations*, caused no less than Robert Benchley to remark, in his amazement that one so young could act so blasé, that he had never seen such *savoir faire* on a stage before. But while Benny's suave subtlety came like a whiff of oxygen to stages inured to more stereotyped fare, he had still to find the medium that would rocket him to the institutional status he would later sustain for more than forty years.

When he had made his first radio appearance on the Ed Sullivan interview programme with the now notorious opening gambit: 'Hello folks, this is Jack Benny. And there will now be a pause for all of you to say, "Who cares?",' he had no idea that within a few weeks he would have a regular show of his own, one which would in time surpass those of all his rivals in staying power, buoyant on the air waves for twenty-five years. For a generation of Americans, no performer would come to be more evocative of that embryonic period in mass entertainment redolent of musty bakelite, the greasy velour of well-worn armchairs, and listening intently. But Benny was

85

more than the right talent in the right medium at the right time: he soon grasped the full potentialities of that medium. No comedian would exploit the in-your-lap realism and intimate vicariousness that radio allowed more convincingly than Benny. Moreover, it did not require the spendthrift facet of his persona to realise that the so far conventional approach of funny man to microphone—the feeding of one incessant string of zany incident and joky vaudeville monologue into an insatiable atmospheric maw—would in time reduce good gags to gold dust.

With genuflection to the success of the *Amos 'n' Andy* soap opera series, and with the guidance of writer Harry Conn, introduced to Benny by George Burns, he plotted a formula which would revolutionise comedy broadcasting. Now the interaction of situation and a complete repertory of stock characters was paramount; jokes and pay-off lines were subsidiary and only valid in so far as they were relevant to the main theme pursued at a leisurely, conversational pace. As Fred Allen put it, tuning into the Benny programme was eventually like tuning into somebody else's home. He omitted that it often involved coming face to face with a blatant demonstration of infinite regress whereby all Benny's domestic activity seemed to revolve around the preparations for that week's programme, the programme the audience was supposedly listening to. The following exchange with Rochester was typical:

Rochester:	You didn't forget your broadcast, did you?
Benny (bitterly):	How could I forget? . . . the broadcast, the broadcast, always the broadcast. Year after year, every Monday I think of ideas—Tuesday I meet with my writers—Wednesday, Thursday and Friday we write—Saturday I rehearse. Then on Sunday I do my programme, and in one short half hour it's all over—all that work for just one half hour—And for *what*, I ask you? For *what*?
Rochester:	For a lousy million dollars.

It is a measure of the realism he created that the public never seemed bothered by the fact that according to strict logic it never heard in its entirety the total half-hour for which he was being paid such an exorbitant sum.

Like a good host, Benny had the grace coupled with shrewd comic instinct to know he could raise as much laughter by making himself the butt of ridicule, as distinct from the exasperating cavalcade of supporting characters which, meandering in and out of his house and office, provided a constantly shifting background against which to set his own personality. In that sense they were all extensions of that personality, defining it, enhancing it, interchangeable pieces of a jigsaw of an identity card. Not surprisingly, some of the names to those pieces recall themselves with a straight-edged clarity.

Mary Livingstone, real name Sadie Marks, had been inducted by Benny into first marriage and then show business from her position behind the hosiery counter in a Los Angeles department store in the mid-'twenties. Having played a Gracie Allen rôle in some of his stage sketches, she transferred to the air when Benny, let down by a contract player, urgently needed an actress to read a letter addressed by a fan, a Mrs Livingstone of Plainfield, New Jersey, to her daughter Mary. Her nervous giggle not only got her through the ordeal, but imparted a trademark to the characterisation of fizzy nervous assurance which she sustained for twenty-five years before reverting to being Mrs Jack Benny and cutting herself off from the performing side of show business completely.

The elephantine announcer, Don Wilson, joined the Benny caravan two years after Livingstone in 1934, the purveyor of a Perry Mason-style bonhomie as expansive as his girth. There was Phil Harris, Jack's brash, bubbling, broad-shouldered band-leader-about-town, a womanising, beer-drinking electric eel of vitality, summed up once by the sedate Benny himself as 'the kind of guy Frank Sinatra thinks Errol Flynn is'. Frank Nelson played one omnipresent clerk prone to giving swivel-necked emphasis to his distinctive combination of sneer and smile as he bedevilled Benny across desks of bureaucracy the breadth of the country. Their ubiquitous feud attained mythical status the week Nelson, as a ticket clerk, aggravating Benny's frustration in his attempt to get his own ticket validated, gave precedence to a stranger who wanted to know if the train on platform seven was the one going to Pasadena, Anaheim, and Glocca Morra. Nelson hissed obligingly in the affirmative, whereupon the stranger launched into a spoken rendition of the complete lyric of 'How Are Things in Glocca Morra?', the clerk became a talking gazetteer of the Emerald Isle and the comedian burned and burned and burned.

Mel Blanc, like Nelson a man of many voices, became immortalised as Jack's constantly protesting French violin teacher, and as a Mexican street-vendor with whom conversation seldom reached a level more meaningful than his enquiry in a needling accent as to whether Benny wanted his hot dog 'with the peekle in the meedle and the mustard on top' or 'the mustard in the meedle and the peekle on top'. Somewhere near was always a purveyor of song masquerading as an insulting employee, initially Frank Parker, who was later replaced by Kenny Baker, who was in turn replaced by Dennis Day, the deep earnestness of whose lyric tenor completely belied the dumb crazy stealth of his perpetual Peter Pan, ever poised to plague his master.

Towering head and shoulders above all the members of the Benny retinue was Rochester, his Negro valet, as played by Eddie Anderson. They first crossed each other's paths in 1936 when the Benny radio script called for a Pullman porter to be in attendance as Benny supposedly journeyed by train from California to New York. The shuffling, croaking rascality of the burly Negro, a porter and so far not an actor in real life, proved the perfect complement to Benny's disdainful inadequacy and soon means were contrived for a Pullman porter to visit him at home. His success was such that within weeks logic had to be thrown aside and Jack hired him as his radio manservant. It would be impossible to imagine the relationship between Benny and Rochester flourishing in the more liberal climate of today. But if, superficially, the valet with his water-melon grin, rasping lilt, and kaleidoscope eyes did profess an element of Uncle Tom caricature, he still in the 'thirties and 'forties represented a refreshingly un-stereotyped black man. Not only did he not talk in 'Down South' jargon, but far from degrading the dignity of his race with his apparent subservience, he was smarter than, and thoroughly disrespectful of, his employer. With irony coming full circle, when they found themselves sharing a bedroom on a Pullman together, it was Rochester who rushed in first and grabbed the lower berth, leaving Benny to endure the discomfort of the upper one. And however raucously, if ineffectually, Benny might holler at him, there always existed between them an unwritten bond of mutual affection. Moreover, when a Cleveland lawyer criticised Benny for his parsimony towards the valet, and hinted at taking legal action on Rochester's behalf, Benny could confidently, if irately, reply that he was prepared to wager that he paid Rochester, even when the show was off the air, more money in a week than the lawyer could possibly make in a month. But at the same time Benny must have been secretly flattered by the suspension of disbelief the criticism entailed.

As we have seen, the borderline between truth and fiction in a Benny programme was blurred considerably. The frequent presence on his show of the Ronald Colmans as next-door neighbours, even though they actually lived eight blocks away; the pet parrot, Polly, like all else unfriendly towards him; the constant mechanical feud with the broken-down 1918 Maxwell jalopy, which he refused to replace; the vault, incongruous in size with its suburban setting, where he hoarded his money; the toupee which in real life he never had occasion to wear; the meanness; the conceit; all contributed in their continuous presence to a mosaic, specific and tangible, which paved the threshold where make-believe became reality. No comedian ever amassed a more copious personal folklore, and because of this no comedian was ever funnier in his own absence. Each facet listed above was a shorthand cut to his invisible presence in interludes when his writers, to change the pace, had him depart from the centre of the stage to become the conversation point of others.

As a measure of how important his credibility became to his sponsors, in 1940 General Foods devoted more than three quarters of its advertising budget for 'Jell-O' to his show. Perversely, the commercials were the one aspect of the production which Benny refused to take seriously. In order, however, to make comic capital from them, he had to integrate the advertising within the actual programme. He claimed he obtained the idea for comedy commercials from the sly undersell of the cigarette advertisement that read 'No smoking—not even an Abdulla', a prominent fixture of British public places in the 'thirties. He adapted this same principle for an early show sponsored by Canada Dry Ginger Ale, in which he detailed the activities of their salesman who covered the Sahara Desert. It so happened that one day he came across a caravan of forty people who were dying of thirst, whereupon he gave them all a drink of the appropriate beverage, and 'not one of them said it was a bad drink'. The sponsors, annoyed at first by what they regarded as negative advertising, changed their judgment at the subsequent affirmative response from the public.

From that moment, no sponsor was sacred as far as Benny was concerned. When sponsored by a cigarette company he would walk on stage prior to the recording puffing a giant cigar at the audience, and then, brandishing it in the air, exclaim 'Welcome to the Lucky Strike programme'. No product derived greater benefit from his kidding, however, than 'Jell-O'. The subliminal salesmanship would begin with his opening line, 'Jell-O again'. He

made a recurring comedy motif out of Don Wilson's back-breaking attempts to sneak in a mention of 'Jell-O's six delicious flavours' on any conceivable pretext. The product could be mentioned as often as fifty times in a single half-hour show; but the sum of those mentions would still be far less obtrusive than the stereotyped hard sell of intermittent block advertising. By the time Benny moved on to another sponsor, 'Jell-O' had not only helped him to the top of the ratings and itself superseded 'Royal Jellin' as America's number one dessert, but far more impressively it had also become the accepted generic household word for all similar gelatine products. And all because Benny refused to give way to broadcasting as a selling medium pure and simple.

The technique of promotion by way of mock-defamation extended into the feud between Benny and Fred Allen, instigated according to Benny by characteristic accident when Allen insisted on making derogatory remarks in the sanctity of his own show about his rival's playing of 'Schubert's "Bee".' As mutual insults proceeded to ricochet from show to show, their individual sponsors became additionally grateful for the way the feud re-affirmed public interest in each other's programmes and brought their products to the attention of possibly new-found listeners. In this respect, Benny, the more homogenised in his appeal, gave the bigger boost to Allen, whose inspired nasal projection of sharp, satirical self-confidence had long been caviar to the general as far as the mass American public was concerned. One can now see a tinge of poetic gratitude, if not justice, in the way so much of Allen's legacy of most quoted one-liners is Benny-oriented. When Benny was nominated to inaugurate a March of Dimes campaign, Allen twanged in retort: 'The dime hasn't been minted that could march past Jack Benny.' Benny himself, with an undisguised blend of affection and mock-petulance, often recounted in his stage act Allen's query when he heard the news that the elm planted by Jack's home town of Waukegan in honour of its famous son had died: 'How can a tree live in Waukegan, with the sap in Hollywood?' At any point in their feud, Benny would have conceded the crown for impromptu ad-libbing to Allen. Once, however, when Allen had accused him of deliberately cultivating a tan so that people would mistake him for Rochester, after the valet had walked away with the best notices in several of Benny's films, Benny did manage to top his rival: 'Hmmm, you wouldn't speak to me like that if my writers were here!' What Allen knew only too well, however, is that where a Benny line had the undisputed copyright of its comedian, an Allen line with Benny as its butt was the joint property of both marksman and target, deriving its comic impetus from Benny's fully developed professional character.

It is ironic that the single most characteristic Benny moment from his entire cinema career, the necktie sequence already mentioned, was itself a cameo contribution to a Fred Allen vehicle, *It's in the Bag*, also known as *The Fifth Chair*. It is equally apt that the most famous of all his films should be *The Horn Blows at Midnight*, the one which flopped most resoundingly at the box-office, and the last self-vehicle which he made for the cinema. Refusing, however, to waste any situation that could be turned to advantage, he took this far-fetched saga of Benny as a visitor from heaven, sent on a mission to annihilate planet earth by sounding a trumpet at midnight, and assigned it to a prominent place in his own personal pantheon of self-denigration. As a result, more than twenty-five years after the film was made and rushed into oblivion by Warner Brothers, any American over forty knew intuitively what Benny was talking about by his most cryptic reference to its title. Once it was announced that Benny was to star in a special television version of the film. He did so, but not before Jack Warner had appeared on Benny's own television show with the plea, 'Don't do it, Jack. Leave us alone. We're making money again now.' He offered a bribe, and once again Benny was trapped in a self-made dilemma.

Over the years the running gag has, to Benny's discredit, not only disguised the fact that until *The Horn Blows at Midnight*, all the films in which he appeared in a star rôle made money, if only on the strength of his radio success and a public anxious in a pre-television age to discover the face to fit the disembodied voice of its hero. Also obscured was his appearance in *To Be Or Not To Be*, the one film which today reserves for Benny a special cult following in France, a country as aware cinematically as it is oblivious of his stage and broadcasting achievements. Sadly, though, one views such recognition in retrospect not merely as reward for personal triumph, but as compensation for his participation in a vehicle unfortunately, though inevitably, ill-timed. The film, in seeming to extract comedy out of the Nazi occupation of Warsaw, found itself in 1942 pinioned to the same shaft of criticism with which Chaplin's *The Great Dictator* had had to contend two years before and would in fact appear even more callous, more daring after the discovery of the concentration camps. But as the director, Ernst Lubitsch, was subsequently anxious to point out, his aim had been merciless satire and not celebration of 'the Nazis and their ridiculous ideology', as well as 'the attitude of actors who always remain actors regardless of how dangerous the situation might be'. This latter observation gave a piquant edge to Benny's stock characterisation, transplanted from cosy Beverly Hills domesticity to a company of Polish repertory actors perilously close to the Hitlerian centre of events. But his rôle was tailor-made for Benny, like smiles on a nurse, and his magnificent low-key performance—one recalls the serene complacency of his counterfeit Gestapo officer: 'Oh, they call me Concentration Camp Erhardt, do they?'—only pinpointed what one had always suspected, that in comedy the most effective hamming is a product of subtlety, stealth and implication, and not a 'Berle by the horns' technique. Benny had shrewdly paid far greater heed to that Abdulla advertisement than the obvious by-product, his own television commercials, would have suggested.

Every precise detail of Benny's physical presence lent itself to this theory, not least the sure-footed, sauntering pace of his delivery. With that voice capable of acid-drop consternation he picked his way through a monologue determined that the audience should grasp the precise contribution which he willed each word or pause to make, here to prompt a belly laugh, there to deposit the merest fragment of his characterisation as a minute detail in the total effect. Nothing revealed the extreme sensitivity of his craftsmanship more than his unerring judgment of not merely when to pause, but of how long to hold that pause before speaking again. He was the first comedian of the mass media to make a comic prop out of silence. With unconscious deference to Chekhov and looking forward to Pinter, he made that silence telling, meditative, pregnant with meaning, as in the radio show in which he was called to the phone by the president of the American Tobacco Company:

> *Benny:* Oh, oh, my sponsor . . . Hello, Vince . . . Vincent? . . . Oh, Mr Riggio. What can I do for you, Mr Riggio? . . . You've been listening to the show? . . . Wasn't it great? . . . Oh . . . I shouldn't have what? . . . But I had to fire them; that quartet was the worst . . . You don't think so? . . . Well, everybody's entitled to his own opinion. That's why they put rubber mats around cuspidors (*silly laugh*) . . . What? . . . I guess you're right; it didn't get a laugh here either. But about that quartet, Mr Riggio, I felt that . . . I know but . . . But, Mr Riggio . . . I know, but . . . Yes, but . . . You might be right, but . . . But . . . But . . . But . . . But . . . I know, but . . . But . . . But . . . But . . . . But . . . But, but . . . But . . .

On Benny's reading, the space between his two most separated 'but's' amounted to no less than fourteen and a half seconds.

His stage appearances proved, however, that he didn't need the extraneous device of an imaginary telephone conversation to make silence funny. Indeed, what Mr Riggio might have said is irrelevant. Far more to the point was the picture of that blank frozen stare curdled by gall that accompanied the silence. Certainly his knack of being able to play with a live audience's reactions, as if they were trout on a line, rested as securely upon his facial deportment as upon his vocal technique. That famous affronted look, once said to resemble 'a calf that had just been struck between the eyes with a sledgehammer', stayed there, lingered, hung on, and went on, until his audience was convinced that no man could hold an expression for so long. As it defied you not to laugh, you became convinced that the motes in the Benny line of vision were not going about their conventional erratic dance, but advancing on his pupils like storm-troopers. And as they drew nearer, so the deprecative Benny eyebrows arched infinitesimally higher, their owner helpless in his resignation that battle would have to commence.

There were routines when this bifocal look of humility and exasperation was seemingly Benny's only contribution: as when he was unexpectedly interrupted in mid-joke by an ear-splitting pop-group or, on the occasion Max Bygraves dropped in on his Palladium act to tell an even better joke, by a rival entertainer. When normality returned and Benny himself, with a faint shrug to heighten the effect, resumed his own joke where he left off, as if nothing had happened, it was the look that remained seared on the memory. And for all he just stood there, his entire body was, throughout, unobtrusively reinforcing this brilliant theatrical joke. He would bite his lips, knead his fingers; the elegant porcelain hands would paw his face before wandering aimlessly from stoical arms-folded pose through a mazy procession from pocket to pocket to pocket; and always with the studied, precise interplay of gesture for maximum effect. From his first entrance onto the stage with that carefully modulated, spring-heeled, arm-swinging stride to what he regarded as the ludicrous strains of his signature tune, 'Love in Bloom'—

93

'Isn't that a ridiculous song for a comedian?'—he convinced you that he not only possessed style, but to a greater degree than any comparable comedian. There was a manicured precision in the ball-bearing wrist movement of his nervous hands, in the stance that suggested, but never became, an elegant slouch, one leg exclamation-mark erect, one leg crooked. But, unlike Durante's, his appearance stopped this side short of caricature. Benny's comment on his own favourite humorist, Stephen Leacock, has a telling aptness here: 'I've seen pictures of Leacock, and he was a very dignified-looking guy. Why, do you know he was a professor of economics?'

Without at any time encroaching upon the more dubious preserves of camp humour, Benny, with his finesse, his hand gestures, his effeminate petulance, his excessive concern over his looks and years, did much to corroborate Kenneth Tynan's theory that comedy, as it sets about its task of exposing those ambiguities within our personalities and the social fabric which society would have us disguise, is in part rooted in 'the exposure of all that is womanish in man, the unveiling of feminine traits beneath the masculine exterior'. Maybe the film critic C. A. Lejeune was anticipating Tynan when upon Benny's starring rôle in the 1941 film version of the Brandon Thomas farce, she wrote:

> Can you think of any
> Reason why Jack Benny
> Should play 'Charley's Aunt'?
> I can't.

Significantly, the following year, for the film *George Washington Slept Here*, based upon a Kaufman-Hart play about a married couple who buy a crumbling old country house, it was agreed that Benny as the husband should be assigned the sharper, more peevish lines spoken by the wife in the play, with Ann Sheridan now taking what amounted to the original husband rôle. Where Benny on stage gave a subtle twist to Tynan's theory, however, was in his subtle implication that he knew we had caught on to his secret, that he must make amends. Hence his femininity was far from unguarded, extra effort made throughout his routine to convince that inside his own professor of cheese-paring economics was not merely an ageing spinster but a drug-store Casanova screaming for escape. The motif of sexual excuse was predominant throughout the act. In welcoming his wife's presence in the audience, he would explain how she didn't usually travel with him: 'She trusts me—it's kind of *sad* that she *can*.' He insisted that he was very happily married: 'I don't fool around. I'm not a wolf or a playboy. Oh—occasionally I glance through the African section of the National Geographic. You know, whatever I *need*, I see *there*.' But if this was the actuality, on stage it soon became transparent as camouflage to the potential tiger within. He insisted that years of playing Las Vegas had prevented him from becoming a prude: 'I guess I feel the way you folks feel—it all depends on *who* is in the nude.' He would reminisce about a lavish French revue imported from the Paris Lido, painting a mental picture for every full-blooded male in the audience: 'There were sixty topless girls—let's see—or was it sixty-one?' He took time off to do his mental arithmetic before committing himself: 'It *was* sixty. I must have counted the redhead twice.' He left one in no doubt that he'd got it correct to the last nipple. When the soubrette attached to his show described for him the scene from her new film where she had to be chased nude by a naked man across a field, Benny sighed and gave all away: 'Gee, if I could only run.' It would be misleading, however, to think of his stage routine as a catalogue of vicarious sexual experience. Rather it was a rambling montage exploring every cumulative facet of the character that had grown around him, like so many rings in an oak, over the years, and now rendered individual jokes relatively unimportant. The reality of his advanced years in no way impeded the flair of his performance. When he walked on stage, reflexes took over, the vibration of the audience rushed through his bones, and he could physically have shed twenty of those rings. What he cunningly refused to let slip however was the added definition those years had given to his characterisation.

Benny's plan in orchestrating his stage routine was to predetermine the first fifteen minutes. Then, he would insist, anything could happen. But no sooner had he delivered his opening line, prompted by the now foregone conclusion of a rousing reception ('I swear I won't be *that* good'), than one was launched down a slipway of conversational ease where no element would jar. With the performer himself by definition a better joke than any he could tell, jokes as such were virtually non-existent. His forte was by way of reportage, in turn by way of self-disparagement, as when he would ramble on for happily disproportionate length about George Burns and the one infuriating aspect of their friendship; namely, that off stage 'he can make me laugh, but I can't make him laugh'. On one occasion Benny sent Burns a telegram containing the funniest joke he could think of. Burns' reply was crisp and curt: 'Don't worry. I won't show your wire to anyone.' A few years later Benny was literally driven to extremes. While they were staying together in a hotel in Minneapolis, Jack, receiving word from Burns in the lobby that he was on his way up to his suite, determined to make one last desperate attempt to make him laugh. Shedding his clothes, he took up his position in the centre of the room with a book balanced on his skull, a glass of water in one hand, a rose in the other. There was a knock on the door, but Burns had scented mischief, and sent the maid in ahead of him. He followed after a suitable interval, poker-faced in his usual dignity. 'Now, how do you explain to a maid that you're waiting for George Burns nude? Until I opened my mouth she thought I was a lamp!'

On stage, his violin and bow played their own part in the mime. He would stand there holding the instrument, his playing of which sounded, according to Fred Allen, 'like the strings are back in the cat'. He had first asked for it long ago, whereupon it was thrown in a no-nonsense parabola from the wings to crash into splinters at his feet, fit only for some scarecrow Tevye, the sacrilege of some uncultured stagehand who had maybe mistaken it for the monkey wrench Benny's father is alleged to have given him together with the instrument in childhood—the violin in the event of his son possessing talent, the monkey wrench in case he didn't. But as he stressed a whole intermission later, 'You're gonna get this, whether you want it or not'. The fiddle served a prism capable of reflecting the entire spectrum of his persona. 'It's a Stradivarius', he would insist. 'At least, I *think* it's a

95

Strad. If it isn't, I'm out a *hundred* and *ten* bucks.' With pained stoicism he recounted the drunken ad-lib hurled at him across a cabaret floor when he explained to an audience that it was made in 1729: 'Did you buy it new?' Having buttonholed our complete attention, the moment he brushed trembling bow against taut string, he revealed himself as Grock might have if he had been a member of the Algonquin Round Table.

Like the classic clown at his piano, he used his music to portray man's struggle with fate, and nowhere more effectively than when that fate touched the raw nerve of his own exposed vanity, as in the engaging sequence where, interrupted on stage by a young girl anxious to obtain his autograph, he was torn between showing off before an audience of a thousand and succumbing to the flattery of an audience of one. Affronted, he carried on playing for as long as he could entertain both prospects, but on her slightest move to turn away recalled her: 'As long as you're here, I'll sign it.' Blinded by such adulation, he would hand fiddle and bow to the girl so that he may scribble more easily. Not that he could rise sufficiently to the occasion to spell her name right:

> *Girl:* You spelt Toni wrong. There are two ways: TONY for a man, TONI for a girl.
> *Benny:* I spelt it with a 'Y'?
> *Girl:* No, with two 'E's'!

By the time he had got round to correcting his mistake, however, she had herself started to play, whereupon Benny burst into his 'now-cut-that-out' fury, kept in reserve for occasions when even his stare would be too mild: 'Give me that violin. Why didn't you tell me you played?' 'You didn't ask me', replied the girl. 'That's the silliest answer I've ever heard!' yelled Benny. At her suggestion of a duet and his rejection of Bach's Double Concerto ('It's been done to death'), they segued into an up-tempo version of 'Getting to Know You'. But by now the tables were completely turned. When he had asked her earlier if she could play like him, the reply had been barbed: 'I used to.' The proof was in the playing; the girl could not resist interpolating cadenzas at every opportunity, until came their encore— 'Just play it straight'—their bows literally became crossed swords in this cause. Then with momentary affection Benny allowed her to bask in her well-won applause, until she was clear of the wings: 'Imagine—fourteen years old— she's thirty-one if she's a day!' And he still had in reserve the snappy, sub-Grappelli jazz solos with which he all but closed his act, and the unique version of Mendelssohn's Violin Concerto which turned unaccountably into 'Love in Bloom'.

Unlike most comedians who attempt to send up culture, Benny was not outflanked, as his successive concerts with the leading symphony orchestras of the world proved, by lack of contact with the subject itself. By the same token, the most outrageous of desecration services will need to be conducted by a priest. The comment by the classical virtuoso, Isaac Stern, to his friend helps to explain how Benny sustained his violin routine for so long: 'When you walk out on the stage in tails, you actually look like one of the world's great violinists. It's a shame you have to play.' Even Stern would have to admit, however, that when Benny sawed away, his target was as much himself as the art of music, the humour based on his shrewd understanding of his own helplessness when set against the accepted levels of musical accomplishment. With or without violin the joke never ceased to be against Benny, and he never ceased to ride the storm of self-denigration with anything less than sublime dignity. The close of his act was its own metaphor for this cool, majestic repose. As he dreamily played 'Goodnight, Sweetheart', he would ask the audience, 'Do you wonder what really goes through an entertainer's mind at the end of a show?' For the rest of the routine it was a sound-track reproduction of his voice that held one rapt:

> Well, guess that's about it . . . I can't get over the way that lady down front kept staring at me . . . Guess it's my eyes . . . They *are* rather sexy for a comedian . . . sort of a lazy-lagoon blue . . . I think sex appeal is important for an entertainer . . . It's important for a butcher if you want to get basic . . . What shall I eat after the show? . . . I'm so sick of cornflakes . . . even with strawberries . . .

Still he played, while his mental soliloquy verbally signed off for the night. The blend of trivia and eloquence, naïveté and style was quintessential Benny. He could never follow its so-simple, but so-devastating theatrical effect. The information it confided was unimportant, but the *ennui* that lurked beneath its presentation was a perfect coda to the act of this most passive of comedians, a last strained attempt at polite resignation by a man too tired to protest his innocence any further.

Few professional funny men have shown a more sensitive understanding of the character they portray, a more certain choice of what is right for that character. His fellow professionals acclaim Benny as being the greatest and most durable editor of comedy material in his lifetime. Certainly the superfluous moments in his act, as in his programmes, were as likely as stray spots on straight dice. In his native country he attained the status of a popular folk hero. Several years ago when a journalists' poll was held throughout North America to nominate the 'outstanding radio personality' of the previous twenty-five years, he beat no less than Franklin D. Roosevelt into second place. Once, when Roosevelt had to make an important policy speech over the air during a national emergency, Benny, in competition, achieved double his rating. In his radio heyday it is said that on a warm Sunday night at 7.00 p.m. Eastern Standard Time you could stroll down any residential street in any town in the as yet un-airconditioned United States and miss not a single word of the Jack Benny programme as it was relayed through the open windows of the nation. His audience was so large because it was never once underestimated by the comedian. He once explained his philosophy: 'I have never believed in playing down to people or in saying, "Well, the 'masses' will like this". I always had a feeling that if the real intelligent people liked what I was doing, then everybody did.' Few were not heartened by the dry warmth of that mid-western drawl, edged even closer to acceptance as the Universal Voice of America by Benny himself. No one could fail to identify, however tenuously, with at least one of the cluster of peccadilloes to which he laid exaggerated claim.

Unlike Will Rogers, the rope-spinning humorist who summed up his philosophy in his assertion, 'I never met a man I didn't like', Benny long recognised the value of playing the suspicious straight man to every character who crossed his path. One feels that the character he played never met a person he wanted to like if that person wasn't prepared to like him, even though there were times when personal greed and vanity demanded that he sustain an outward show of familiarity. Who else would go out of his way to organise a contest, as Benny did, in which competitors were asked to relate in no more than fifty words why they found him excruciating? More than 277,000 took up this challenge to insult, tempted by 10,000 dollars in prize money.

As a corollary to his deliberate cultivation of several objectionable streaks, no popular comedian has more often acted as a sounding-board for speculation as to where the public self stops and the private individual begins. A measure, in fact, of his complete lack of professional jealousy could be found in his guffaw-prone enthusiasm for other great funny men; of his actual generosity in the fact that he was the first funny man to give credit to his writers, or in his instructions to Eddie Cantor, when Benny couldn't attend an important charity event: 'Eddie, fill in this cheque for whatever you need', whereupon Cantor filled it in for 25,000 dollars, as he explained in his autobiography, 'The least Jack would have given—and with joy'. If there was, however, one aspect of his comic characterisation that rang true on meeting this calm, mild, contemplative man, it was his undisguised love of the spotlight and applause. But it was apparent not as mock-conceited hauteur, but as genuine exhilaration at the prospect of each new curtain-call. There was a sweet naïveté in the way a performer of such stature, who had been everywhere, met everyone, won every appropriate award, on the eve of a performance at the London Palladium in his eightieth year, perused the souvenir programme for the event with the true excitement of an apprentice comic getting his first big break. Benny never lost sight of the sense of wonder that sustains all great theatre from his own, as much as the audience's, side of the footlights. He was supposedly in Britain on a working holiday, and was adamant in expressing his hatred of vacations *per se*: 'Vacations without work are empty. The fun is playing, to be a ham and show off a little bit. The thing is never to lose your enthusiasm, never let the excitement get away. You must never become blasé. Big you can become, as big as you like, but you won't sustain it without keeping the excitement hot.'

It is arguable that on a cold, statistical computer-basis, which would take into account over fifty years of performing before live audiences, twenty-five years on radio, twenty-four years on television, not to mention *The Horn Blows at Midnight*, treating an individual's experience of each successive show or broadcast as a single unit, he performed to a larger total audience than any other comedian. There is, however, a subtle irony to the other side of this coin, namely that, in a career dominated audience-wise by the mass media, individually on a per joke, *per caput* basis, no comedian's laughs ever cost their audience, his sponsors excluded, less. It is at once the ultimate joke against this Fifth Avenue Scrooge and the finest testimony to his achievement in popular terms.

Fred Astaire

Top hat, white tie, and tails

Noël Coward once remarked to his sometime dancing tutor 'Freddie, when I see you dance, it makes me want to cry'. A clue to Astaire's style is that one need only hear that line to know that Coward's tears sprang not from jealousy or a sense of personal failure, but from an intense joy reflecting the sheer ecstasy of his friend's dancing. For Astaire, the dance and life itself were indissolubly blurred. This dancer did not just explore the whole scope of the dance, he interpreted the whole scope of existence through his dancing. His need to dance was the gyroscope's need to spin. And in this world of compulsive movement, so it seemed his hoofing could express no less than 360 different degrees of emotion. Both the ups of gaiety and romance and the downs of frustration and depression were grist to his toe-tapping mill. Venting his anger against a chair, his kick would become the prelude to a dance, as valid rhythmically as lyrical embrace or jaunty stroll. At no time was his walk ever more than one step removed from a dance routine. His whole world—one of chairs and tables, walls and ceilings, bars, ballrooms and bandstands—became a trampoline of three all-encompassing dimensions. His knack of tuning into rhythms which pass the ordinary man by can only be matched by the readiness with which the trained naturalist will discern life and movement where, to the under-privileged gaze of the layman, they simply don't exist. For Astaire there was no aspect of life, however disagreeable, that could not be redeemed at least part of the way by his intuitive ability to choreograph his whole being. Here was as much a sense of humour as of rhythm, often witty, always exhilarating.

Life began for Astaire on 10 May 1899, in Omaha, Nebraska. He was just over a year younger than his sister Adèle and their early career together is marked by that combination of haphazard causality and never-look-back momentum which for so many movie-goers would come to symbolise the eternal backstage musical, with its creaking plot and whirlwind montage. The dancing career of the screen's greatest hoofer began as no more than a postscript to his sister's own ballet lessons, to which he would be dragged along reluctantly at the age of five. A more colourful influence on his life was the decision by his home town in 1906 to enforce prohibition as a local option long before there was any threat of the whole country going dry on a coast-to-coast basis. Until then their Viennese immigrant father had been a prosperous beer salesman; now financial expediency found him casting a more acute eye on the success, if only at local church hall level, being enjoyed by his two children. Under their mother's care they were despatched to New York to be enrolled as pupils of the Claude Alvienne Academy on 8th Avenue, the result of a small classified advertisement spotted in a theatrical trade paper, the *New York Clipper*. Within a year, their name now legally changed from the Austrian Austerlitz to the more theatrically acceptable Astaire, brother and sister were launched upon the fiercely competitive world of professional vaudeville in Keyport, New Jersey, under the winsomely prophetic billing, 'Juvenile Artists Presenting an Electric Musical Toe-Dancing Novelty'. Astaire may not have been born wearing a top-hat, but here he came so close to the embryonic ideal that the legend may be allowed to persist. As a miniature bride and groom in full evening dress they danced on and around two colossal 'wedding cakes', their steps activating the 'Dreamland Waltz' chimes and fairy lights cunningly installed in and around the ersatz almond-icing. As a climax he and Adèle made quick changes into lobster shell and champagne glass respectively, the prelude to a more eccentric dance duet. Even then the humour, if forced, was in evidence, but not nearly so much as the sugar-plum artificiality of the setting, to be repeated later in the improbable fairground fantasy of those countless Hollywood ballrooms and piazzas.

Over the years the wedding-cake routine and others would acquire both the grime and the expertise synonymous with touring's tedious provincial haul. In his autobiography Astaire reminisces about the recurrent nightmare of going on in the number one or two spot and having to perform to a half-empty house with additional accompaniment provided by the banging-down of seats. It is perhaps surprising that the nightmare did persist, was never exorcised as the obvious theme for a dance. But Astaire had not yet found the casual stride which could shrug off what he found irksome with cool rhythmic understatement. And yet the seeds were there. His earliest attitude to dancing was one of reluctance: 'Dancing was merely something my sister did . . . I let it go at that and the hell with it.' The reluctance, however, was tempered with an uneasy resignation, made more tolerable perhaps by jealous curiosity, to go along with his sister and what she did. In 1916, as their vaudeville days were drawing to a close, the *Boston Record* reviewed their act: 'Fred and Adèle Astaire gave a fine exhibition of whirlwind dancing, although it could be wished that the young man give up some of the blasé air which he carries constantly with him. He is too young for it and deceives no one.' Young he may have been, but it was an understandable front for one who, having endured a compulsory apprenticeship that had entailed at its most humiliating his portraying the girl Roxanne to his sister's Cyrano, now found himself playing second fiddle, or at best straight man, in an act the reviews of which constantly telegraphed the same message: 'The girl is superior to the boy.' The pose of bored indifference, nonchalant superiority, was a cultured way of registering protest at being carried by her professionally; of giving, by way of self-justification, some dramatic purpose to his tell-tale background position; of breaking away, yet maintaining family and professional ties in spite of it. Astaire said later of those early years: 'I must have been a tiresome little boy.' In their book *Jazz Dance*, Marshall and Jean Stearns, having deduced this for themselves, go on to articulate his attitude even further: 'Okay, Adèle's the star, so I'll help her out, but I'm bored to death.' And yet, all the time, as Astaire came nearer to finding his own form, so conceit would mellow.

In 1916 they were offered parts in the Broadway musical *Over The Top*. It would still, though, be six years before they could claim not merely a real hit, but one written with them in mind, *For Goodness Sake*. In 1919, one critic reviewing the show *Apple Blossoms* and misled by their surname, had decided they must be French and applauded their 'Parisian chic'. In so far as the Continent did call, however, it was from London; at the insistence of Noël Coward they took *For Goodness Sake*, retitled *Stop Flirting*, into the West End. Their initial success had a hurricane impact and in the socialite circles of a capital which embraced them with champagne-slack arms, Astaire found the perfect finishing-school for his special brand of insecure insouciance. Over ten years later, riding high on the success of his new film career, he would be greeted by Douglas Fairbanks Senior in the Savoy Grill: 'What do you mean by revolutionising the movie industry? I've just seen *Flying Down to Rio* and you've got something absolutely new.' The accolade was appropriate not merely for its truth but for where it took place, at the fashionable focal point of the society amongst which Astaire had burnished his style in the 'twenties. In return London had demanded and got their subsequent Broadway hits, *Lady Be Good* and *Funny Face* and then, in 1932, as if to put Astaire to the crucial test, claimed Adèle herself on her marriage into the British aristocracy as Lady Cavendish.

More often than not, those admirers lucky enough to have enjoyed the whole span of Astaire's career claim that his sister was the best girl partner he ever had. Although he had by now proved himself in his bedazzling solo routines, so far he had never done a show without the girl whose animal grace and intriguing charm had essentially dictated the material that had taken him, as well as her, to the top. Anxious to take a decisive step that would forestall the comparative oblivion which he now feared threatened, he plunged into Cole Porter's *The Gay Divorce*. Sadly, the shock of seeing him solo in a generally uninspired production and the foregone conclusions of critics (who made out that half of his performance was aimed at the wings in the hope that the ghost of Adèle might be there to rescue him) distracted audiences from the one big breakthrough contained in an otherwise only moderate personal success. In his 'Night and Day' duet with Claire Luce he achieved what he wanted, 'an entirely new dancing approach', in short the first purely authentic romantic *adagio* dance of his career. The plots and dances shared with Adèle had all scrupulously avoided any intimation of incest. Their forte was light comedy, and any suggestion of love between them was completely asexual, stamped with the seal of gentle burlesque.

With the satisfaction of having broken this new territory he turned his attention to the cinema. He had so far distrusted the new medium for depriving dance of its essential three-dimensional quality and, in spite of Paramount's talk of filming *Funny Face*, had only committed himself to celluloid twice before, with Adèle in a Mary Pickford feature of 1915, *Fanchon the Cricket*, and again for a Vitagraph short sixteen years later. It is more likely, though, that he had realised that in films, whatever his skill as a dancer, he would never rise above the lesser-than-star billing of mere featured speciality player without some capacity for romance. Once he had proved that capacity to himself, there was no stopping the man whose dancing would at times appear to provide the screen with its own fourth dimension. The notorious legend supposedly attached to his screen test for Paramount— 'Can't act; can't sing; slightly bald; can dance a little'—could stand now as the motto for the very quality of understatement that characterises his style. Happily its author's advice went unheeded by R.K.O. Radio to whom he went in 1933 to make *Flying Down to Rio*, but not before a rival company had accorded him the most stylish introduction ever given a new recruit to the screen. When production on *Rio* was held up, he was lent to M–G–M for the Joan Crawford vehicle, *Dancing Lady*. Astaire's name may have been at the bottom of the cast list, he may have danced only one number, but it was an auspicious début if only because he was cast as himself. Even more significantly, he was actually introduced on screen with his own name. When Clark Gable, playing the choreographer in a backstage story, casually explained to Crawford: 'I've got Fred Astaire here from New York to dance with you. Oh, Fred, would you come here please?' he was enacting more than the prelude to one of the cinema's greatest success stories. The device had its own subtle overtone of flamboyance mixed with reserve, and as such aptly mirrored the style of the man it introduced. That the general cinema public, to whom Astaire for all his stage success was still unknown, should become grateful for the name, only served to emphasise the futility of an industry that, whatever the wishes of the two performers concerned, could afford to have disregarded the talent of both himself and his sister for so long.

If Astaire found the silver screen strange territory, the girl chosen by R.K.O. to be his own special partner not only had several years experience of playing in the movies already behind her, but had actually resolved never to make another musical when offered the rôle opposite Astaire. Ginger Rogers was determined that this would be no more than a one-time thing, and made sure that Astaire realised: 'I don't want to do any more musicals, but I guess it'll turn out all right; anyway, we'll have some fun.' She could not have known then that they would dance their way together through no less than nine movies in six years. After several minor film appearances, her joky, headstrong ingénue had captured the popular imagination as the precocious, monocled, Pekinese-hugging 'Anytime Annie' in *42nd Street*. Those initials were too much of a coincidence not to suggest to those who noticed that anything approaching a mere single-show relationship with Astaire was very much against the choreographic cards. Astaire had worked, if not danced professionally, with her before, staging her 'Embraceable You' number in *Girl Crazy*, the Broadway show which made her a star and the talk of the town at a mere nineteen; for a while they had continued to know each other socially—and in this capacity had danced together, but strictly for fun. Rogers' initial attitude may no doubt have been swayed by a desire to relive these old times, although as their career together progressed it became no secret that off-screen they were not each other's favourite person, as even a superficial 'between-the-lines' reading of Astaire's autobiography will show. By the time they came to make the last of their 'thirties films, *The Story of Vernon and Irene Castle*, Mrs Castle was jealously defending her own anxiety at seeing Rogers portray herself to Bosley Crowther of the *New*

York Times: 'Fred had begged me not to let her do it.' That she could get away with such a line without causing a sensation can only suggest how blasé the relevant sections of the public had become to the off-screen rumours.

At first appearance they were far from compatible. Ginger was twelve years his junior. Emotionally they were as positive to negative, her all-out onslaught on life and its problems directly at odds with his reticent, tangential style, the Queen Bee and the butterfly. But between them there flourished a hyper-sensitive rapport, a togetherness, far more meaningful than that implied by the famous aphorism variously credited to a faceless studio executive and to Katharine Hepburn: 'He gives her class and she gives him sex.' It needed Astaire to bring out the soft marshmallow vulnerability that hid behind her smart cracknel façade; it needed her to transform his Stan Laurel gigolo into fully fledged Knight Errant. He would later dance with partners who projected sex far more blatantly than Ginger, and indeed, for all Ginger's verve, were far more accomplished dancers, but only this relationship succeeded in making the metaphor of dance for romance from courtship to afterglow appear spontaneous, and hence believable. The sexual tension was only underlined by their respective dancing abilities. By training, Rogers was little more than a Charleston dancer. Whereas Astaire effortlessly breathed the dance, she gasped at it. The difference in their skills complemented that in their personalities. Away from the dance floor he was as unassuming as she could be impetuous, but as soon as the dance began, he subtly assumed an unspoken sexual and psychological advantage. And yet however complementary they proved to be, this must not disguise the Punch and Judy interplay that always acted as prologue to the *raison d'être* that was the dance. However accurate the claim of dance-historian Arlene Croce that Astaire and Rogers transformed the dance into a unique 'vehicle of serious emotion between a man and woman' that never happened at such a sustained level in the cinema again, the love affair was always born out of a basic antagonism. However early he was himself captivated by her charms, she teasingly kept herself in reserve. He became the puppet to her 'hard-to-get' whims and wiles until, slowly relenting, she was somehow tempted into the choreographic overture to a happy ending. What began on the dance floor as a cautious clash of opposites ended in the dreamy ecstasy symbolised by those immortal spins and subsequent exhaustion, but not before the whole ordeal of courtship had been skilfully translated into choreographic terms. Her attempts at abandoning him could be as restrained as the flicking of a silk scarf, as reckless as striking an apparent blow which sent him spinning or sliding way across the floor. The depth of feeling contained in their interpretation of numbers like 'Night and Day', 'Cheek to Cheek' and 'The Way You Look Tonight' would have been significantly undermined without the initial zig-zagging which was her last effort to evade his Svengali-like beckoning, without that hesitant, suspense-laden pause towards the end to suggest loving fear of eventual consummation. The studio copy about their 'dancing across the screen, the nation and into the hearts of the world' was a refined way of saying that their success stood for the most optimistic, the most imaginative expression of the basic mating instinct the cinema had yet brought to the public. Every girl who ever fancied her chances at 'catch-me-if-you-can', every guy who ever saw himself as less than Adonis but still determined to try, saw themselves in the whirling couple, as surely as Fred and Ginger were reflected in the bakelite floor on which the art-director insisted they spun.

After Ginger, Astaire never had a regular partner again, and anyway the potency of the myth they had created together would have forbidden it. Although ten years after the Castle movie Judy Garland's sudden indisposition afforded them the opportunity for a reprise in *The Barkleys of Broadway*, in the spring of 1939 Fred had to face the reality of a second professional separation. The stature he had by now acquired in the film world coupled with his own determination partner-wise never 'to get into that sort of predicament again' invested his personality with a new-found energy. When he is asked today to name his favourite partner, tact prompts the reply 'Bing Crosby: he worked hard, learned the steps, and never complained about his costume.' But there is no need for him to resort to obvious humour to avoid embarrassment. For all the precision and dynamite of Cyd Charisse, the vibrant, if mismatched, technique of Rita Hayworth, the self-possessed athleticism of Eleanor Powell, as well as Ginger's special magic, the quintessential Astaire remains solo Astaire. And if here he seemed to pool the effort and skill of two dancers, then that is another way of saying that the best dancing partner he ever had was his own imagination.

Alistair Cooke possibly came nearest to the point when he suggested that the only rightful partner for Astaire in the eyes of God was Miss Minnie Mouse herself. Certainly it would require an inhuman device of vast plastic scope to match all his moods, moods which made him something more than the supreme ballroom dancer he revealed in his partnership with Rogers. There was the fiendish finesse of the 'Say it with Firecrackers' routine from *Holiday Inn*, in which he threw torpedoes to explode in synchronisation with his feet, which in turn with visible flashes ignited strings of firecrackers wired across the stage at strategic points of his choreographic plan; fiendish not merely for its visual Lucifer effect, but for the devilish way it provided a satisfactory outlet for extra emphasis on the beat without risk of shin-bucking or toe-bruising. He could seemingly coax a human response out of inanimate objects, as with coat rack and metronome in *Royal Wedding*. But it would be wrong to imply that his brilliant dramatic instinct for combining the spontaneous and the unusual in his solo work had not been present in his films with Rogers. Golf game and sword dance are ingeniously dovetailed in *Carefree* as 'Since They Turned "Loch Lomond" Into Swing'. Here, clubs crossed on the ground act as an invitation to a Scottish reel, its own prelude to a dazzling succession of six straight shots only enhanced by his fast shuffle between each tee. Only Astaire could play harmonica during all this and still remind one of 'smart places' as distinct from fairground side-walks. Equally ingenious was the humanised triptych of three silhouettes in his tribute to Bill 'Bojangles' Robinson in the film *Swing Time*. As Astaire, black-faced for the only time in his career, dances in and out of sync with his flickering shadows, one finds oneself endorsing Robinson's own assessment of Fred as an 'eccentric dancer'. No longer, however, is the phrase one of unenthusiastic dismissal. Here 'eccentric' spells unique as never before in the dancing canon. Later in *Blue Skies* the brilliant counterpoint of this number would be amplified to the point where Astaire is 'Puttin' on the Ritz' in front of a chorus of no less than eight images of himself, the multiple-screen technique—the cinema's own answer to the three-card-trick—having come up trumps with the screen's greatest magician. Astaire would several times resort to the cherished arcana of the special effects department to enhance his routines. 'Shoes with Wings On' in *The Barkleys of Broadway* is just that, with Astaire as a cobbler carried away when the objects of his toil assume a life not normally expected of them until firmly fixed on the feet of someone with his own lightning-flash legs. At one point in *Royal Wedding* his high spirits even lead to dancing up walls and along ceilings.

It would be inaccurate, however, to give undue emphasis to the part played in his routines by mere hardware gimmickry at the expense of his fluid physical presence and the sheer force of imagination. The archetypal Astaire solo remains his performance of the title routine from *Top Hat*. The dance has its own personal trademarks: Astaire outlining with his cane the arcs of magic circles such as soothsayers would describe with a wand in the sand; the subtle serpentine indecision of the lone dancer reacting, when lights and music are lowered, to the invisible threats shrouded by the dimness; the visual metaphor of cane for machine gun, the male chorus reduced to ducks in a shooting gallery, the tapping foot now the gun's report. Ironically, the latter idea went unnoticed five years earlier when created by Astaire for a number ('Say, Young Man of Manhattan') in *Smiles*, the Ziegfeld show of 1930. The inspiration for the *Top Hat* routine characteristically came to him at four o'clock in the morning. Hermes Pan, his lifelong partner in choreography, has explained how ideas would besiege the fertile Astaire mind in the most unlikely manner in the most unlikely places. Legendary were the parties disrupted by Astaire having to dash to the studio to give practical rein to his imagination. A child skipping in the street, a shoeshine boy snapping his duster, a matador's swerve, all acted as the impetus for new creations. For the 'Slap That Bass' routine in *Shall We Dance?* the chugging tempo of a cement mixer seen on the lot the day before was translated into a cunning rhythm section of steam engines aboard a battleship. Each dance he created had to pass the test of just such an idea, a *raison d'être* that could vary from novelty angle to evocation of specific mood to distinctive characterisation. Dancing in a vacuum was not enough.

'Top Hat, White Tie and Tails' also serves as the finest showcase for what became the special emblem of the Astaire style. It was not that the Puckish sprightliness of his lean, wiry frame needed its white tie and tails, nor the sardonic, sad-grin, clownish face its top hat, to convey the almost diffident yet precise elegance that was a cornerstone of that style. They did, however, seem to intensify the special colour Astaire brought to what W. H. Auden described as that 'low, dishonest decade'. The aristocratic attire never stood in the way of his basic image of the ordinary man, identifiable at all levels, both rich and poor. Indeed, one of the fundamental reasons for his popularity was that for someone with such 'class', he never aligned himself with any particular class code. Ironically, in the depression years of the 'thirties, no uniform could have been as classless as white tie and tails. If he appeared at times to spend all his life in evening dress, he was carrying out an act of semi-wish-fulfilment both for those to whom the lusher 'twenties had

allowed the idea of dancing-the-night-away as a life-style to become a reality, and for those to whom it had never been anything more than a paper-thin image of unattainable luxury. In retrospect one can even see the attire as a metaphor for his genius. He remained ordinary when dressed up to and even beyond the nines, in the same way that however extra-terrestrial his talents may have appeared, he never ceased to be one of us, the little man urging his audience to explore their capabilities, rather than a show-off obviously flaunting his own.

Astaire, however, was equally Astaire whether as soldier, sailor, sportsman, or even semi-clad. In his autobiography, he highlights his special enjoyment in making *You'll Never Get Rich* for the simple reason that he could wear service uniform most of the time, a welcome relief from 'those damned tails'. The test-case, however, was in his early solo routine, 'Looking for a Needle in a Haystack' from *The Gay Divorcee*. Here he is employed in the actual process of dressing and one can see that the Astaire style is something more still than the clothes he wears and the way he wears them. The subtle low-key finesse with which he sheds tie and dressing gown and assumes new tie and jacket, all the while finger-drumming the mantelpiece, foot-tapping the floor, vaulting over the sofa and on to chairs, executing *entrechats* throughout the room, was enough to hint what later films would prove, that as far as Astaire was concerned the simplest action, whether leaning against a door to light a cigarette, or putting a nickel in a telephone, would be invested with his unique blend of attitude and instinctive rhythm. At the end of the routine he catches his hat, and twirls his umbrella with a juggler's bravado, as if to confirm what we already know, that to go out into the world with this refined exuberance is to be prepared for all comers.

No one put his finger more successfully on the precise nature of the 'devil-may-care' strain in Astaire's work than James Cagney. Astaire himself affectionately volunteers the informed verdict of the master gangster and song-and-dance stalwart: 'You know, you-so-and-so, you've got a little of the hoodlum in you.' It is as if the outlook that influenced Astaire's initial introduction to the dance as a boy had persisted. Talking of his early ballet training, he comments: 'I never cared for it as applied to me. I wanted to do all my dancing my own way, in a sort of *outlaw* style. I always resented being told that I couldn't point my toe in, or some other such rule.' The 'outlaw style' would admirably serve several gangster rôles in later years. But the impulses in question are as relevant to the lyricism of *The Gay Divorcee* as to Mickey Spillane-pastiche. The cool detachment, the self-composure are ever present. Cagney's perceptive assessment came from watching Astaire in action. One wonders, however, if it was ever influenced, however slightly, by hearing the astonished reaction of Jack Warner to Mervyn LeRoy's idea to transfer the stage show *The Gay Divorce* to the screen, long before R.K.O. actually realised the project: 'Who am I going to put in it—Cagney?'

In his celebration of singular physical ability aligned with a basic normality, in his projection of that perky optimism that forbids worry until hit in the same place twice, Astaire fulfilled for the Depression audience a service similar to that offered by Fairbanks in the years immediately before and during the First World War. Even if the hoodlum had been non-existent, his cavalier would surely have convinced the sceptic that this hoofer exuded a distinct masculinity at odds with the uneasy image usually associated with male dancers. However erroneous the fallacy that overstates homosexuality, or at least effeminacy, in this most arduous of professions, there are psychologically sound reasons for supposing that Astaire was one dancer to give substance to the fallacy—on the evidence alone of the emotional blueprint of his earlier years, mother-fixated, sister-oriented, and often bereft of a father's company. And yet nothing could be further from the truth. His only serious rival amongst dancers of the silver screen, Gene Kelly, also proves the exception to the groundless rule. But whereas Kelly always seemed to go out of his way to emphasise the fact that there was nothing suspect about dancing as a male pre-occupation (the title of his first television show in 1958 tells its own story: 'Dancing—A Man's Game') with Astaire this was implicit from the word 'go'. Whereas Kelly projected an athlete's strength, an arrogance of attack in his rôle as dancer, Astaire allowed nothing to override his basic delicacy and yet still remained more vividly than Kelly in strong physical contrast to the generalised female partner. Not surprisingly, when the two masters partnered each other on screen for the first—and last?—time in the Gershwin number, 'The Babbitt and the Bromide' for *Ziegfeld Follies*, it was a meeting of two diplomats from different planets, each eyeing the other cautiously as they joked about their professional rivalry to the detriment of the individual brilliance of their respective dancing. The incident is best treasured now for its 'collector's piece' rarity; any attempt to compare and contrast the two within its context is as futile as a comparison of their whole careers. Their aims, styles, and personalities are so diverse that any such exercise becomes meaningless. In Kelly's own words: 'I was the Marlon Brando and he the Cary Grant.'

In a recent edition of *The Andy Warhol Interview*, an extensive interview with Astaire appeared side by side with a feature on Tommy Tune, the brilliant young tap-dancing star from Ken Russell's film *The Boy Friend*. Asked if he thought he possessed magic, Tune replied: 'No, magic possesses you.' This was a clearer signpost to the special secret of Astaire than anything said by the magician himself during the longer interview. Magic cannot be pinned down in words, hence Tune's elusive modesty. One does know, however, that the quality he had in mind was one shared by Astaire and Nijinsky amongst few other dancers, a quality beyond the performer's control. To an extent it involves the sheer will-power of believing yourself into the impossible, as evidenced by the fact that Nijinsky was supposedly able to suspend himself in mid-air to delay his fall during a leap. It is akin to the alchemist's gift to transmute the mundane into the sublime. Astaire's lithe stick body became its own magic wand. The magic of his routines was intrinsic, transforming mere gadgets and gimmicks out of all recognition. It is not simply that all but a few dancers are incapable of accomplishing what to the layman are impossible feats. Set a competent hoofer on a giant typewriter for the first time and he may well bewilder with his steps on the keys. What would set Astaire apart, however, is that he would instinctively tap/type out the lyric of the song he was singing at the same time.

Everyone will have his favourite fantasy projection of Astaire, whether as Mickey Mouse or D'Artagnan, Al Capone or Cardini. And yet, for all his spontaneity, no storybook veneer should disguise the muscular reality

112

behind his gazelle-like leaps and those pirouettes in which his outside leg would seem to wrap itself around the other at double the speed of the torso to which it was attached. Many lyricists celebrated in song the ease with which Astaire seemingly achieved his effects, but only Lorenz Hart in 'Do It The Hard Way' from *Pal Joey* came close to the secret: 'Fred Astaire just works so hard . . .' Astaire has his own views on this: 'My routines may look easy, but they are nothing you throw away while shaving. It's always murder to get that easy effect. I don't try to make things look easy. I'm human enough to want people to realise the hard work that went into them.' His failure pays tribute to his perfectionism. A seemingly simple throwaway trick like dislodging his hat with his cane and catching it on his foot in *Funny Face*, required the arduous grind of three weeks' rehearsal and thirty takes before Astaire was content. In April 1935, for a rare article on the self-effacing star, *Photoplay* secured an exclusive scoop report on the dancer's rehearsals for *Top Hat* for which it set the scene as follows:

> Practice makes perfect—and Fred Astaire practises. He rehearsed nine weeks before he made one dance shot for *Roberta*. He rehearsed every day of the nine weeks—Sundays and holidays. On Thanksgiving, Christmas and New Year's Day, after stewing about in the morning, he telephoned a lissome gentleman named Hermes Pan and arranged to practise two hours in the afternoon. Each time he confided to Mr Pan that the dance numbers worried him so much he couldn't possibly enjoy the holidays. The only way to stop worrying was to rehearse.

Is it surprising that he had so many dancing partners after Ginger, when one recalls her own assessment of Astaire as a 'hard taskmaster' who 'always got a little cross with me because my concentration was not as dedicated to the projects as his was'? His sister Adèle had once christened him 'Moaning Minnie' for this very reason. Hermes Pan observed that 'except for the times Fred worked with real professional dancers like Cyd Charisse, it was a twenty-five-year war'. Astaire, revealing a ruthlessness that sits uneasily on his light fantastic shoulders, has never disguised the blood, sweat and tears: 'The tears came from the girls. If they cried at rehearsal, I was sure we had a hit.' In spite of the arsenal of four-inch stiletto heels, flowing sleeves weighted with lead, choking, sneeze-inducing ostrich feathers, blinding sequins and bangles available to his leading ladies by way of reprisal the main war was, as director Rouben Mamoulian sensed, nothing if not selfcentred: 'Fred is a terribly complex fellow, not unlike the Michelangelos and Da Vincis of the Renaissance period. He's a supreme artist, but he is constantly filled with doubts and self-anger about his work—and that's what makes him so good. He is a perfectionist who is never sure he is attaining perfection.'

Astaire brought more than a meticulous devotion to the film medium. If it was only after entering films that he was able to consolidate any sort of reputation he had won in the theatre, he did so partly because he was the first to realise that there was no need to abnegate his theatrical legacy in exploiting the dance in essentially filmic terms. Until then the dancer had always been photographed piecemeal, the physical co-ordination of expression and limbs a by-product of the cutting room, and when Astaire insisted upon being filmed full-length in one take he was criticised for not being cinematic enough. And yet the elegant sweep of the camera revealed in the final product, unimpeded by distracting reaction shots, well signified the conquest of space achieved by a dancer no longer restricted to the confines of a theatre stage. Whereas at one time he had feared that the flat surface of the screen might rob the dance of its three-dimensional quality, he soon found that the camera could in fact enhance it, closing in on him for the intimate effect, backing away when he wanted space, throughout preserving a fluidity, a logic denied the celluloid patchwork of his predecessors. Which is not to say that he did not wield the scissors here and there. Astaire has volunteered no less than the 'Top Hat' routine as just one instance of 'more than meets the eye'. But the subtlety and skill with which he allowed the public eye to see only what he wanted it to see are all part of his genius. His hair's-breadth sensitivity in the cutting-room is evidence of a man as master of his medium as never before. Arlene Croce tells how he could detect when sound and picture were out of sync not merely to the frame (the speed of the film being twenty-four frames per second), but to the sprocket hole (there being, say, four sprocket holes per frame). When he saw *The Story of Vernon and Irene Castle* at Radio City Music Hall, he sensed something was amiss. Grabbing a telephone he summoned the studio in Hollywood: 'Get someone out here right away. The film is five frames out of sync.'

One needs little perception to see that he pioneered the breakaway from the dehumanised, abstractionist patterns, masquerading as dance, of Busby Berkeley—a style which Sir John Betjeman, in a brief spell as a film critic, described as 'drunkard's dream'. The integration of dance with plot championed by Astaire had a lasting effect on the film musical, to be exploited with greater realism by Vincente Minnelli and Gene Kelly during the 'forties and 'fifties. What he kept to himself, however, was the sheer filmic quality of his dancing style, whether on stage or screen. Marshall Stearns described that style as 'particularly fond of abrupt transitions from flowing movements to sudden stops, posing for a moment before proceeding to the next step—stop and go, freeze and melt'. The description could almost stand as the brief scenario for a cinematic sequence. No terminology could have been more apposite to show that Astaire did not need the *blatant* use of cutting-room techniques. The diversity achieved on film by cutting or frozen-frames, mixes or dissolves, was intrinsic in the very nature of *his* dance itself.

No assessment of Astaire should allow his talents as dancer and choreographer to overshadow his flair as a singer, and yet thankfully the fact remains that as a singer he remains a dancer. The spry, springy voice, suggesting tonsils that are cushions of air, gives itself away as soon as it is heard. But there is more to the comparison than the general buoyancy with which his voice skims across the surface of a lyric. Beneath the overall effect is a precise detailed interpretation of that lyric which will chart its own dance in the most adamant wallflower of a mind. One recalls his tentative advance—phrase by phrase—towards the special girl of Berlin's 'Change Partners': 'Must you dance—every dance—with the same fortunate man?—You have danced with him since the music began—won't you change partners . . .?' and then, after he has gained confidence with each step, the nervous backing down implicit in the now muted suggestion, 'and dance with me?' Equally telling is the mounting *joie de vivre* he instils into his one hope, his suggestion that she sits this dance out and while he's alone, he'll get the waiter to tell her partner 'he's wanted on the . . .'—and then the peak of breathless exhilaration at the mention of the *deus ex machina*— '. . . telephone'. There is his cautious approach as he gropes his way through the beginning of Gershwin's 'A Foggy Day'; the carefree lackadaisical jaunt he makes out of Berlin's 'Isn't This a Lovely Day?'; the way he makes certain syllables tap out their own tattoo in the same song's 'Let the rain pitter patter but it really doesn't matter'; the breathtaking shuffle of Gershwin's 'Fascinatin' Rhythm'—'Just like a quiver'; the monosyllabic momentum of Berlin's 'Puttin' on the Ritz'; the breathless vocal climb in the same writer's 'Cheek to Cheek'—'and my heart beats so that I can hardly *speak*'.

Oscar Levant once observed that Astaire 'is the best singer of songs the movie world ever knew'. He certainly had few rivals. If Crosby's special knack was in singing his songs as if he were speaking them, Astaire with his slightly hesitant but still controlled phrasing sounded as if he were the lyricist putting them to paper for the first time. The lyricists themselves must have been impressed. Certainly no popular vocalist, with the debatable exceptions of Crosby and Ethel Merman, ever had more great standards written specifically for him or her than Fred Astaire. His unique vocal style, coupled with the necessity for the songs to be danced to, encouraged composers to reach rhythmic heights they would never have achieved without Astaire as a spring-board. The *Photoplay* article already quoted gave a revealing glimpse of how his choreography could in fact prove a crucial creative factor of the final composition:

> Music isn't necessary to him in creating a dance. The dances for *Roberta* were rehearsed for two weeks before Jerome Kern's score arrived. Astaire adapts the music to his steps, not his step to the music. Kern's music has been re-arranged to suit Fred's rhythm. In it have been inserted spontaneous 'tum-tiddley-tums' hummed by Fred while rehearsing. Hal Borne catches them on the keys of a tiny, battered theatrical piano, and scribbles them down . . . Somehow, they always fit in.

Composers appeared to have no qualms about this process, even though it dispensed with their safeguard of a conventional musical arrangement before the number passed to Astaire. Irving Berlin insisted that he would rather have Astaire introduce his songs than any other vocalist; the notoriously fastidious Jerome Kern commented, 'Astaire *can't* do anything bad'. Certainly the songs which the usually folksy Berlin wrote for the ritzy Astaire remain his most invigorating, including 'Top Hat', 'Let's Face the Music and Dance' and 'I'm Putting All My Eggs in One Basket', in addition to those cited above. With Kern the process worked in reverse, his quintessential Astaire number 'I Won't Dance' added to the film version of *Roberta* in 1934, having been composed for the London show *Three Sisters* with thoughts of Astaire far from Kern's mind. Later, however, would come the equally flippant 'A Fine Romance' and 'Pick Yourself Up', and the submissive 'The

Way You Look Tonight', in collaboration with lyricist Dorothy Fields; and then the mellower 'You Were Never Lovelier'; 'I'm Old-Fashioned', and 'Dearly Beloved' with Johnny Mercer. The *Three Sisters* number uncannily reflected the mood of cool, surface detachment that was a basic ingredient of Astaire's romantic chemistry, and it is this aspect, delicate but unsentimental, that Kern came to exploit most effectively in their relationship.

Although, by comparison with that of Kern and Berlin, the contribution to the cinema of Cole Porter and George Gershwin was marginal when seen against the perspective of their total careers, it is not surprising that the achievement of Fred Astaire should figure prominently within that contribution. Of the fifteen films made featuring the music of George Gershwin, only four were based on original scores for the screen and luckily Astaire starred in two of them. *Shall We Dance?* produced its title song, 'They Can't Take That Away from Me', 'They All Laughed' and 'Let's Call the Whole Thing Off', while *A Damsel in Distress* yielded 'A Foggy Day', 'I Can't Be Bothered Now' and 'Nice Work If You Can Get It'. And this is not to mention 'Fascinatin' Rhythm', introduced by him and Adèle on Broadway in *Lady Be Good*. Porter also enjoyed the distinction of writing an early theatrical vehicle for Astaire. However, when *The Gay Divorce* was transferred to the screen as *The Gay Divorcee* only one song by Porter survived, 'Night and Day'. Seven years later in 1941 Porter would make amends with 'So Near And Yet So Far', 'Shootin' the Works for Uncle Sam', 'Dream Dancing', and 'A-stairable Rag', all from *You'll Never Get Rich*. But by then Porter had already immortalised 'the nimble tread of the feet of Fred Astaire' in somebody else's song.

In recent years the songs quite as much as the dancing have, by courtesy of film archives and individual memory-banks, kept the flame of his legend fiercely aglow. The veneer of past achievement, however, should not disguise the contribution to that legend of his later years. No one has done more to disprove the cruel hard fact that the life of a dancer is the shortest artistic life in the world. Perhaps because dancing was to Astaire a natural breath of life, rather than a mere discipline applied from without, he could as late as 1968 invest his solo routine in *Finian's Rainbow* ('When the Idle Poor Become the Idle Rich') with a freewheeling panache that not merely disguised the slower pace, but provided the most dazzling of all curtain-raisers to a seventieth birthday. If one did detect a dash of caution as he ricocheted his way up a mountain of packing cases, swung from the rafters, twirled the walking-stick, it added a welcome edginess to the old verve and precision without detracting in any way from the basic elegance, untarnished throughout a film career of thirty-five years. And if this time he didn't get the girl, he did get the rainbow. In spite of its metropolitan gloss and the plot-motivating intrusion of a whole gallery of Harpies and Lotharios, the world of the standard Astaire musical had remained throughout nostalgic and witty, innocent and basically uncorrupt, where true love really did run smooth. In this respect it served as a valid contemporary projection of the pastoral myth. There was then a comforting irony in the way he came with *Finian's Rainbow* to arrive, as if full circle, at a truly rural Arcadia.

Throughout his career Astaire has been like a blade of grass. If you cut the top off most plants, they either die or take ages to recover. Grass, however, seems to thrive on the surge of regrowth that cutting encourages. It is this capacity for constant regrowth and revitalisation that in retrospect characterises Astaire's continuing success story. It involves the endless search for choreographic originality, the flawless ability to master each new technical advancement, the patience and intuition required in meeting the demands of each new partner, each new director. Astaire never had to endure any desperate career trough. It is significant, however, that his characterisation in *The Band Wagon* of a failing Hollywood hoofer intent on a Broadway comeback, should prove to be the pinnacle of his entire solo—as distinct from Adèle- or Ginger-oriented—career, coming as it did at a period when his last few films had been purely minor successes and he must, at the age of fifty-two, have been anxiously concerned for his own future. Towards the end of the day, however, the brightest token of his capacity for regrowth remains the enduring popularity of his less active years, consolidating as it does a lifetime's legacy of challenge well met. Cult-hero is too restrictive a word to use of an entertainer who like no other dancer before or since danced down the imaginations of his public. The imagination craves the incredible and Astaire never disappointed. He even got to dance on the radio and then there was no limit to the public's interpretation of the compact 'string of ricky-ticky-ticky-tacky-ticky-tacky steps' he specially devised to compensate for leaps that could neither be seen nor heard.

Astaire himself remains totally unimpressed by his reputation as a living legend. It is an attitude that disappoints many of his admirers and yet it was inevitable. The very qualities of self-effacement, modesty, and insatiable desire for new horizons which helped to found his popularity are precisely those which now prevent him from accepting the burden of his fame with anything but reluctance. In April 1973, he was fêted at a gala in his honour at Lincoln Center under the auspices of the New York Film Festival in co-operation with the City Center for Music and Drama and the Museum of Modern Art. Astaire used the press conference for this singular occasion as an opportunity to enlarge upon the notoriously modest reply he once gave an interviewer who asked him about the origins of his style: 'I just dance.' If tolerant amusement is a fit response for his confession to the press that 'I've always hated white tie and tails. They're so uncomfortable and I try never to wear them', it is with something approaching desperation that one listens to his wish, emphasised with morbid illogicality in the subsequent Warhol interview, that all his films should be destroyed, no permanent record of himself should survive. One could dismiss his own dismissal 'I just dance' with the qualification that Olivier just acts, Sinatra just sings. But the influence ranges wider. Seldom has such a happy mean been struck between work of such intense aesthetic quality and sheer popular appeal. For all its Keatonian wit and elegant precision, the sheer hard grind and mental discipline, Astaire's achievement never ceased to appear within easy reach of any Sidewalk Joe who ever fancied himself waltzing out in top hat, white tie, and tails. But if the self-deflating attitude towards his own talent appears at times to reach the madcap dimensions more usually associated with the excesses of the publicity machinery which encouraged the attitude in the first instance, nothing can or will undermine the legend now. As George Axelrod pointed out, 'Astaire' has added a new word to the language.

Bing Crosby

Where the blue of the night . . .

Aᴛ ᴀ ᴛɪᴍᴇ when slapdash is often palmed off as nonchalance, Bing Crosby has elevated the civilised quality to the status of a virtue. It is not enough, however, to suppose that life has just come easily to him. This would imply a lack of personal control, of moral strength. He has made disinterestedness appealing because at the same time he remains in total command of his life. He may never have raised his eyebrows in surprise, but then he has never compromised either. He may distrust the outward display of emotion, but that distrust stands as an affirmation of the deepest concern. For all his modesty, he above all knows his own worth, with his own shrewd understanding of what James Agee meant when he wrote in 1945 that he would enjoy Crosby 'probably even if he did nothing more than walk across a shot', a not-so-glib tribute to the most unassuming of entertainers who became his own one-man embodiment of *laissez-faire*.

His social manner now is naturally relaxed, a synthesis of all the qualities that have contributed to show-business immortality, of flawless self-possession and gentle humility, of masculine strength and sympathetic warmth. Most indicative is his smile, its own combination of impudent joy and deep, deserved satisfaction, a joint celebration of both the present and the past. As he puffs contentedly on the jutting pipe that is a natural extension of his short, lean silhouette, one is soon caught up in the easy rhythm which informs his acting, his singing, his total personality. For all that he would have one believe otherwise, it is inconceivable that a success as phenomenal as Crosby's should not have been built upon a sometime foundation of practice, sweat, tears, if only in the constant polishing of that casual charm. Nothing said so far, however, should obscure the fact that this ease and equanimity are nothing if not ingrained in the first instance.

His lazy independence was the linchpin of a special style which at the peak of his popularity no less than half of the world's impressionable male white population would seemingly strive to emulate. In 1964 he came out of quasi-semi-retirement to make the film *Robin and the Seven Hoods* with Sinatra and Dean Martin. One of Bing's three songs had the latter pair chiding him for his lack of 'Style', whereupon straw-hatted, tuxedoed and with cane poised he sprung effortlessly into action, leaving them right back at the starting post. The performance was the more remarkable for being untypical. In earlier years loose-fitting sports clothes—reputedly to accommodate his golf swing—and not Fifth Avenue elegance had provided the perfect sartorial complement to his attitude, underlining his indisputable claim to being 'just one of the fellows', adding weight to C. A. Lejeune's claim that Hollywood was at its best at its most human. The most perfect expression of his style, however, had no need to be seen—namely, his voice. In an entertainment era dominated by radio and the gramophone quite as much as by the cinema he would have made an impact whatever he wore. The singer was as he sang, and that was as if there was all the time in the world.

His initial impact was the fortuitous culmination of a unique set of historical circumstances. His musical coming-of-age coincided not only with the advent of mass media—radio, electrical recording, and 'talkies' in that order of immediate personal importance—perfectly suited to convey his low-key warmth and intimacy to the widest possible audience, but with the subdued, yet desperate aftermath of the frenetic 'twenties, the immediate sequel to the Jazz Age or, in the words of Scott Fitzgerald, that 'children's party taken over by the elders'. On the threshold of the Depression years, at a time when, in spite of the evidence of Wall Street that life like the bowl of cherries in the song had its own hard centre, many people would still have difficulty in convincing themselves that the fun days were over, Crosby was exactly right. His cultured, manly baritone, in marked contrast with the high-pitched, other-worldliness of his crooning forerunner, Rudy Vallee, added a dash of responsibility to his devil-may-care. He could juggle the home-spun with the sophisticated, the jazzy with the sentimental and keep all the balls up in the air at the same time. More than this, Bing had an instinctive feel not merely for the kind of songs his public wanted sung, but also for the way they wanted them sung. Never did his treatment of a number betray the sentiments one would have expected from his audience on becoming acquainted with its lyric *per se*. He also possessed a sense of humour, a quality unusual for a popular singer if only because of the limitations placed on displaying it. Because it allowed him to do just this, radio was an ideal medium; but there were other reasons quite as much in character: 'You didn't have to worry about putting on any wardrobe or any make-up or anything. Just there's the script and you knock it off and you're out and away laughing and scratching.'

National popularity came to him almost overnight after his first appearance for CBS in an unsponsored daily fifteen-minute programme on 2 September 1931, the result of a chance transatlantic hearing by the network chief, William S. Paley, of Bing's recording of 'I Surrender, Dear', upon which he immediately cabled to shore with instructions that Crosby should be contracted. The air waves provided full scope for his distinctive hands-in-pockets conversational style, a hybrid of slack slang and polysyllabic surprise. In the Crosby phrase-book skis became 'society slats', a group of 'co-eds' 'a covey of culture-vultures'. A duet with a fellow performer was always an opportunity to 'cross cadenzas'; but it would never 'wow the audience', merely 'crumple the folks'. But with a voice like his, he didn't need the carefree lingo to convey the relaxed hammock swing of his personality.

Singing is as natural to Crosby as sweetness to honey, in spite of his insistence that he is 'not a singer—more a phraser'. But while he differentiates at his own expense between himself, the 'journeyman sea-level baritone' of his own description (who as a boy gave up the vocal lessons his mother had arranged as soon as the baseball season began), and the trained classical singer, it is the latter who must often stand in awe of Bing's own unerring sense of rhythm and ability to stay effortlessly on pitch. Pushed to explain what he means by 'phraser', he admits to paying constant attention to the words he's singing, to the extent that melody will become subsidiary to message. He will twist a tune around to accommodate a lyric to the rhythms of normal conversational speech, leaving a number well alone should the tune resist. And here the dividing line between the old 'groaner' and the opera virtuoso does become valid. The latter, in striving towards a surface display of technical mastery, has less need to attach thought to the words. The casual rhythmic phrasing of Crosby not only demands it, but also reveals a distinctive creative facet that plays its own part in explaining what has made Crosby unique in the most overcrowded profession in the entertainment world. One has only to listen to his rendering of a punchy, up-tempo number like 'Now You Has Jazz' with Louis Armstrong from the 1956 film *High Society* to realise that his voice had a snaky flexibility far beyond the little catch in the throat that first caught the public ear in his early 'scat' days. While he talks freely about the vocal technicalities now, during the period of his peak success he devoutly believed in the art that conceals art. Then his explanation for his singing success was coyly commonplace: 'It's not difficult to imitate me, because most people who've ever sung in a kitchen quartet or in a showerbath sing like me.' But he would not, and never will, give away the exact extent of the practice required to make each number succumb to his ideal of relaxed perfection. He had shrewdly made sure that security on his own bathroom was the tightest anywhere in the world.

While the material rewards of success would have been enough to convince Crosby of the immediate impact of his casual artistry, it is doubtful if he ever sensed the far-reaching influence his style would have upon popular singing in the years to come. In time it became a sort of model for a group of hopefuls that would include Perry Como, Dean Martin, Andy Williams and Sinatra himself amongst a thousand others. Bing brought a breath of best golfing air to a musical arena dominated by the image of the stiff-shirted tenor or dramatic baritone with his square phrasing and artificial diction. His supremacy as simply a singer of songs is and doubtless will remain irrevocable. Over a quarter of a century from the early 'thirties when he first hit his stride with the mass public, he has starred in more successful films and until now sold more records than any other singer, including Jolson, Sinatra, Presley and the Beatles. For ten years he was consistently voted the most popular film actor, nine of his films enjoying an exalted position amongst *Variety*'s poll of all-time grossers, a success overriding all changing musical trends. At the last count his total record sales were computed at no less than 375 million. What escaped most of the world's notice as its breath was being taken away was that this figure represents his sales on the Decca label alone. It fails to take into account the records he has made for eighty-seven other labels. And the figure is all the more impressive in that most of those sales were achieved during the commercial calm before the storm of high-pressure plugging and personality pushing. But even now it is unlikely that either Presley or the Beatles, in their capacity as performers, will surpass him, neither having yet enjoyed such a wide general acceptance as Bing.

The danger with any appraisal of Crosby is that it will become swamped by statistics, figures so gargantuan as to prove impersonal. One is consequently grateful for the humour of Bob Hope for putting the wealth attendant upon such figures in a nutshell, wealth so immense as to cause the man variously described by Crosby as 'ski-snoot' and 'scow-prow' to quip: 'Bing doesn't pay income tax anymore. He just asks the government what they need.' One is likewise grateful for the near-mythology that always accrues to people who have endured extreme hardship for placing in humane and proper perspective the full extent of his personal appeal. When a division of American soldiers was trapped on Bataan towards the bitter end of 1942, General Douglas MacArthur radioed to the White House that the man his men most wanted to hear at that most torturous of moments was the very man whose surname not only rhymed with, but virtually spelt 'carefree'. Appropriately, on the Japanese surrender at the end of hostilities, General George Kenny was heard to remark amid the celebrations aboard the battleship *Missouri*: 'Well now, if we just had Bing Crosby here to sing a couple of songs, it'd be perfect.'

Crosby openly admits that he would never have achieved such colossal sales figures without casting his net so wide as to encompass no less than 2,600 separate 'single' recordings from the day he first entered a recording studio in 1926. At the badgering insistence of Jack Kapp, the head of Decca Records, who contributed considerably to toning down the early 'boo-boo-boo' affection of Crosby's singing style after his first flush of success, he recorded every possible type of song, from Stephen Foster to Gershwin, Brahms to Victor Herbert, cowboy ballads to hymns, semi-classical to blues, even patriotic readings and playlets with Orson Welles. He proved that there was hardly any kind of material he could not master and in so doing stood revealed at his peak as the synthesis of the many strands of the American popular music tradition. And if this way he also notched up more flops than most of his contemporaries, it would be unfair to accuse him of blatant lack of discrimination. Crosby himself chose the song which was not a little responsible for confirming his early radio success and has remained his signature tune ever since: 'Where the Blue of the Night Meets the Gold of the Day'. He did in fact change the original lyric by Roy Turk before the number caught on and is now officially listed as one of its authors. Likewise Crosby himself spotted his first million-seller, 'Sweet Leilani', while it was being played in a hotel lounge in Hawaii. On his return he had a struggle convincing the producer of *Waikiki Wedding* that the song was the lullaby they were after for him to sing to a Hawaiian child in the film. Bing played hard to get and went back to the golf course where he invariably won the day.

Given the unwritten rule that there are some songs which become the copyright performance-wise of one singer, which no other singer should sing, he vies, not surprisingly, with Astaire and Sinatra for top overall priority. Certainly top songwriters have composed more hits with Crosby in mind than for any other performer with the arguable exceptions of Merman and his *Holiday Inn* co-star. Amongst the songs he has introduced, and which have become standards in part because he happened to sing them originally, are Cole Porter's 'I Love You, Samantha', Irving Berlin's 'Be Careful, It's My Heart', Rodgers and Hart's 'Easy to Remember', Arlen and Mercer's 'Accentuate the Positive', Hoagy Carmichael's 'Stardust', Burke and Van Heusen's 'Busy Doing Nothing' and 'The Second Time Around', Burke and Johnston's 'Pennies from Heaven' and 'One, Two, Button Your Shoe', in addition to 'Please', 'Love in Bloom', 'Love Is Just Around the Corner', 'June in January', 'The Waiter, the Porter, and the Upstairs Maid', all from less distinguished writers. He can claim to have introduced more Oscar-winning songs than any rival, including 'Sweet Leilani', 'Would You Like to Swing on a Star?' by Burke and Van Heusen for *Going My Way* and 'In the Cool, Cool, Cool of the Evening' by Mercer and Carmichael for *Here Comes the Groom*. And all this makes no mention of the *pièce de résistance*, namely the number Irving Berlin penned for *Holiday Inn*, 'White Christmas'. This song of seasonal schmaltz, which transcended even hymn status to become no less than an anthem for peace during the most desperate years of the Second World War, not only won a fourth Oscar but proved to be the biggest-selling record by any performer ever, having sold as many as thirty million copies so far.

In keeping with such a momentous success story, no performer can claim a more multi-faceted pedigree of musical influence than the singer who was born Harry Lillis Crosby in Tacoma, Washington on 2 May 1901 (three years earlier than the date given in all publicity throughout his career). He was rechristened eight years later as a result of his adulation for and passing resemblance to Bingo, the Charlie Brown-type hero of a comic-strip entitled 'The Bingville Bugle'. The change of name was instigated by a childhood friend whose equally exotic tag of Valentine Hobart, with its Mark Twain connotation of Mississippi riverboat gamblers, Bing had long coveted for himself. But if childish independence craved the unconventional, Bing had only to look to his line of ancestry which went back to Denmark (Crosby is a phonetic Danish equivalent of 'town of the cross') on his father's side and County Cork on his mother's. It is a family tree which, after successive transplanting from Denmark to Ireland, England, and finally the United States, can boast upon its paternal branches William Brewster, a signer of the Mayflower Compact; Captain Nathaniel Crosby II, Bing's great-grandfather, who sailed around Cape Horn in 1849 and was one of the founders of Portland, Oregon; Blind Fannie Crosby, the legendary authoress of countless hymns and gospel songs; and maternally, from Ireland via Canada, his uncle, George Harrigan, a would-be saloon troubadour who helped to popularise the Cohan song, 'Harrigan, That's Me' on a local Tacoma basis.

But Bing's attention was soon side-tracked from comic strips and the prospect of genealogical tables. From the early moment when his father, Harry Lowe Crosby, bought one of the first commercial phonographs, or 'Victor Talking Machines', the family life of the musically enthusiastic book-keeper, his wife Kate Helen, and their seven offspring, of which Bing arrived fourth in line, revolved literally around this miniature platform for the distorted vocal talents of the day. Bing himself cannot recall a time when he was not able to conjure sounds genie-like out of the machine. He has certainly never played down the influence it had on him: 'Everybody in Spokane knew when I was coming because they could hear me singing or whistling. I suppose that was because of having a dad who was always bringing a new tune into the house on sheet music or on record—I had a constant succession of them in my head. And I had to whistle or sing to get them out.' But the magical if scratchy ease with which entertainment could be summoned did not stand in the way of his noticing that some talent stood out and was especially worthy of emulation. Inspiration was provided by the tender-sweet, lyric voice of John McCormack, with whose Irish descent Crosby could proudly identify; by the even greater impact of the personal electricity of Al Jolson, whom he had the additional advantage of watching live when he took a part-time job as property assistant at the Auditorium Theatre in Spokane, where the family had moved in 1906 (it was at this theatre that Crosby recalls 'the first priming coat of show business rubbed off on me'); by the vibrant jazz and blues singer Mildred Bailey, known affectionately as 'Rockin' Chair Lady' after her first big hit.

At twelve, Bing was already appearing at local concerts singing a premature medley of ballads about lilacs on graves, running brooks, twilight and the pain of unrequited love, to be climaxed by a comedy number about his dog, Rover, for which he would walk on stage dragging an empty leash. The dog had a habit of disappearing sufficiently often for the young Crosby to admit: 'Sometimes I wish I were a tree,/Then Rover would have to look for me./Oh, where's that doggone, doggone, dog of mine?' In time he found himself reading law at Gonzaga University, but while he was studying by day, he kept singing and playing drums in local clubs by night. The ribbing he took from colleagues, who at that time found it sexually suspect for a supposedly full-blooded male to be singing songs like 'One Fleeting Hour' and 'Peggy O'Neill', did not stand in the way of his decision to drop his studies and make a full-time career out of music, any more than the fact that he was grossing more in a week from singing than the solicitor to whom he was articled earned from the law. His first professional engagement was at his local cinema and entailed providing an appropriate vocal prelude to the big movie, sea shanties for a naval epic, country songs for a western, and so on. By night he was still busking at local gigs with 'The Juicy Seven', later renamed 'The Musicaladers', and eventually in 1921 he teamed up with their leader and pianist Al Rinker in a double act, 'Two Boys and a Piano—Singing Songs Their Own Way'.

If Crosby was disheartened at this stage by the opposition he met from his parents, there was compensation to be gained from a fairy godmother, in the person of no less than Mildred Bailey herself, who apart from being an everlasting influence on the young song stylist was also the sister of Al Rinker. Launched on their way by her promise to give them some useful contacts, they found themselves at the start of a mutual adventure that would prove as picaresque as any subsequent *Road* picture.

In 1925 they set out for Los Angeles in a battered old model T tied together with string, with twenty dollars in their pockets, and landed a lucky audition to play the Fanchon and Marco cine-variety circuit with their double act. This led to rôles in Will Morrisey's travelling 'Night Club Revue', which eventually folded through lack of company discipline as well as total lack of public interest. Within eighteen months they had progressed to the Paramount-Publix Circuit, alternating between the Metropolitan Theatre in Los Angeles and the Granada in San Francisco. At this time their act featured up-tempo numbers like 'Mary Lou' and 'In a Little Spanish Town', with a sprinkling of spicy novelty items with final lines like 'Oh, you must have slept like Aphrodite,/Because you didn't take your nightie'.

At the Metropolitan their act was brought to the notice of Paul Whiteman, then America's most popular band leader, who was playing the Million Dollar Theatre a block away. Summoned to his hotel room, they auditioned for all three hundred and ten pounds of his imperial silk-swathed presence as he sat eating caviar and sipping champagne, redolent with eau-de-cologne. However, by the time the master-showman introduced them to their first mutual audience at the Tivoli Theatre in Chicago the picture had changed: 'I want you to meet a couple of boys I found in an ice-cream parlour in Walla Walla.' While not true, the introduction exactly set the carefree, humorous tone of their act.

The further they moved east, however, the more antagonistic audiences became to their material, until, came the band's big début at the newly opened New York Paramount, Bing and Al flopped so badly that they were not merely removed from the rest of the run but, when 'Pops' opened his new nightclub on Broadway, were reduced to table-waiting service. Crosby's increasingly excessive drinking and wild-oat-sowing tendencies at this time were such that Whiteman was forced into giving a guarantee that any future contract for the Paramount would contain a 'no-Bing' clause. The maestro, however, was as shrewd as he looked formidable. Crosby's youthful recklessness tested his tolerance, but, because he sensed Crosby's priceless if as yet embryonic gifts, not least his capacity for audience identification, he persuaded a confident young singer-composer-pianist named Harry Barris, who billed himself 'Young Mister Show Business Himself', to play down his own ego and complete a hat-trick that would henceforth be known as 'Paul Whiteman's Rhythm Boys'. They toured the Keith circuit under his invisible aegis, their snappy presentation promoted as pioneering the 'swing style' vocal technique.

On Whiteman's return from a tour of Europe the trio became integrated into the band and now, as audiences began to single out the minstrel with the effervescent *vibrato* and 'come-into-my-parlour' grin, the full significance of Whiteman's patronage became apparent. The fact that Bing was given a silent rubber-stringed fiddle to 'play' as he sat in the band line-up is a clue. Until Whiteman spotted Crosby, the singer who sang with a band was a musician whose versatility enabled him to double on an instrument, which was momentarily put aside as he demonstrated his middling vocal prowess. Crosby was the first to be employed on the strength of his personality and vocal ability alone and as such the first of the 'band singers' as the public came to know them. But even his extraordinary vocal talent wouldn't bring Whiteman to dispense with the illusion of versatility the dummy instrument was meant to encourage. In fact the fiddle was at once penance as well as means to an end. Originally Bing was given a succession of wind instruments which he had to pretend to blow. To Whiteman's mounting fury, however,

he couldn't resist blowing an inopportune 'oompah' to complement a spectacular arrangement. Hence the screech-less violin. Otherwise the only
instrumental ability he was allowed to show was in his sock-cymbal
accompaniment to the comedy numbers that were always a stand-by of
the 'Rhythm Boys' routine and in the occasional spell on kazoo for a trick
trombone effect.

However many restrictions 'Pops' placed upon his youthful ebullience,
Crosby would never be able to complain of his years with Whiteman. He
admits that 'if I have any ability as a song stylist or have made out musically,
it's largely because of the associations I formed while I was with the band'.
Certainly no singer ever enjoyed a more impressive nursery. If in emulating
the vocal looping-the-loop, if not the emotional exaggeration, of his early
idol, Al Jolson, he had absorbed the instinctive timing of the vaudeville art,
the secret of its special attack, it was in working with such jazz legends as
Bix Beiderbecke, Joe Venuti, Lennie Hayton, Eddie Lang and the Dorsey
Brothers that he acquired the added subtlety of tricky jazz phrasing. Incredible as it may now seem in retrospect, they were all at one time part of
Whiteman's rank and file. One indication of the lengths to which 'Pops'
would go to ensure that the most progressive arrangers and the most stunning performing talent of the day was at *his* disposal is that in January 1928
his weekly payroll came to no less than $9,400—*then*. And out of that Bing
was getting more than a mere percentage: 'I hung around them day and
night. I listened to them talk. I picked up ideas. Although I wasn't a
musician—I'm still not one—I learned to appreciate good things when I
heard them and to recognise bad things and avoid them.' Unconsciously at
the time, he would strive to make his vocal inflection fit the way Beiderbecke
would himself phrase his solo melody on that golden cornet, Lang on that
throbbing guitar. It would take several years for the Crosby style as it was
known at the height of his fame to crystallise and superficially no one would
in vacuo describe it as that of the jazz singer. But on close analysis, few
voices have more subtly reflected the environment of their formative years
and in the process more surely laid claim to that title, and that in spite of the
fact that his own success helped to pull down the blind on the Jazz Age
itself. His own sense of identification with the Whiteman period is best
measured now by the glow of enthusiasm which suffuses his personal account
of the jazz immortals. Moreover, one soon realises from his insistence that
the over-romanticised Beiderbecke was not least a serious student of
Stravinsky, Ravel, Debussy, the avant-garde classical music of its day, and
from his joy in paralleling the volatile Venuti's skill on violin with that
fiddler's prowess at blowing rafter-shaking raspberries, often substituted for
the last note of the song which he had no right to be singing anyway, that
Bing was not only exposed to a complete spectrum of inspired musicianship,
but that no one could be more contentedly grateful for the experience.

For three years Crosby recorded with both Whiteman's band and others
in the menial 'with vocal refrain' capacity of band vocalist before his name
was given precedence over that of the orchestra for his 1929 recording of
'My Kinda Love'. The following year saw the filming of *The King of Jazz*,
an elaborate showcase for Whiteman and his stellar group of soloists, for
which Bing sang the opening song, 'Music Hath Charms', and, with the other

two Rhythm Boys, featured their novelty 'So the Bluebirds and the Black-birds Got Together' in tinted silhouette. Once shooting was over the boys struck out independently and became affiliated to Gus Arnheim's Orchestra. The Arnheim radio show brought Bing the wider public exposure he required and soon a contract with Brunswick Records was his. After ten stupendous months with Arnheim at the Cocoanut Grove in Los Angeles' Hotel Ambassador, the trio held out for a higher salary, was refused, walked out, and found itself blacklisted by the Union as a result. With this the Rhythm Boys went their separate ways, Barris subsequently pursuing an independent career as an accompanist and Rinker as a radio producer. Bing's own big break into radio, in the late summer of 1931, has already been described and within months he was booked as the big attraction into the New York Paramount. His career had come full circle. Ironically, the Paramount was the theatre where five years previously Whiteman had been barred from using his services. Now Bing was allowed to stay for a record-breaking twenty-six weeks and to collect a weekly salary of no less than $7,500 in the process. The most significant development of his success on both air and turn-table was that now Hollywood began to consider him for parts in major films. He was given the lead in *The Big Broadcast of 1932*, a revue on celluloid held together by a slender story-line and featuring the big radio names of the day including the brilliant Burns and adorable Allen, buxom Kate Smith, the Mills Brothers and the Boswell Sisters; within two years he was rivalling Mae West as Paramount's biggest box-office attraction. The baroque eccentricity, the banal extravagance of both Hollywood and its people seemed to throw into welcome relief the relaxed artistry he had acquired during the long slog of touring and playing incessantly to live audiences.

The attempts made at the time to make him conform to the preconceived Hollywood ideal of a romantic idol are now well known. The make-up department initially spent so much time gluing those jug-handle ears back against his head, securing a toupee or what he calls his 'scalp-doily' to that thinning scalp, that comedian Jack Oakie christened Crosby 'The Robot of Romance'. The heat of the studio lights, however, soon sent the ears springing back to give Bing, in his own words, the look rather of 'a whippet in full flight', the look that to his relief eventually persisted on the screen. Meanwhile the toupee was proving sufficiently irksome for him always to be plotting ways of playing a scene, even a love scene, with his hat on; no Catholic actor was ever more desirous of playing a rabbi's rôle. But the processing was irrelevant. What no studio had realised, as Crosby began in pictures, was that the advent of sound had made looks subsidiary to talent and personality—certainly as far as the leading song-and-dance men were concerned. In the silent days the only alternative for the balding, ear-flapping actor who refused romantic grooming, however artificial, was to play character rôles. But the people who had changed the times were the last to realise it. As Arlene Croce has indicated, the list of male singers and dancers who became big cinema stars—she witnesses Chevalier, Astaire, Dick Powell, Sinatra, Kelly and Lanza, in addition to Bing—is 'very largely an assortment of ageing, balding, skinny, tubby, jug-eared, pugfaced and generally unprepossessing men'. With Bing, however, the least conventional romantic of them all, the resistance to appearing any other way is an actual token of his style. He doesn't care—with care. When the toupee was dislodged during a violent quarrel with Carole Lombard in *We're Not Dressing*, he not only requested that they keep that shot in to avoid re-shooting, but won the day, as the final print proves.

His cinematic career went from strength to strength, eventually revealing hidden emotional reserves as a straight actor in films like *The Country Girl* and *Little Boy Lost*. At the outset, however, success was primarily in spite of the quality of the vehicles he was given, with two glaring exceptions—those of his religious and of his *Road* phase. He received an Oscar for *Going My Way* and his portrayal of the crooning Irish-American priest of a slum community, St George thrusting his lance through the dragon of big-city cynicism. The key to his success here was that he did not act like a priest at all, at least not the stereotyped, foregone conclusion of a priest that existed in the public mind. What his audience did not realise was that the chief influence on his rôle was his time spent as a youth amongst the Jesuit Fathers of Gonzaga High School and Gonzaga University, which subsequently awarded him the honorary degree of Doctor of Music in 1937. Subtle yet tough, devout but debonair, his Father O'Malley absorbed more than a lightning flash of mentors like Father Kennelly, or 'Big Jim', weighing in at 280 pounds and feared for his frequent recourse to a cassock-concealed chain twelve feet long with keys attached which he would flick out with an angler's panache to sting a misbehaving pupil where it would hurt most, or Father Gilmore with his head-in-the-clouds line in hair restorers in which he failed to interest the young Crosby.

The assured quality of his performance, which skilfully treads a thin line between seriousness and sentimentality, is in fact less surprising than his acceptance of the rôle in the first instance. When Jack Kapp originally asked him to record 'Silent Night', eventually one of his biggest selling records, his immediate reaction had been, 'Who do you think I am, Lily Pons?' He at first greeted the idea of *Going My Way* with a similar fear of sacrilege, but was eventually persuaded by director Leo McCarey, with an improvised run-down on the plot which had little in common with the eventual film, that the idea of Bing in long, black, buttoned-down robe was not so wild as it might have appeared. And if one regrets that this priest has an improbable number of show-business contacts to whom to turn for help in getting his choir to make a hit record of their own, then showman's licence may be claimed *quid pro quo* on the grounds that Bing himself was only won over to the 'Silent Night' recording on the grounds that its total royalties be donated to charity. The film was so successful that in *The Bells of St Mary's* it bred that rarity in cinema history, not merely a successful sequel, but one which did even better than its forerunner. Both films were banned in South America, where objections were raised to a priest wearing sweat shirts and playing baseball, but any guilty Hollywood conscience was assuaged by a message of encouragement from Pope Pius XII, gladdened by any attempt made to humanise the priesthood.

Going My Way also re-emphasised what the success of the *Road* series had already proved, Crosby's exceptional sense of rapport with his fellow artists. The antagonism, however, struck up between his bland religious novice and the peppery old priest of Barry Fitzgerald, enthusiastically living up to his irascible image, was no mere 'second take' of the Hope-Crosby relationship. The ever-present qualities of modesty, warmth and ease enabled him to serve admirably as foil, without at the same time appearing as anything less than equal, to a whole string of co-stars. One recalls the exciting contrast between the sherbet fizz of the Satchmo personality and the dry wafer biscuit of Bing's. But eventually it was a capacity channelled to maximum effect in the direction of comedy. In his autobiography he characteristically played down this talent for mixing:

> An entertainer who is seen or heard too much is like the pitcher which overplayed its luck at the well. If I'm fortunate in being associated with a Bill Fields, a Fred Astaire, a Bob Hope or a Barry Fitzgerald or some other talent-loaded individual, it's like hitting a triple parley at the races. It helps the pictures—in which I have a financial stake—at the box office; I don't have to work so hard; if the picture's good, I get more credit than I would have if I'd knocked myself out in a turkey.

Elsewhere, however, he did volunteer: 'Once or twice I've been described as a light comedian. I consider this the most accurate description of my abilities I've ever seen.' This was intended as a self-disparaging assessment of his total acting ability, but does in fact throw light upon a most neglected aspect of his talent.

Whereas in the eyes of most singers a superficial display of bonhomie does pass, albeit mistakenly, as a substitute for comedy itself, Bing's qualifications for entry into the inner sanctum of true comedians are more deep-rooted and secure. They amount to more than the knack of delivering a humorous line in idiosyncratic style; more than the sense of humour that would distort bedtime stories for the four sons of his first marriage so that Little Red Riding Hood became a jockey, The Grandmother the racing commissioner, and The Wolf a crooked starter; more than the ability, when, as frequently happened, he forgot his lines at a recording session, to ad-lib a lyric like:

> *Castles may tumble and fade after all,*
> *Life's really funny that way.*
> *Sang the wrong melody,*
> *We'll play it back,*
> *Hear what it sounds like, hey hey.*
> *They cut out eight bars,*
> *The dirty bastards,*
> *I didn't know which eight bars they cut.*
> *Why don't somebody tell me*
> *These things around here?*
> *I'm going off my nut.*

No singer who ever aspired to his stature could boast of a comedy apprenticeship with the Mack Sennett studio, with which he made—or improvised—a series of comedy shorts in the early 'thirties. The songs, like 'I Surrender,

Dear', 'At Your Command' and 'Just One More Chance', after which the films were named, and the hackneyed romantic plots around which the physical action revolved are irrelevant in this context; but not the professional comedian's assault course of quick-rising dough and escaped lions, uncovered fish ponds and harum-scarum automobiles which put Bing into comic trim to tackle the countless miles of *Road* ahead. Also working for him was a close friendship with W. C. Fields, or 'Uncle Bill', with whom he appeared in *Mississippi* in 1935. At the preview, when Fields saw that this was one picture he hadn't completely stolen, he passed his own rasping comment on the rising Crosby phenomenon, that 'underhanded sort of fellow, who churlishly relies on the illegitimate device of singing'; but the remark belied the almost paternal affection he held for the neighbour and sometime golfing companion, whose fondest memory of the great comedian is of him practising his juggling on the shore of Toluca Lake and then complaining that he had to quit because the geese were hissing at him. No comedy experience, however, could prove too much for the double act he was about to sustain with Bob Hope both on and off screen over half a lifetime.

Although they would not make *Road to Singapore*, their first film together, until 1940, they had known each other since December 1932, when they shared the same bill at New York's Capitol Theatre. And yet the mythical feud they would now develop to great effect on their individual radio appearances over a period of seven years reached the cinema screens only by chance, when Fred MacMurray rejected a script written for him and Jack Oakie, as two nomadic young blades in devious pursuit of Dorothy Lamour. The combination of *Boys' Own Paper* picaresque and sneaky sexual shenanigans suited well their spontaneous, easy-going rapport and helped to sustain success at the box office via *Zanzibar*, *Morocco*, *Utopia*, *Rio* and *Bali* over a period of fourteen years, with the exclusion of a miscalculated attempt at reunion via *Hong Kong* in 1962. The adrenalin of their relationship was provided by the friendly cut-and-thrust of any two pals vying over money, sex, age and looks. And yet if Hope, with his over-anxious air of urbane frenzy was indisputably the clown, Bing was far more than the duck's back for the water of Hope's humour. If Hope's comic persona represented an intriguing amalgam of honesty and duplicity, of male sexual bravado and effeminacy, of cowardice and bumbling aggression, Crosby was funny in his own right because of the subtle acknowledgement he always seemed to pay the situation just this side of camera range. To put down Bing, Bob would resort to lines like 'You collapsible Como, you' and 'He's going to sing, folks —now's the time to go out and get the popcorn'; Crosby had only to cast that almost subliminal sideways glance of friendly disdain, before his lips even released their famous 'tut-tut' and Hope even knew what was happening, in order to get his own back.

W. H. Auden once gave two reasons why the ordinary man is dissatisfied on those occasions when he most feels like singing and is brave enough to make the attempt; namely, the difficulty in producing a pleasing sound and the impossibility of composing a song on the spur of the moment expressly to fit its mood. Both reasons provide a clue to Crosby's popularity. In the public mind his own voice with its self-styled bathroom resonance is the most potent force of persuasion in the history of popular music that the man in the street can produce something approaching a pleasing sound of his own; and so comprehensive is the range of material that Bing has recorded that there is for his admirers, of whom Auden was one, a song for literally every occasion, the next best thing in the circumstances to a capacity for composing at the drop of a mood. His sexual appeal represented another two-pronged assault on the popular imagination, both a universal feminine infatuation with the soothing caress of his voice, and a strong masculine identification with the golfing, hunting, fishing image of a man who once accepted a dare to swim ten lengths of a pool with that lighted pipe in his mouth—and won. But however many levels there may be to his appeal, they are all overshadowed, however much he might protest to the contrary, by arguably the most prodigious talent the world has ever known for making hard work look easy. Maybe Astaire just beats him here. In spite of that, no performer has shown himself more honestly grateful for the element of luck that, of course, does enter any show-business success story. He still seems slightly bewildered by the extent of that success. His surprise is natural, and a guarantee that the modesty which cites his willingness to listen to the advice of others as the second main reason for his prosperity, is wholly genuine and not inverted pretension. One has no qualms, then, in ending this profile with the epitaph by which he has revealed he would most like to be remembered: 'He was an average guy who could carry a tune.'

Marlene Dietrich

Falling in love again

ER ENTRANCE IS as sensuous, as tantalising as that of any great lady of the theatre. Halting momentarily on the threshold of the wings with a mischievous look that suggests no goddess is ever taken for granted, she proceeds with a slow, svelte swagger and the teasingly quizzical suggestion of a smile to glide towards the centre footlight. She stops, but at no point does her body, swathed in a helter-skelter of swansdown, ever cease to weave its own distinctive rhythm as conveyed by the slightest thrust of a hip, the faintest shuffle of a shoulder, its own irresistible proof that the dance is no exclusive preserve of the legs and feet. Her shimmering white compels the spotlight beam towards her with gravitational force, to subject to the severest scrutiny the quality which in 1936, half a lifetime ago, Graham Greene referred to as her 'Absolute Beauty'. One goes back further to the day when film director Josef von Sternberg first found in her 'a face that lives—really lives'. He could at last see a way of meeting the Herculean challenge of translating credibly to the screen the beauty of saloon-singer Rosa Frölich, re-christened Lola-Lola, a beauty so overwhelming, so prodigious as to lead the title character of Heinrich Mann's sardonic novel *Professor Unrath* to sacrifice his position and self-respect. Since then, words as copious and scintillating as the sequins on the clinging gown she now reveals have been summoned to describe her timeless charms. One can certainly catalogue the high cheekbones, as elegant and clean as paper sculpture; the wise expansive forehead; the deep-set, questioning eyes beneath filigree brows; the fragile orchid hair; the glistening lips poised wittily between humour and disdain. But her true beauty transcends the verbal identi-kit of such a list. It resides in the ethereal excitement generated by her total presence, something beyond visible contours, however closely linked.

In the absolute aristocratic control over both voice and gestures which never lapses into patronage, one detects that Germanic conviction of superiority, telling one that not for nothing did she come from a stern Prussian military background. Catch her face at a certain angle and it appropriately suggests the cool severity, the iron will of a female guerrilla fighter. If the image appears harsh, it is not to the exclusion of the chanteuse who recounts all man's sorrows; it plays its own part in the message she would have one take closest to heart, that however great one's suffering, survival should be the grail. Inseparable from the strength and relentless determination are an honesty and purity which prevent her own survival from being branded as callous. The same qualities invest the steely precision of her technique with credibility, if not absolute spontaneity. Every movement from the hand shielding the eyes to denote despair to the lift of an eyebrow to indicate surprise is directed at a specific effect. Dietrich has rigorously emphasised such discipline as the key to the challenge facing the solo entertainer: 'Technique and control, they are all that matter. In every single bar of my music, every single light that hits me—I know it and can control it. In films, too many people, too many intangibles. Here, if it goes wrong, I know whom to blame—me . . . On stage I can be myself. Nobody cuts or dubs or edits me afterwards.' Self-assessment of this kind, however, does less than justice to the 'intangible' in her own appeal. One will not find the secret of her mystique in single-mindedness alone. What makes her sense of purpose so precious is the network of opposites in which it is inextricably and unconsciously enmeshed.

It is a paradox that an assurance so resolute, a technique so stoutly defined, should stand revealed as the spiritual backbone of an image so protean; therein lies the germ of her mystique. Relentless yet gentle, opulent yet concerned, practical yet playful, she sways like an ultra-sensitive pendulum between poles of behaviour that are far apart. This applies not least to the most basic human polarity of all. Tynan wittily summed up her stance *vis-à-vis* sex when he remarked that Dietrich came close to representing the opposite of the old joke which insists that most women have gender, but no sex: 'She has sex, but no particular gender.' Her drive, her authority have long been provocatively mannish, a facet that did not escape the attention of Sternberg, who tastefully directed sequences with her clothed in white tie and tails for *Morocco*, a pilot's overalls in *Dishonoured*, and the uniform of the leader of the Russian cavalry in *Scarlet Empress*. In public life she flaunted trousers long before it was the accepted feminine fashion to do so, her much-publicised visit to Paris in 1932 bringing the chief of that city's police to refer to an old ordinance that forbade women dressing in masculine apparel on a moral issue. What it did prove was that Dietrich's erotic appeal did not hinge upon the open display of bare flesh; that she professed an implicit masculinity that appealed to women themselves, who on the wish-fulfilment principle could identify with a member of their own sex who, like the characters she played, seemed happily immune to domestic drudge, male chauvinism, and menstrual pains. Meanwhile men, mesmerised by her sheer sexuality, fell prey to the myth in which beauty and danger become interchangeable, enhancing each other. Their minds will go racing back to the plea articulated on their total behalf by Victor McLagen at the mercy of her seductive spy in *Dishonoured*: 'You trick men into death with your body . . . You put something into war that doesn't belong there. If I stay, I'm not only in danger of losing my life, but of falling in love with you, you devil.' One recalls the pronouncement of the deranged Emperor Caligula to Claudius in Alexander Korda's unfinished *I Claudius* (directed, incidentally, by Sternberg): 'I sentence you to death in the most beautiful way', and realises that Dietrich would have made the ideal Messalina. But if she still affects men in this way, awakening their most latent self-destructive impulses, there can be no room for complaint. She gave full strident warning as early as 1930 in *The Blue Angel* when Lola sang 'Be*ware* the amazing blonde women'.

The sexual conflict in no way needs the sartorial definition of masculine attire to make its effect. The quick change from diamonds and furs to tie and tails which used to be a highlight of her stage act has long been discarded, but without at all damaging her aura of ambiguity. Interestingly, it was dropped not, as one might have supposed, as a concession to age but simply because the girl capable of making the change in a rapid twenty-two seconds flat left to get married and a suitable replacement could not be found. Before an audience her age itself is not exempt from that ambiguity, although here the pendulum does incur a bias. For all one moment she may remind one of a child, as when she steals a peek-a-boo glance under the piano at her musical director in the midst of a sweeping bow to him or with a girl guide's enthusiasm scoops back the hefty curtain to prompt our applause for the orchestra, the more lasting impression, however much her looks attempt to diminish it, is of an individual who has digested all human experience. It is arbitrary whether she has taken seven, seventy, or a thousand years to do so, just as it is reassuring to know that whatever devastating catastrophe the future may hold, she has been through worse and survived. That her skin has retained its bloom is only the second greatest testimony to her achievement; the first is that at no stage of her performance does one lose sight of the attitude on which the achievement is founded, one fashioned from the grazed scar tissue of experience.

Probably more research effort has been expended in an attempt to pinpoint the precise moment in time when life began for this chanteuse than for any other entertainer. Legend, as vague as it is romantic, holds that Maria Magdalene Dietrich was born in Imperial Berlin, sometime between 1901 and 1908; a birth certificate unearthed in Berlin categorically states that she was born on 27 December 1901; in the date reputedly carried by her passport, only the final digit is changed, the year now 1905. The details of her family background are quite as capricious. Arthur Knight, in a retrospective of her career in *Films in Review* for December 1954, tried to give them some semblance of order:

> According to some accounts, she was born the daughter of Louis Dietrich, a lieutenant, later major, in the Uhlan Cavalry. When he died, the story continues, her mother married Colonel Edward von Losch of the famous Hussars. Another version eliminates Major Dietrich and reduces von Losch to lieutenant. In one biography Dietrich *père* retires after World War I, in another he dies on the Russian front; von Losch dies variously on the Russian front in 1915, or in Germany shortly before the end of World War I. Dietrich's mother is either of French descent, or 'daughter of the head of the great Conrad Felsing jewelry firm', a concern founded by Marlene's great-grandfather which carried in its window the legend: 'Purveyor to His Majesty the Kaiser'.

What cannot be disputed is the severe discipline to which she found herself subjected throughout such an upbringing, with its stark insistence that any outward display of temperament or emotion was beneath human dignity. In restrospect it would appear to augur badly for success in a profession which, at its highest level, demands of its members unrestricted public access to their entire backlog of emotional experience, if—that is—one did not know of the forthcoming intervention of Sternberg himself. Her upbringing was a key both to their relationship and to her earliest success, the preparation that would enable her in time to submit more unquestioningly than she would later be prepared to admit to the discipline of the Svengali figure who would impose upon his vision of her a personal philosophy at once fatalistic and sexually harsh.

Dietrich herself has shown a tendency to dismiss her career before *The Blue Angel*, claiming in her act that she was still a student when Sternberg discovered her, on a separate occasion that she was 'nothing in films until handled by von Sternberg'. She had certainly studied at Max Reinhardt's Drama School, eliding her two christian names into Marlene on entry around 1921. But there were almost ten years of creditable activity on Dietrich's part before she played Lola. Her fascination for the theatrical had first been stirred by reading out aloud the words of the German poet Weimar during a self-imposed period of introspection after her ambition to become a concert violinist had been thwarted by muscle damage sustained by her arm on the eve of her first public concert at sixteen. Weimar's words provided the text for her successful audition with Reinhardt, the launching pad for a cluster of small parts on both stage and screen. In 1922 Reinhardt himself cast her in his own stage productions of *The Taming of the Shrew* and, as Hippolyta, *A Midsummer Night's Dream*. A total of approximately seventeen films embraced a single line in *Die Freudlose Gasse*, an early starring vehicle for Garbo, and eventually starring parts of her own in *Wenn ein Weib den Weg Verliert* (*Café Electric*), *Prinzessin Olala*, *Ich Küsse Ihre Hand, Madame* (*I Kiss Your Hand, Madam*), *Die Frau nach der Mann sich Sehnt* (*Three Loves*), and *Das Schiff der Verlorenen Menschen* (*Ship of Lost Men*), the last three all made in 1929, the first two the year before. Her stage career had already blossomed from the cliché-spoilt moment in 1926 when she was brought in as a last-minute replacement for the star in Reinhardt's production of the Abbott-Dunning American musical, *Broadway*. In 1928 she was seen again on the Berlin stage in a production of Shaw's *Misalliance*; and then came the satirical revue *Zwei Krawatten*, in which, auspiciously, she was given the chance to speak a few lines of English. It was here that Josef von Sternberg saw her for the first time.

The director would later write of the occasion: 'Never before had I met so beautiful a woman who had been so thoroughly discounted and undervalued.' It is more likely, however, that any relative neglect discerned by Sternberg could be traced to Dietrich's own state of mind, rather than to the opinions of a German entertainment industry that had already bestowed star, if not legendary, status upon her. Acquaintances from those early days have recalled the insecure, tentative approach she displayed towards her work, an attitude now borne out by her dismissive treatment of those early years. As soon as she began to work for Sternberg, he proceeded to strip away the inhibitions which one can now see pinned her beauty like a butterfly's wings to the paper on which her earlier photographs had been printed. His transformation of Dietrich transcended the elementary concepts of both an actor's impersonation on her part and a director's rationalisation on his. He saw within her all the ingredients of a heady personal dream and, as her presence had caused that dream to float up from the depths of his subconscious, so he now used every means at his disposal to make those ingredients surface physically within Dietrich herself. In many ways it was sculpture in the purest sense. Sternberg himself has put it another way: 'I put her into the crucible of my conception, blended her image to correspond with mine, and pouring lights on her until the alchemy was complete, proceeded with the test. She came to life and responded with an ease that I had never before encountered.'

The process was in no way complete with their first film. So far his aim had been restricted by the specific characterisation demanded by *The Blue Angel*. There was still a wide gap between the plumpish, unsvelte 'petty bourgeois Berlin tart' and his own more universal vision of Dietrich as a 'pictorial aphrodisiac'. As if to indulge him with a blank page on which to create his fantasy Paramount withheld the earlier film from release in the United States until after the opening, a month earlier in December 1930, of his first Hollywood film with Dietrich. Without damage to the overwhelming success of *The Blue Angel* elsewhere, Sternberg was allowed with *Morocco* to convey to the most important, because largest, national audience in the western world his own undiluted image of the star as *femme éternelle*, without in any way risking the unfair censure carried in the wake of the disappointment that comes when fond memories are not revived. This was a Dietrich untied to time or place, with the facility of a mirage for appearing unexpectedly in strange, but always romantic places. As Alistair Cooke pointed out, 'It is because she is this sort of international essence of sin that she exotically blinds the senses of conventional man with a job to do in a definite place; it is because she has no home, no passport, no humdrum loyalties, that the memory can hold her only in permanent soft-focus, which is the regular way of presenting her screen image.' At the end of *Morocco* she sets out in pursuit of legionnaire Gary Cooper across the vast infinity of the desert in no more than cocktail dress and high-heeled sandals. The intensity with which Sternberg realised his dream created a milieu in which even here the suspension of disbelief became a norm, the senses triumphed unhesitatingly over reason.

Sternberg pursued his obsession through five more films during the next five years: *Dishonoured, Shanghai Express, Blonde Venus, The Scarlet Empress*, and, most aptly titled of all, *The Devil is a Woman*. The latter is her own favourite, 'because I looked more lovely in that film than in any other of my whole career'. Certainly Sternberg had lost no momentum as from film to film, in an attempt to heighten their allure, he shrouded the looks of his Trilby in the increasingly erotic atmosphere he discovered he could conjure out of lenses, shadow, gauze, feathers, even cigarette smoke. But Dietrich's opinion was one-sided. To many he had now not merely surpassed himself, but gone over the top. His flesh and blood ideal had been reduced to so much extra statuary amongst an already over-elaborate décor. Whereas the receipts from *Morocco* had helped to save a Depression-teetering Paramount from near collapse and *Shanghai Express* would go on to gross three million dollars, success in box office terms had already begun to slide. Paramount would complain of what they saw as the director's reckless expenditure, while the Spanish government, claiming misrepresentation, underlined the film's failure with the request that it be removed from circulation. But Sternberg had already made up his mind. During shooting he released a statement to the press: 'Fraülein Dietrich and I have progressed as far as possible together. My being with Dietrich any further will not help her or me. If we continue, we would get into a pattern which would be harmful to both of us.'

Dietrich, hearing of his decision from a third party, was distraught, but had in fact less cause for tears than Sternberg. His career as a director had now passed its peak; but that pinnacle had been to reveal Dietrich herself as the stuff of which legends are made, to send every other studio in Hollywood combing Europe for its own Dietrich equivalent, to distil from her an individuality that not only made such missions futile but would continue to elevate every film, however bad, in which she ever played. That said, however, no director would ever again capture her presence on screen with the personal lyricism of Sternberg. The highest achievement for which her audience could hope was the originality of a new dimension that would excitingly complement its preconceptions. For Frank Borzage working under Ernst Lubitsch in 1936 and then for Lubitsch himself in 1937 she made *Desire* and *Angel* respectively, revealing in both a teasing sense of humour that added relish to her sex appeal and, as throughout life, prevented her legend from slipping into the limbo of caricature. In spite, however, of a thriving popularity amongst the intelligentsia and the loyal readership of fan magazines the close of 1937 revealed that she rated only *126*th at the box-office, low enough for Paramount to pay her between 200,000 and 250,000 dollars not to make the one film she was still contracted to do. There followed a two-year absence from the screen before the tide turned and then ironically Sternberg was not uninfluential in seeing that it did.

Universal were anxious, as part of an economy drive, to resuscitate Tom Mix's *Destry Rides Again*, this time as a satire on westerns themselves. The producer cabled Dietrich, holidaying on the Riviera, with an offer to play the part of the brawling bar-room singer, Frenchie. It so happened that Sternberg was also on a Mediterranean vacation. His advice rang crystal-clear in her ears: 'What Joe Pasternak has in mind will be very effective. I put you on a pedestal, the untouchable goddess. He wants to drag you down into the mud, very touchable—a *bona fide* goddess with feet of clay—very good salesmanship.' Her success in the rôle revitalised her entire career. Over the next five years she might find herself enacting the same stereotype of a saloon songstress more often than she might have wished, but the formerly unexpected casting provided her with a direct access to the public's affection which, in the more aloof days with Sternberg, had been unimaginable. And the timing could not have been more fortuitous. A war was raging, one result of which was that the cinema would take second place in her career to the deliberate cultivation of a live audience, a task made easier by this subtle shift in her screen persona.

Her Hollywood career had been paralleled by the rise of Nazi militarism in her native country. The imminence of the Nazis' rise to power had in 1930 impelled a cautious Sternberg to omit the political overtones from his film of Mann's novel, in which the Lola-Lola figure acts as unofficial agent to a political group identified in all but name with the Fascist party, by whom

143

Unrath himself is then used. In the ensuing American years, a love-hate
relationship would evolve between actress and fatherland. Attempts by the
German film industry to woo her back at any price in 1932 were blocked by
the nausea induced in her by political events. Germany retaliated by ban-
ning *Blonde Venus* from its screens in July 1933 on the moral grounds that
it undermined the sacred institution of marriage. Yet the invitations would
continue to come, one in 1937, so rumour has it, at the instigation of Hitler
himself. The Fuehrer's infatuation for the star was no secret, even after she
had delivered the most smarting of counter-strokes by taking out American
citizenship. In November 1937, a month after her action had been attacked
by the infamous Jew-baiter, Julius Streicher, in his paper, *Der Stuermer*,
the German news agency carried a brief disclaimer on Hitler's instructions:
'The assertions [in Streicher's article] in no way reflect the facts.' Streicher
had made vicious play of the Jewish judge who had sworn her in, of the
Jewish friends she frequented in Hollywood. She not only shouted him down
in public, but, when a rumour circulated that Hitler was going to present
her with an award, she disclaimed it in advance in no uncertain terms.

When war broke out she was able to translate her frequent tirades against
the behaviour of her countrymen into positive action, by embarking upon a
gruelling schedule of front-line appearances to entertain allied troops under
battle conditions throughout Europe and Africa. She has since described
these activities as 'the only important thing I've ever done'. But their importance would extend far beyond the humanitarian level which led de
Gaulle to appoint her a Chevalier of the Legion of Honour on the liberation
of Paris and earned her the Medal for Freedom from the U.S. War Department. The theatre of war provided Dietrich, never a part of the Brecht/Weill
Berlin cabaret scene as many people suppose, with her first real platform as a
solo entertainer. In a recent interview with Sheridan Morley in *The Times*
she revealed a surprising mentor:

> I had a great teacher—Danny Thomas, the American comedian. I was
> in troop concerts with him in Italy, 1944, and he taught me everything:
> how to deal with an audience, how to answer if they shout, how to play
> them, how to make them laugh. Above all, he taught me to *talk* to them.
> I used to do some conjuring tricks Orson Welles had shown me. We
> were working off the back of a lorry and one night some soldiers began
> to jeer and interrupt. Somehow I dealt with it and afterwards Danny
> said, 'That's it—that's all I have to teach you.' Soon after that he left
> me to go back to America and I was on my own in the concerts and that's
> how it's been ever since. Once you have caught the attention of the
> front-line troops who know they may be about to die tomorrow, then
> you can catch the attention of anybody anywhere.

She would continue to make films but, often nothing more than gratuitous
attempts to cash in on the glamour of her name, they became less important
than her personal appearances as a prestige attraction for fabulous sums
throughout the capitals of the world. Here, her own producer and destiny,
she was able to deploy all the knowledge of lighting and costume she had
acquired under the wing of Sternberg to project her own version of the myth

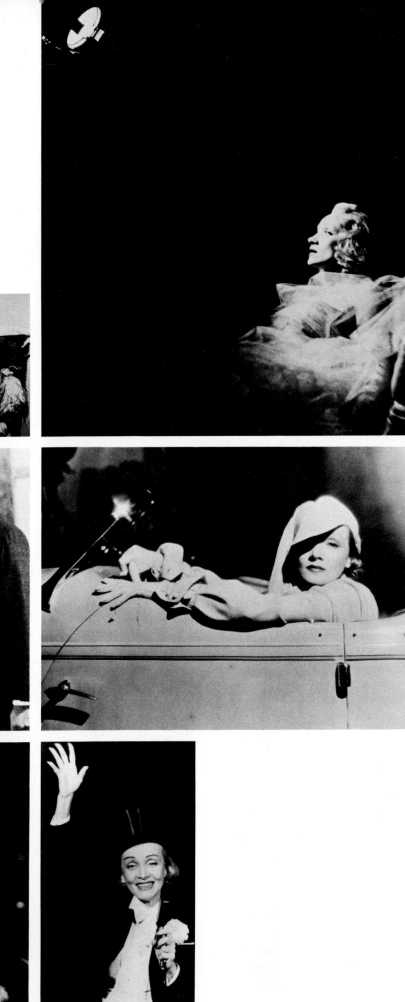

146

he had helped to create, tempered now with a delicate self-parody and the extra dimension of wisdom and worldliness that had accrued from the buffetings of the intervening years. For the clearest measure of her success in her new rôle one returns to her native land. She held off appearing in Berlin until as late as 1960. Even then hostility was rife towards her in many quarters, yet she not only still played to packed houses, but on her opening night took no less than sixty-two curtain calls.

No solo performer gives a more categorical impression of presenting her material on her own terms. Each song, complete with autobiographical introduction, represents a vocal snapshot from her past which in less assured hands would amount to no more than yet another tedious link in a chain of so many domestic transparencies. And yet tinted by the sepia of her throaty, siren purr, thrown into relief by an imagination which, denouncing a mere parrot-fashion delivery, even now backs up her words with a clearly defined mental reality, and lit up by her sheer idealism, her material transcends majestically the level of scrap-book trivia. Her voice, in part anticipated by Fitzgerald when he wrote of Daisy Buchanan singing 'in a husky, rhythmic whisper, bringing out a meaning in each word that it had never had before and would never have again', has limitations to which she admits before any critic. Her skill is in the ease with which she negotiates the vocal snares in any one number. She has always insisted that perfection in achieving the high notes is subsidiary to emotion and meaning, and so she relies on her own arcana comprising sudden guttural emphasis and amplified murmur, militant shout and playful chuckle, halting sob and world-weary sigh. Her vocal technique may be, indeed has been, dismissed as '*Sprechgesang*', yet the term tends to obscure the skill, founded on dramatic instinct, with which she can transmit the most brittle of ironies, the most elemental depths of passion, the full range of light and shade, humour and depth.

Her control over her audience is so complete that while a large proportion is almost certain to possess a knowledge of her life more encyclopaedic even than her own, they will be among the first to forgive the passing inaccuracy in an otherwise immaculately presented repertoire. It ceases to be important that the first song she ever recorded was one called 'Peter' in 1927, and not the one, as she insists, 'about a girl on the telephone—calling her man—asking him to come over. If he is not free in the evening, the afternoon will do'. 'Johnny' was, in fact, first recorded in 1929, repeated four years later on film for Rouben Mamoulian in *Song of Songs*, and has never been translated into English. She swerves into the lyric, conveying a sluttish mischievousness, a provocative and sensuous performance that ensnares you, dangerously against your better moral judgement. On more innocent ground (although innocent by Dietrich standards can only be about as innocent as a knowing Shirley Temple receiving her first screen kiss as Morelegs Sweetrick in an early parody of her success in *Morocco*), she sings the song she sang to Sternberg at that early audition for *The Blue Angel*: 'You're the Cream in My Coffee.' Arms rigid, tongue hesitant, she first mocks her earlier nervous effort, explaining that she won the part, but 'surely not because I sang so well'. In her voice then, however, he may well have discerned the hint of sexual ambiguity he would build upon in later years. Certainly the sultry drive she puts into this number now strikes an appropriate balance between

147 masculine timbre and feminine fragility, qualities which also inform her treatment of other favourite American numbers, like 'I Can't Give You Anything But Love, Baby' and 'My Blue Heaven'. But, before she crossed the Atlantic to an 'Amewica' jazzing to such tunes, there was the film which her audience will obligingly concede as 'the first film I ever made'. She volunteers the jaunty 'Lola' from *The Blue Angel*, at once teasing those who favour and now have to wait for that film's other anthem, 'Falling in Love Again', and masochistically throwing down her own sternest challenge. The song is the first practical test for all but Sternberg's ghost as to whether her earliest spell is still potent. Where his camera had moved in to focus on her black-stockinged thighs as top-hatted she sat alluringly upon a beer-barrel throne, so now the collective memory of a large part of her audience zooms back to that earlier cabaret stage, with its harbour backcloth, hazy lighting, and ornithological décor. She more than lives up to her challenge, and it is no slight upon her success, rather a token of her lifetime's achievement, to qualify it by saying that the adoration and nostalgia of an ardent public go half way towards meeting the challenge on her behalf.

Other songs telescope together from other films to provide a shifting montage of varying moods: the winsome *'Quand l'amour meurt'*, inseparable from the moment in *Morocco* when as another cabaret entertainer, Amy Jolly, this time with tails to complement her top hat, she tossed the white carnation to Gary Cooper; the strident 'See What the Boys in the Backroom Will Have' complete with vocal bump-and-grind and racy grin from *Destry Rides Again*; the coy self-mockery of 'The Laziest Gal in Town' from *Stage Fright*, penned by Cole Porter twenty-three years earlier in 1927 with a prophetic irony that would later provide Dietrich and her closest fans with a sneaky tongue-in-cheek, even if fictitious, excuse for why in this film she had a rôle that was no more than subsidiary to Jane Wyman's.

Almost as prominent a motif as her film career in the cause of stage-autobiography is that of friendship. When she essays material that is not distinctly Dietrich, it is often as a mark of friendship; and it is her tribute to the friend in question that her special talent never fails to do it justice. She announces that she will sing Charles Trenet's composition 'I Wish You Love', 'but as a love song sung to a child', and then proceeds to make it sound both erotic and a lullaby at the same time. The fact that she was not allowed to sing *'La vie en rose'* in France during the lifetime of Piaf, its creator, should not obscure the depth of their friendship, nor that in Piaf Dietrich found, in her own words, 'everything Paris means to me', nor that to a wider international audience the song became almost as identifiable with her as with her French counterpart. She is most moving at this level when in German she evokes the memory of friend Richard Tauber, with his haunting *'Frag Nicht Warum'*, 'a song of goodbye and tears and of long parting'. Ernest Hemingway once said of Dietrich, 'I think she knows more about love than anyone'. He could have qualified his assertion by adding what becomes agonisingly clear with this number, if it had not already done so before: that she knows even more about love at its saddest, sourest moment, that moment when poignancy becomes physical pain. This knowledge informs Dietrich's style whether, as here, she sings of a separation which love itself might well survive or, as in her solemnly defiant treatment of an old American folk song, 'Go Away From My Window', when love's defeat proves irreversible.

A similar knowing informs her songs of war. Her introduction to 'Lili Marlene' as a song that she sang 'for three long years, all through Africa, Sicily, Italy, through Alaska, Greenland, Iceland, through England, through France, through Belgium and Holland, through Germany, into Czechoslovakia', may, as Peter Bogdanovitch has suggested, owe something to Hemingway himself. In *A Farewell to Arms* he wrote:

> There were many words that you could not stand to hear and finally only the names of places had dignity. Certain numbers were the same way and certain dates and these with the names of the places were all you could say and have them mean anything. Abstract words such as glory, honour, courage or hallow were obscene beside the concrete names of villages, the numbers of roads, the names of rivers, the numbers of regiments and the dates.

But while she invests her geographical roll-call with dignity, it would be asking too much to expect pure objectivity at the same time. As she remembers country after country her weary inflections build to suggest the mounting futility of war itself. As she sings the song, her distant croak swings her back into line with a million tramping feet. She becomes the archetypal good-time girl, who, at once callous and heart-broken, has leaned helplessly against a million barrack doors as men whose emotions she has engaged have been led forth, maybe not to return, reduced to so much dispensable cannon-fodder. It is reportage of brilliance, not least because of the cynical overtones which Dietrich conveys, a cynicism derived from her secure knowledge that a quarter of a century before her war the fathers of those shell-shocked troops whose hearts she would break had themselves hummed 'Lili Marlene' at the height of 'the war to end all wars'; and that fifty years later, for the Somme one could read Saigon and realise that nothing had changed.

Her revulsion at the timeless absurdity of war is best expressed in her version of the simple children's 'round' song, 'Where Have All The Flowers Gone?' with its accusing refrain, 'When Will They Ever Learn?', first made popular by Pete Seeger. Staring into blankness she recounts how the flowers have been picked by the young girls to give to the young men who have gone off to the war. In turn as soldiers they have 'gone to graveyards, every one', and it is at this point that her voice stands revealed as the living parallel of her name as it was interpreted by Jean Cocteau: 'at first the sound of a caress, then the crack of a whip.' Her disenchanted whisper is suddenly transformed, snarling in anger as if a knife had become whetted on a stone lodged somewhere amongst her vocal chords. Her defiance now is more than that of a camp-follower who so happened to view the last world war at close hand, but of a woman who in 1945, only a few days after the horrors of Belsen were revealed, was searching for and mercifully found her sister among the survivors, and who at the beginning of the war had lost her German husband to internment in France. At no point does she ask for sympathy, merely goads one into questioning one's apathy. She sings a song, 'White Grass', about a soldier who returns home from the war to find his wife killed and his home destroyed, even though he is on the winning side. But there is no need for further persuasion: her 'Mother Courage' figure has already pierced one's marrow to the point where acquiescence is a foregone conclusion.

The close of her performance fulfils a promise intimated earlier, to sing the 'other song' from *The Blue Angel*, not as she once claimed she had originally wanted to sing it, 'sentimental with lots of German soul', but as Sternberg insisted she sing it, as a creature freed from all constraints of morality or conscience and on the prowl for love, alone on which she thrives. After the passionate urgency of her plea for mankind, to hear 'Falling in Love Again' contains its own irony. But one is not surprised, for her whole act bustles along on this quality. Her celebrated abrupt dismissal of the past to Rex Reed—'I am an international theatre star now. It's so boring, all that talk about the legendary Marlene and the legendary films of von Sternberg . . . Don't make them important. I do not like to be interviewed any more by pansy film-fan writers'—conflicts with the simple fact that the greater part of her theatre act is in open acknowledgement of her early career. Aware of the contradiction, she must at her own expense poke gentle fun at her achievement and, in her teasing approach, at those in her audience who set greater store by it than she does. In so doing she reveals a tantalising glimpse of the real Dietrich, her irony and sense of humour merely strands in a down-to-earth practicality not at first identifiable with one of the great romantic images of the twentieth century. Yet it is an image in which poets and critics, carried away in their intoxication, have tended to see an incarnation of other-worldliness or, at her most earthly, a symbol of the human soul. That her normal reaction to such eulogy is allegedly contempt is not surprising when one calls to mind her claim that she would most happily have become a milliner had she found herself too nervous to go on the stage. *This is the Dietrich* who, according to Tallulah Bankhead, had no qualms about going around Las Vegas by day with her hair in curlers for all to see; who at the end of the day 'whipped up the most delicious scrambled eggs and tomatoes you ever tasted'; who in the Hollywood of the 'thirties became self-appointed nurse to a little-known, influenza-ridden and always grateful David Niven ('She then went to work and herself cleaned the whole place from top to bottom, changed my bedclothes and departed. She came back every day till I was well.'); who will travel on the London underground to beat the traffic jams; who when rained upon by a surprise shower of rose petals valued at £500 at the culmination of her 1973 London season, later asked her impresario to have them swept up and shipped abroad for use at subsequent concerts. With her feet firmly on the ground, she has always kept her legend in proper perspective, never mistaken it for reality. Cocteau may well have compared her to a frigate, a figurehead, a Chinese fish, a lyrebird, and the Lorelei; but there can be little doubt that she found Noël Coward's introduction to her performance at London's Café de Paris in the 'fifties far more acceptable:

We know God made the trees
And the birds and the bees
And the sea for the fishes to swim in.

We are also aware
That He has quite a flair
For creating exceptional women.

Coward was well familiar with her blend of humour and common sense; indeed he once called her 'a realist and a clown'. It is her combination of the two qualities, coupled with a basic vitality, which has prevented her legend from becoming an aged caricature in the eyes of those who still want to, still do, believe in it. The more she appears a human being and less an exalted goddess, the more eager one is to accept her limitless understanding of life and the human heart, an understanding uncontaminated by false sentiment and cloying self-consciousness, and, paradoxically, the easier it becomes to understand why so many have set her upon that Olympian pedestal in the first instance.

Bob Hope

Thanks for the memory

IT IS DISCONCERTING that at the age when entertainers of stature and durability become ripe for reassessment Bob Hope should find his own achievement shrouded in the mist of his recent identification as a standard-bearer for the American political right at its most hawkish, even more so since his actual status as a member of that masochistic breed known as stand-up comics has long been dismissed by the intellectual and critical élite. In recent years the pricks endured by the image of this once most buoyant of funny men would appear to have reduced him to a slightly shrivelled version of his former self, Michelin man in semi-collapse. None could have been more pointed than the barb administered by Groucho Marx, an early idol of Hope himself, who, when asked for his appraisal of the younger comedian in a recent rare interview, quickly hopscotched to the next question with a curt 'Hope? Hope is not a comedian. He just translates what others write for him'. Whether intended as sincere criticism or prompted by quasi-political spite, the remark, as it dropped from Marx's dour lips, gave fresh impetus to the one aspect of Hope criticism most deserving of cliché-rating, the man as loudspeaker to a joke-telling machine fed by an army of scriptwriters. But, on the principle that Sinatra has never been rebuked for singing songs he didn't write, so one would have thought there must be something more to Hope, some special talent literally between the lines that has contributed to his becoming the richest entertainer history has ever known.

At one Writers' Guild benefit, all the writers who had ever worked for Hope were asked to come up on stage. Over thirty trod the rostrum. But if such stories lend a ring of truth to the sense of hyperbole that leads Hope himself, or at least a scribe on his behalf, to refer jokingly to the departure of his writers from a room as resembling the opening scene from *Exodus*, it is unlikely that he will now have more than seven regularly employed at any one time. At the peak of his radio career there was an even dozen; a film on top of his normal schedule might necessitate three or four more. One should not, though, allow the sheer mathematics of the operation to disguise Hope's own involvement in their work. He manipulates them and his own needs with the expertise of a card-sharper shuffling a stacked deck. When he was active in radio, each writer was expected to submit a full script on the same subject for that week's show. The final script was the comedian's own distillation of these several versions. And only when it was eventually transmitted did the recorded programme come out at thirty minutes; until then both writers and performers, as well as the live studio audience, had been bound to the more gruelling discipline of a ninety-minute duration. His editorial instinct was unerring, each decision a natural extension of the major one taken at the fulcrum of his career when as a struggling vaudevillian at the turn of the 'thirties he realised that his forte rested not in eccentricity, nor visual humour, but in his delivery; that continual success would depend upon an ever-flowing stream of topical material, material that would need to be written. More recently Hope has seen both his gift and his popularity in telling political perspective: 'It's like getting elected to office. You're going to get elected if you say the right things—but only if you say them *right.*'

Hope's delivery is far more subtle than the over-worked epithets—'rapid-fire' and 'machine-gun'—would imply. Certainly it is fast, and bound after a round of verbal ammunition to hit more than a few targets, but such terms exclude the delicate precision, the knowing attitude behind each performance. His tongue recalls the whip of the circus performer intent on lashing the cigarette out of the profiled lips of his trembling partner. Not every flick will succeed, but most will, and those that fail only add to the mounting anticipation of the next attempt. And just as the whip never errs on the side of injury, so there is little chance that a sub-standard Hope one-liner will evoke the rancid groans reserved for a lesser exponent of timing. Caught up in the snap-crackle-and-pop of an overall verbal texture, it is immediately covered by the next, if not swamped by the laughter of its predecessor, the worst reaction it can achieve being that indifference which evaporates into forgetfulness within seconds. Inherent in his delivery is a refreshingly dismissive attitude towards the material itself and hence, with subtle irony, to the writers responsible. It is the implication gathered from his speed that no joke is as good as the one that follows, that each one is a fresh start until that too is discarded in favour of the next. He represents a swivel-tongued 'master' salesman of the American Dream, parading so many insurance policies, each the ideal, the one-and-only.

Hope has said of his own comedy technique: 'You have to get over to the audience that there's a game of wits going on, and that if they don't stay awake they'll miss something, like missing a baseball someone has lobbed to them. What I'm really doing is asking, "Let's see if you can hit this one!"' It is a game which it is fascinating to watch him play; an exercise for the interested bystander in spotting the gambits used to telegraph to the audience that they should be laughing here, that that was a joke there. Often there are no obvious places in his delivery for laughter—until one looks. Imagine Hope at the Oscar ceremony: 'We have a special prize for the losers—a do-it-yourself suicide kit. And I want to tell you . . .' Those last six words are to Hope what the controlled twiddle of his cigar is to George Burns, the opportunity for an unwieldy audience to absorb and respond. It's going out of his way to sneak in a joke in an almost un-jokelike context—'I stepped up to the ticket office of an airline and said I'll take two chances to London'—and get that extra decibel of laughter which is really the audience complimenting itself upon not merely getting, but also spotting the joke in the first place. It's the incisive sting in the tail imparted by the negative approach that transforms a line like 'The plane we came in was so ancient that . . .' into 'I won't say the plane we came in was ancient, but . . .', his observation seeming now more acute, more worthwhile than the more stereotyped speech-pattern would have allowed. It's actually stepping outside of his routine to criticise his own performance: 'I found that joke in my stocking. If it happens again, I'll change laundries'; or, by way of re-assurance, a relatively unresponsive section of the audience: 'You get the jokes later and enjoy them longer.' Throughout, the breezy confident tone with its bubble-gum twang hints at a game being played. But so far, in an age when computers can be programmed both to speak and to play, little that has been said above need elevate Hope, for all his brilliance, above the status of machine in the most sceptical of minds. This even applies to the one un-disputed aspect of his comic talent, that given any single line with claim to comicality no comedian will on average be more certain through his delivery alone to achieve for that line the maximum comic effect which it deserves on its own merit. It is the ability that makes a once topical line, like his reply to the query 'Do you believe in reincarnation—you know, that dead people always come back?' in his 1939 film *The Cat and the Canary*, 'You mean like the Republicans?', still sound funny, even though the political context in which the film was made and then enjoyed has ceased to bear meaning to an audience viewing it today.

To add the necessary flesh, as it were, to the mechanical bones, one could specify the cool dignity of his bouncy, Bennyesque stride to the centre of a stage, the proud, plumped-sofa-cushion stance with hands clasped before him when he gets there. But one must look to the face with its man-in-the-half-moon profile for the most vivid physical complement to his unique ver-bal style, the visual punctuation to the jokes. It is a face which compels the eye, for long stretches of his act the only mobile item on display. Here is the haughty sweep of the hook nose; the timely jut of jaw; the studied licking of tongue over upper lip; the roving glare of those twinkling eyes, at once searching and defiant; the sudden apprehensive glance; the equally furtive crack of a smile tucked slyly away in the corner of the lips. The unmistakable features have become a shorthand reference to the psychologically consistent persona which critics have tended to deny him since his earliest days in radio. Then they had some justification. Unlike Benny, Fred Allen, and Edgar Bergen, his principal rivals over the airwaves, Hope relied almost entirely for popularity on the monologue with which he opened his show, eschewing personal characterisation and the potential offered by the new medium as an assault course for the imaginations of his listeners. Within a short time, however, his film career enabled him to acquire a fixed personal-ity that extended at all angles away from the line that linked his tongue to his writers' brains. Indeed, he was almost certainly the only stand-up, or talking, vaudeville comedian to grow substantially as a result of his cine-matic experience; the others either transferred intact without loss of face (like Fields and the Marxes), or, as in most British instances, lost consider-able impact, not to say often floundered dismally, on the change-over. If the Hope character still appeared shallow to many, that may be because his vehicles never allowed him the deep realistic relief afforded W. C. Fields or the great silent comedians. Still, however much the on-stage Hope retained his early one-dimensional air as a paragon of self-confidence, it now became inseparable from the alter ego of the silver screen who always appeared poised on the brink of catastrophe. Old jokes took on new meanings, while the writers had to work that one degree harder to give an added dimension to some of the new ones.

One line from *The Cat and the Canary* comes close to summing up this basic duality in the Hope persona: 'I always joke when I'm scared: I kid myself that I'm brave.' Certainly cowardice would appear to be one of the more prominent human failings turned to comic advantage by the comedian. But whereas with Harold Lloyd or Keaton their actual predicament *in extremis* was sufficient cause for laughter, Hope, with the added resources of sound, can't resist joking on top of the situation, however unnatural and unlikely in real-life. This is the desperate safety valve of a man who has been forced to admit 'Even my goosepimples have goosepimples'; who has time before at last passing out to comment 'Some fun!' when pinioned to a door by a knife through his coat shoulder; who, feeling uneasy in a tough hoodlum bar along *The Road to Utopia*, with mock-pugnacity quickly adds an amendment to his order of a lemonade: 'In a *dirty* glass.' It is possible, without too tortuous a stretch of the imagination, to see every stage performance he has ever made since becoming identifiable with this trait as a metaphor for extreme perilous circumstance. For all his outward display of self-assurance as joke after joke tumbles across the footlights, the snappy urgency of his delivery now becomes a comment upon the sheer guts, not to mention desperation, needed to become a stand-up comedian in the first instance, the loneliest job in entertainment and, because the only one where audiences will never forgive mediocrity, the most difficult.

The ambivalent quality best informs the act beneath the surface. On more than a few occasions, however, Hope has laid bare the wound:

> There's a fellow walks into a psychiatrist's office—has a rasher of bacon over each ear, and he takes off his hat and he has three eggs on top of his head and the psychiatrist takes a look and says, 'What can I do for you?', and the fellow says, 'I'd like to see you about my brother'. That's it!—Play, hurry, play—see, the fellow had a rasher of bacon and he has three eggs on the top of his—ooh, this is murder here—keep the motor running . . .

But always there is the false confident, nervous chuckle to catch in his throat, to remind one that his self-assurance will somehow always bounce back upright, however often it is toppled. Hope never gives in, never loses his namesake quality, the virtue that expands frontiers and most redeems him in the eyes of his fellow countrymen. As one of his P.R. men said recently: 'Bob is sort of the American Falstaff . . . He really believes the cavalry is going to come charging to his rescue any minute.'

The scope he offers for self-identification is vast. While the memory of his cowardice lingers with the persistence of Benny's tight-fistedness, he similarly has come to reflect a whole glossary of basic human failing, which his writers have skilfully annotated throughout the years. Here are greed: 'I never should have eaten that last duck . . .'; conceit: 'It's only me. Only me?! That's the understatement of the year!'; lechery: 'I never give women a second thought. My first thought covers everything'; jealousy: 'It's not that Jack Benny's cheap; he just hates to give away money after he's memorised the serial numbers'; and, in the line that rings true of Hope with the same resonance that 'Any man who hates children and dogs can't be all bad' rang true of Fields, 'I do benefits for all religions—I'd hate to blow the hereafter on a technicality', a wise-guy opportunism always on the lookout for the main chance, perfectly in tune with the civilisation that would adopt him as an Uncle Sam figure in stars-and-stripes motley.

It would be unfair to demand intrinsic character illumination as a critical *sine qua non* of his material. An unwritten law of American show business was that when a big news story hit the headlines everybody wanted to know how Jack Benny would react to it and what Hope was going to say about it. It was as an essentially topical comedian that his reputation was first made, partly through the refinement of his distinctive dry, brittle delivery that it became secure. It should not be accounted a value judgment that always the larger part of his routine has reflected the environment in which it is told, the newspaper that has preceded it, rather than the man who was telling it. As a topical humorist he represents a bridge between Will Rogers, America's rural conscience of the 'twenties and 'thirties, who used to crack 'There is no credit in being a comedian when you have the whole government working for you', and the irreverent new wave of intellectual urban satire led by Mort Sahl in the 'sixties: 'Now, is there any group I haven't offended?' When he is assessed amongst this freewheeling inventive company, it does grate that Hope's style should require writers like a diabetic needs insulin, however real his ability to project their material as if it came from the inspiration of the moment. His rapier-sharp delivery, however, while less ruminative, provided a much needed advance from the slower jovial rusticity of his rope-spinning forebear, its taut compression its own comment on the gathering frenzy of the times. The crackerbarrel philosopher found himself succeeded by the crackerjack. It would be another generation, though, before this pungency would be reflected in content, as distinct from style. According to Thurber's definition of a satirist as a man who takes risks, Rogers, only biting for a fraction of the time, could not exclusively be regarded as such; Sahl with his 'anything goes' contempt for everything that spells 'establishment' qualified all of the time; but Hope never did.

Since his initial success he has known seven presidents, all of whom, to use Rogers' phraseology, have worked for him, from Roosevelt, on the occasion of a mid-Atlantic conference with Churchill ('World strategy means where and when we will attack the enemy and what'll we do with Eleanor') via Nixon: 'His plan for settling Vietnam is to let Howard Hughes buy it and move it to Las Vegas.' But sponsor-hedged and anxious to please most of the people most of the time he has made no secret of toeing the presidential line throughout his career. The jokes are all harmless fun, the stuff of which White House banquets are made, exercised with a discretion as sharp as their delivery. This may be to underestimate him. Many of his gags have achieved a topical notoriety of their own, as on his much publicised visit to Moscow to film a television special in 1958, when lines like 'They have a national lottery here. It's called living', 'Anybody without a stiff neck is a traitor', and 'The workers love Khrushchev very much. He hasn't got an enemy in the entire country. Quite a few under it', actually succeeded in raising the temperature of the Cold War. In Thailand in 1972 this same habit of distorting the customs of the country he is visiting, such as comparing the shaved heads of a group of Buddhist monks when seen from above to a cantaloupe convention, led to a formal apology to the Thai government from the American ambassador. Such comment, however, is too far removed from the surgically incisive treatment of the more sensitive areas of Middle American life needed to place him in the line of stand-up social commentators that can claim Sahl as pioneer and Lenny Bruce as martyr. It takes more than a lapsed diplomat to make a national satirist.

With the brash singularity of a fact from Ripley's *Believe It or Not!*, the comedian destined to become an American institution was born not in the United States, but in Eltham, a suburb of London, the fifth of six sons of a stonemason, on 29 May 1903. He was christened Leslie Townes Hope, a situation that led unwittingly to maybe his first wisecrack. In his fourth year the family emigrated to Cleveland, Ohio, where he was eventually enrolled at the local school. When asked his name by one of his playmates, he replied formally, 'Hope, Leslie'. From that moment he became 'Hopelessly', eventually shortened to 'Hopeless', to the entire academy. It is claimed that he first discovered the actual exhilaration of an audience's laughter when his voice cracked while singing 'The End of a Perfect Day' at a family reunion. His mother had, in fact, been a concert singer in her native Wales. She gave him the compass course that would eventually set him on an entertainment career. But first he had to navigate the almost *de rigueur* round of smalltime employment, embracing—first in and then out of school —newspaper boy, butcher's mate, shoe salesman, pool hustler, stockboy in a meat market, golf caddy, motor company clerk, and even, under the name Packy East, a spell in the boxing ring that saw the bell with his defeat in the lightweight semi-finals of the Ohio Novice Championships. That he had a natural bent for the stage had been proved by the prizes he acquired at local talent contests for his impersonation of idol Charles Chaplin—Hope once waited an hour and a half in a blustery New York doorway to catch a glimpse of him—and by a flair for tap-dancing revealed during lessons from a Negro entertainer, King Rastus Brown. At one point he actually ran dancing classes himself. His visiting card held nothing back: 'Leslie Hope Will Teach You How to Dance—Clog, Soft Shoe, Waltz-Clog, Buck and Wing and Eccentric . . .'

The first professional booking came at the age of nineteen as one half of a dance act with a girl friend, Mildred Rosequist. He would make no discernible headway, however, until 1924 when the manager of Cleveland's Bandbox Theatre needed a cheap local act to fill out a bill featuring rotund comic Roscoe 'Fatty' Arbuckle, desperately attempting a comeback after the scandal that had driven him from Hollywood three years before. By now Hope had a new partner, Lloyd Durbin, to be replaced shortly on the latter's death by George Byrne. Their mishmash of tap, soft-shoe, buck and wing, Cleopatra's Nightmare, and vocal rendering of 'Sweet Georgia Brown' that masqueraded under the billing 'Two Diamonds in the Rough' appealed to

Arbuckle, who, oblivious of that ironic twist of fate whereby he would soon fade completely from the screen and Hope would become the cinema's biggest comedy draw, introduced them to Fred Hurley, the proprietor of a small touring musical comedy revue. In 'Hurley's Jolly Follies', Hope found himself not only dancing but playing saxophone and doing black-face comedy. He was at the beginning of an arduous haul of non-stop touring and several shows a night, of 'living on coffee and fingernails, staying in the sort of hotels where the maid changed the mice twice a day'. Somewhere along the way he would change his own name. He would also acquire the experience and expertise which years later, at a rehearsal of Jerome Kern's *Roberta* on Broadway, would lead the composer to ask, 'How the hell did you get this ease on the stage?' and the budding star to reply, 'Mr Kern, you don't know what I've been through'.

Before tackling Broadway in such grandiose fashion, Hope still had to reveal in embryo the monologuist we know today. While working a small theatre in New Castle, Pennsylvania during the late 'twenties, he was asked at short notice to announce the coming attractions at the end of his regular, and now slightly jaded, dance routine. This was the cue for Hope to interpolate several of the Scottish jokes he had been polishing in his spare time: 'Ladies and gentlemen, next week's show, the Whiz-Bang Revue, features a Scotsman named Marshall Walker. He must be a Scot; he got married in his own back yard 'cause he wanted the chickens to get the rice . . .' Within a short time Byrne retired, Hope went solo, and, once persuaded to drop his black-face make-up, minuscule derby hat, and big red bow-tie, obtained a one-week engagement as master of ceremonies at the Stratford Theatre on Chicago's 63rd Street. He stayed for six months, all the while sharpening a genuine instinct for the spontaneous, unrehearsed ad-lib, symbolic of the authority equal to any emergency of the true vaudevillian. This facet of his talent would never receive full credit in his later writer- and cue-card-monopolised years, but, coupled with the most copious of filing-cabinet minds, enabled him to dominate regular question and answer sessions with an audience well into the 'fifties. Hope has never been struck dumb for an answer, not even when one spectator, wilder than usual, volunteered 'Which way does a pig's tail turn, clockwise or counterclockwise?' Could Hope top the laughter the question itself evoked? The reply boomeranged back, 'We'll find out when you leave', and he did. Probably the only time he has been rendered speechless in public was when a group of militant feminist demonstrators bombarded him with ink-bombs during the Miss World Contest at London's Royal Albert Hall in the autumn of 1970. He beat a very dignified retreat into the wings, paused, and then returned, before delivering—unaided by writers—the line that one would have most welcomed within a split-second of the catastrophe: 'I wanna tell you, this is a nice conditioning course for Vietnam.' To the staunchest of his admirers the delay must have carried the same air of niggling let-down experienced by the fans of another American folk-hero, Evel Knievel, on his survival of that death-defying yet disaster-prone leap across Snake River canyon some four years later.

From Chicago it was a short hop to Broadway and, via the Palace, his first full-scale musical comedy as a solo performer, *Ballyhoo of 1932*. The following year the rôle of Huckleberry Haines, the staccato-spoken best

162   friend of the leading man in *Roberta*, made him a star. He stole the show from such notables as George Murphy, Fred MacMurray and Sydney Greenstreet, proving himself a rare combination of funny man and matinée idol. The lightness of his touch was witnessed in his ability to follow—at his own insistence—the declaration of the leading lady, played by a tearful Tamara: 'There's an old Russian proverb, "When your heart's on fire, smoke gets in your eyes" ,' with a line like, 'We have a proverb over here in America too: "Love is like hash. You have to have confidence in it to enjoy it " ,' without detracting in any way from the sensitivity of the moment and of the song for which she had provided her cue. The transition to radio, with its innate bonus of coast-to-coast exposure, was in logical progession. After sporadic appearances on the 'R.K.O. Theatre of the Air', the 'Bromo-Seltzer Intimate Hour', the 'Atlantic Oil Show', and the 'Woodbury Soap Show', a regular seven-to-ten minute topical monologue spot on 'Your Hollywood Parade', featuring Dick Powell as master of ceremonies, brought him both popular and critical acclaim. The show itself in time flopped, but he didn't. No radio comedian had ever made his invisible audience laugh so many times in such a short space of time. It led in 1938 to his big break, sponsorship by the Pepsodent toothpaste company for his own show, a relationship that would endure for fifteen years. But by the end of the 'thirties the cinema had already staked a claim on his services.

In 1934, while still appearing in *Roberta*, he made a short for Educational Pictures entitled *Going Spanish*. Hope, however, benefited more from the coverage which influential columnist Walter Winchell gave his candid comment on his own performance than from the film itself: 'When Bob Hope saw his picture at the Rialto, he said, "When they catch John Dillinger [the current Public Enemy Number One], they're going to make him sit through it twice".' All options with Educational were dropped by mutual agreement, whereupon Hope, between 1934 and 1936, made an inauspicious series of shorts for Warner Brothers. And then in 1938, to coincide with his radio success, there came along what could be regarded as the two most auspicious films of his career. *Don't Hook Now* was a seemingly insignificant short in which Hope played himself at a golf tournament, insignificant, that is, except that here for the first time he appears on celluloid with Bing Crosby. In *The Big Broadcast of 1938*, his first full-length film, he proved that even under the shadow of W. C. Fields he could still communicate from the screen the same light finesse he had cultivated so exquisitely in musical comedy. His mellow warbling, in vocal tandem with screen-divorcee, Shirley Ross, of an intimate review of their marital history became for many the most memorable moment of the film. He brought to their reconciliation scene a wry, meditative quality that belied his principal reputation as a comedian. Damon Runyon quickly volunteered a critique, not of the film, but of the song: 'What a delivery, what a song, what an audience reception!' Certainly not to Runyon's surprise, 'Thanks for the Memory' became Hope's signature tune.

It is ironic, in the light of his fame as a solo comedian, that the individual moments that stand out most distinctly in a career encompassing over seventy films are either those that evoke memories of a song-and-dance apprenticeship or, with Crosby, of the traditional double act. There was his

163

loose-limbed shimmying to the ocarina accompaniment of 'Sweet Potato Piper' along *The Road to Singapore*; Hope as Eddie Foy Senior in *The Seven Little Foys* dancing in table-top competition with Cagney's George M. Cohan, the edge of the former's taps counterbalanced by the lull of the latter's soft-shoe to the point where they come out quits; his saddle-jogging singing of 'Buttons and Bows' to his own concertina accompaniment in *Paleface*; his trilling hymn of praise to 'Home Cookin'' in *Fancy Pants*. The vaudeville heritage is always rising to the surface in his films, a personal frame of reference that implies a bond of assumed intimacy between performer and audience. When asked on the haunted threshold in *The Cat and the Canary*, 'Don't big empty houses scare you?' he boasts timorously, 'Not me—I used to be in vaudeville.' As if to place extra emphasis on the fact, all but the first of the *Road* series with Crosby have him cast as a compulsive performer with a nomadic urge. Taken together, the names he assumed, while nowhere near as outlandish as those assigned to Groucho or Fields, neatly summed up the blend of undaunted ambition and seedy mediocrity so characteristic of that particular calling: Fearless (Hubert) Frazier (*Zanzibar*), Turkey Jackson (*Morocco*), Chester Hooton (*Utopia*), Hot Lips Barton (*Rio*), Harold Gridley (*Bali*) and Chester Babcock (*Hong Kong*).

For both Hope and Crosby all seven *Road* films from *Singapore* in 1940 to the least successful, *Hong Kong* in 1962, must be accounted a 'Utopia' of their own. Both entertainers found themselves treading a road to wish-fulfilment where the great comedian could sing and, as already recounted, the great singer could pursue laughs, and no one—but the other one—would mind. The competitiveness carried in the wake of such a chiasmus, always highly ambivalent in view of the deep if sometimes wary affection each performer had for the other, permeated all other aspects of the life they shared: money, looks, age, and not least the affections of Dorothy Lamour. The rivalry even extended beyond the context of the films themselves to provide comment upon their actual film careers. In *The Road to Bali*, nine years after *Going My Way*, a mirage of Humphrey Bogart leaves behind the Oscar he has won for his performance in *The African Queen*. Hope grabs it from Bing, exclaiming petulantly: 'Give me that—you've already got one!' With typical effeminate self-congratulation he preens himself ready for a make-believe acceptance speech: 'Friends, this is a proud moment for me, receiving this Academy Award. I'd just like to say one word—' At this point the alligators close in, someone shouts 'Run!', 'That's the word!' yells Bob. In the earlier *Road to Morocco*, Bing interrupts Hope's death-speech only to prompt the complaint, 'Why d'you have to spoil the only big scene in the picture? I might have won an Academy Award!' But if the make-believe was to come true, it was no more on the cards that Hope should win an Oscar than that he should win Dottie Lamour. He was the perpetual loser, the aspect of his character with which most of the millions who flocked to the box-office would identify, while Crosby inevitably walked off with the girl without so much as seeming to try.

In 1954 Hope did receive an honorary Oscar, somewhat cloyingly for 'his contribution to the laughter of the world, his services to the motion picture industry and his devotion to the American premise'. But he is ever insistent, 'I'd just like to *win* one'. That he hasn't so far, however, has stood him in good comic stead for the frequent rôle he has played as master of ceremonies at the annual Academy Awards ceremony since 1941. In 1968 he cracked, 'Welcome to the Academy Awards, or—as it's known at my house—Passover'. Sadly the quality of his more recent pictures has not matched the earlier panache of *The Princess and the Pirate, Paleface, The Lemon Drop Kid, Son of Paleface, Off Limits*, and the best of the *Road* series, so much so that it looks as if 'Passover' could well prove self-perpetuating. But there can be little doubt where, Oscar or no Oscar, his heart lies: 'You do a movie and you have to wait to find out if it's any good. But personal appearance tours, that's instant satisfaction.' And yet had he been confined to celluloid throughout his career, he would still provide a comforting and noteworthy link between the rortier tradition of Fields and the Marxes and the light comic genius of Lemmon and Matthau, in spite of James Agee's valid misgiving that at his peak he was relatively undeveloped as a visual clown. In his classic article on comedy published in *Life* magazine during September 1949, Agee wrote of Hope's performance in *Paleface*:

> Bob Hope is very adroit with his lines and now and then, when the words don't get in the way, he makes a good beginning as a visual comedian. But only the beginning, never the middle or the end. He is funny, for instance, reacting to a shot of violent whisky. But he does not know how to get still funnier (i.e., how to build and milk) or how to be funniest last (i.e., how to top or cap his gag). The camera has to fade out on the same old face he started with.

One essential difference between Hope and Crosby has become more clearly defined as the years have progressed. While Bing has been happy to sidle away from the limelight, even if he can't quite bring himself to make that last final break with it, Bob has continued to pursue an increasingly hectic spiral of tours, benefits, television specials and one-night stands, with the relentless energy of a man determined to prove himself younger as he gets older. The word 'workaholic' could have been coined expressly on his behalf, and it is arguable that *Time* magazine did just that. He is the only comedian who can boast that his success truly embraces all the media. His antlike drive, in so far as it amounts to a personal statement of his determination to stay on top, bears testimony to a complete patchwork quilt of past triumphs.

Between 1948 and 1972, most prominent in his dizzying annual round were the trips made at Christmas to entertain American forces at bases throughout the world. The routine was carried over from his morale-boosting efforts in the Second World War which had prompted John Steinbeck to remark 'It is impossible to see how he can do so much, can cover so much ground, can work so hard, and can be so effective'. Steinbeck's comment became more valid each year, with the sad exception of its final claim. It had never been too difficult to see why Hope was so effective in this area. There was a touch of sweet irony in the way a comedian who more than most relied upon cowardice as a principal comic weapon became a government-issue Merry Andrew to the common fighting man: 'We didn't intend to stop here—but we're on our way to Vietnam and some chicken was dragging his feet. I hope the PX has my size shoes.' He articulated what every G.I. was thinking about his lot, but couldn't express quite as quirkily as Hope: about the extreme discomfort of faraway places, the shortage of women, the routine mockery of the ever-present possibility of death, the iniquities of the two-tier class system of service life—with Hope firmly on the side of the ordinary draftee. But in later years the effectiveness wore thin. The response which he had come to expect, a reaction which with its cheers and whistles, shouts and yelps suggested a battle-field of its own, became moth-eaten as the Vietnam conflict escalated and as Hope himself found it more and more difficult to identify with a new breed of soldiers, a breed which, drugged and depressed, had more than ever before begun to question the rôle it was playing. Banners and placards which had once greeted him with 'Welcome to the greatest American since George Washington', now read 'The Vietnam War is a Bob Hope joke', and 'We're Fonda, Hope' (note the cunning comma), with reference to actress Jane Fonda, whose own Anti-Vietnam War group of actors, anxious to entertain the troops with a radical play, had in 1971 been refused visas.

In 1969 Hope had tried to connect more intimately with this audience by making marijuana jokes, like his description of baseball as a game in which 'you can spend eight months of the year on grass and not get busted', and, still striving to be the G.I.'s buddy, 'Instead of taking pot away from the soldiers we should be giving it to the negotiators in Paris'. But their effect on his reputation was surface-deep. At heart the radicals suspected his own ambiguous attitude to the war, his staunch declaration one moment that he was anti-war and yet the next that if he were anti-government policy he would not go; the commercial gain to be derived from the NBC television special, the inevitable celluloid end-product of his trips; his closer-than-closer friendship with Nixon and Agnew. And then at Christmas 1971, he dared a line that was as red rag to the bull: 'You're off the front page back home. The Vietnam war is now tucked away between Li'l Abner and "Chuckle a Day".' The last Christmas present the troops wanted was confirmation of their uneasiest suspicion, that Nixon was playing down their sacrifice to favour his own election campaign. Amid heckling and waves of bitterness Hope was forced to take refuge in the patriotic homily with which he had recently seen fit to close his show. He would praise their rôle, paint them as misunderstood heroes back home, emphasise 'There's nobody more anti-war than I am. There's nobody more anti-war than you are.' To his credit as a performer this did succeed spasmodically in rallying the less extreme element to a standing ovation on his behalf. Yet he could never claim that the reconciliation was total, any more than the average soldier had come to believe that he was in all honesty one hundred per cent on their side.

It would have been the ultimate irony of the Vietnam war if it had succeeded, as it threatened to do, in bringing about the downfall of the entertainer with greatest claim to be styled the Mr Sandman of the American Dream, the most decorated civilian in American history. But if Hope had proved he was not untouchable, he came through the ordeal with his optimism intact, a politically neutral quality characteristic of the American spirit which, if his television ratings are to be believed, may well have led people other than those who merely want their right-wing prejudices confirmed to forget the immediate past and to identify with him still. His politics have been criticised for their proselytising naïveté. It may, however, be unfair to regard the boyish zeal with which, for all his current right-wing tendencies, he has for over thirty years courted the friendship of whichever president is in office, as well as the logbook statistic of six million air miles travelled to entertain American servicemen, as anything more than manifestations of that insatiable craving for affection and recognition from every possible quarter endemic in every entertainer of the school he represents. Although he is arguably the one American entertainer who could not only run for the Presidency, yet win, he has announced that he has no intention of so doing. One is reminded of George M. Cohan's reply when asked how he would most like to be remembered—as an actor, a playwright, or a composer. One can see Hope, ambassador, millionaire, political figure, harking back to his fond origins and identifying with Cohan's answer: 'I guess I'm just a song-and-dance man.' Yankee Doodle Dandy to the Silent Majority, he is shrewd enough to know that as long as he holds that office he will somehow be above even the Presidency.

Judy Garland

Somewhere over the rainbow

S HE MAY WELL have been the greatest star. Certainly no one has ever been able to define with more than ephemeral success what made her unique, to itemise with any guarantee against omission the secret formula that produced the special alchemy a forgiving Gene Kelly had in mind when during the tedium of delayed shooting for *Summer Stock* he remarked, 'I don't care how long I wait for that girl—I'd wait forever for that magic.' Four years later, in *A Star is Born*, against an uneasily harsh background of ear-piercing automobiles and neon signs, James Mason, in character as Norman Maine, attempted his own definition: 'I never heard anybody sing *just* the way you do . . . You've got "that little something extra" Ellen Terry talked about. She said star quality was "that little something extra".' Her brief, incredulous, husky reply, 'Who—*me?*', could only have confirmed 'that little bell' that Maine admits had already rung in his head.

On stage her frailty and insecurity were curiously part of her strength, gloriously defiant as they fed the tension upon which all great performers thrive. The equation whereby theatrical attack and real-life vulnerability produced the surging high-strung vitality that characterised all her performances was shrewdly assessed by no less than Noël Coward, who told Judy in a magazine interview in the early 'sixties, 'Whenever I see you before an audience now, coming on with the authority of a great star and really taking hold of that audience, I know that every single heartbreak you had when you were a little girl, every disappointment went into this authority.' But on one point Coward was over-confident. When Judy in acquiescence confessed to The Master that all the emotional setbacks of a lifetime were compensated by the thrill of making an audience of less colourful people forget their own more mundane troubles, he became almost ruthless in his support of her special talent:

> And if there are people who cannot withstand these pressures, and if they are destroyed by these pressures, then they are simply no good and are just as well destroyed . . . The race is to the swift. In our profession the thing that counts is survival. Survival. It's comparatively easy, if you have talent, to be a success. But what is terribly difficult is to hold it, to maintain it over a period of years.

Maybe his words were meant as a warning. More likely he was unable to entertain a vision of her future that was not circumscribed by the talent and presence he saw then at their bedazzling zenith, and beneath the spell of which he happily succumbed. At the time, however, when her *Summer Stock* finale number with its 'Sing Hallelujah, c'mon get happy! You gotta sing all your cares away' was ringing around the world, no one mindful of her almost self-perpetuating throat-slashing, wrist-lacerating attempts at suicide could have failed to respond to the total irony of Coward's generalisations, nor to their hauntingly prophetic nature when the talent did become eroded, and the pressures did prove fatal. One wonders if during the fraught emotional countdown to the end of her life Coward recalled his conversation with her. He may have regretted it. Almost certainly he would have to concede that Garland was the exception, the last talent that could ever be dismissed as 'no good', one whose own star quality, as her final performances revealed, relied as much upon her personal imperfections as upon any professional technique.

Soon after Judy's death, the lyricist E. Y. Harburg was in London, discussing tentative plans for staging his latest musical based upon the Children's Crusade of 1212, in which 50,000 children were recruited by the twelve-year-old visionary, Stefan of Cloyes. Drawing a parallel between children then and the young of the twentieth century with their increasingly empty lives and vapid mental horizons, Harburg explained: 'What children want is a little glimpse of glory—somebody to give them something to march for or sing for.' He sounded as if he had forgotten that thirty years earlier he and Harold Arlen had provided the children of a world on the brink of war with just that. But if in 'Over the Rainbow' from the film version of *The Wizard of Oz*, he had penned a song which many children would adopt as their special anthem, the child it might have helped most with its message of dreams that really were worth dreaming was already seventeen. The more extreme the measures taken by M–G–M—unable to get Shirley Temple on loan from 20th Century Fox for the part of the twelve-year-old Dorothy—in their attempt to stifle her maturity (strapping down her breasts, encasing her in a steel corset, surrounding her pigtailed figure with extra-tall co-stars), the more she seemed to sing with the knowing authority of a twenty-year-old.

There is a facile school of thought, championed by her Scarecrow co-star, Ray Bolger, which says that Judy Garland never grew up; one must concede to it a degree of truth. As the child who, in *The Broadway Melody of 1938*, outpoured her complete devotion to 'Dear Mr Gable' with a total lack of self-consciousness, she proved herself quite incapable of giving anything less than her all. It was a characteristic that persisted into adult life and once prompted Ethel Barrymore to remark to a studio executive, 'Judy should be brought to work in a large limousine, made to work non-stop for an hour and a half, and then taken home in an ambulance.' Here was a quality as germane to her tragedy as to her success, the lack of self-consciousness later passing for naïveté as she allowed the most intimate details of her private life to pass into public ownership.

It would be even more accurate, however, to say that Judy never knew anything but the life of an adult. Jack Haley, who played the Tin Man in *Oz*, and would in 1974 become father-in-law to Judy's daughter Liza, once recalled, 'I would say, "Well, Judy, if you ever become a star, please stay as sweet as you are", and she would say, "I don't know what could change me, Jack. Why would anything change?" ' A seemingly innocent remark from a child becomes a harrowing indictment of the system that made and perhaps destroyed her, a system that had no emotional truck with childhood, once that system was laid bare. It is feasible that at however early an age Judy had been presented with 'Over The Rainbow' by Harburg, this latter-day children's Knight Errant would have been too late.

Anticipating her legendary routine from *A Star is Born*, Judy was literally 'born in a trunk' on 10 June 1922, backstage at the Princes Theatre, which her father managed, not in 'Pocatello, Id-a-ho', but in Grand Rapids, Minnesota. Her real name was Frances Gumm, and she was the third daughter of Frank A. Gumm, singer, and Ethel Milne, pianist, otherwise known as 'Jack and Virginia Lee, Sweet Southern Singers'. She would later change her surname on the advice of comedian George Jessel who, when they shared a bill in 1935, told her she was as pretty 'as a garland of flowers'. Within a year Hoagy Carmichael had scored a success with his song 'Judy', and the whole name fell into place.

In her third year she made her famous début, tottering unannounced to the front of the footlights to sing 'Jingle Bells' before an amateur-night audience. From that moment a normal development, anything more secure than the ersatz environment of show business, was barred to her. Hurled into touring vaudeville with her two sisters, she would surprisingly in later years retain a deep affection for her father, who died when she was in her early teens. For the mother who came to use her daughter as a vicarious outlet for her own frustrated theatrical ambition, she would voice different feelings: 'She was no good for anything except to create chaos and fear. She was the worst—the real-life Wicked Witch of the West.'

By the age of twelve she had been cut off professionally from her two less talented sisters, who were allowed to go their own cosy, domestic ways. Her parents were now divorced and with her mother clenching her elbow she was marched imperiously into the jungle of the film world, having been spotted by an M–G–M talent scout singing at an *alfresco* campfire show somewhere in New York State. She was now firmly set upon that ghost train ride of experience that would buffet her between hilarity and torment for the rest of her life. No spectres would prove more haunting than those of the executive who when she grew overweight told her, 'You look like a hunchback. We love you, but you're so fat you look like a monster'; or of Louis B. Mayer who, when one doctor suggested she needed a year's rest, coldly refused: 'We have fourteen million dollars tied up in her'; or of the Wicked Witch herself who would menacingly play off the studio against her daughter as a disciplinary threat: 'You behave, Judy, or I'll tell the studio on you.' They took their place in turn amid the inhabitants of a mental chamber of horrors that already included the insensitive newspaper critic who had described her at six as a 'leather-lunged blues singer', and the crass theatre owner who had passed his own judgement on her vocal prowess: 'You may sing, love, but you don't sing good.'

Even in an entertainment world staffed by angels, the emotional strain provided by a routine that demands your appearance on set at five every morning, your constant attention throughout the day, and your attendance at studio parties into the early hours would have been traumatic. The insatiable glare of publicity, the constant requirement to live emotions that are not your own, contributed both to the snare of enforced narcissism, and to the inexorable and now cliché routine of sleeping pills, waking pills, slimming pills, stimulators, tranquillisers, and then the almost *de rigueur* alcohol to wash them down. The nearest her tempestuous early life came to childhood was in resembling a grotesque and seemingly endless game of Snakes and Ladders—sadly one charted not by Disney, but by Dali.

A psychiatrist's puppet, her nervous system shattered, she began arriving for work incapacitated or late; in time she would fail to arrive at all. After two suspensions, she was eventually fired by the studio in 1950. In the eleven years after making *Oz*, she had made no less than twenty major films. What is quite amazing to anyone in full knowledge of the emotional background against which they were shot is to see how remarkably she developed as an actress and performer in spite of it all, from being the intuitive child star through the radiant maturity of *For Me and My Gal* and the wistful sensitivity of *Meet Me in St Louis* to the sophisticated high comedy of *The Pirate*. By the time she came to make her next film, *A Star is Born*, in 1954, her own personal experience of life was gaining more vivid focus in her dramatic work, an integration that enabled her subsequently in 1961 to shun song and turn the small part of a drab Jewish *Hausfrau* in *Judgment at Nuremberg* into a dramatic triumph seemingly miles away from the make-believe, magnolia-scented adolescence of her 'Andy Hardy' days with Mickey Rooney.

In 1950, however, the horizon of Judy's continuing film career was far from sharp. The only offers of work for the moment now came from the live theatre. In April 1951 she played the London Palladium, tripping and falling on stage on the opening night. Few in her audience then were shrewd and sympathetic enough to suspect that in so doing she was unwittingly passing a comment on the system that had just discarded her with used-Kleenex nonchalance, that the fall was no casual mischance, but the tragic faltering of an emotional cripple. But then she sang and in so doing pulled herself back on a more surefooted path that led to her legendary personal triumphs at New York's Palace Theatre, and the whole legend of 'Judy Live'. Like a butterfly released from the chrysalis, she had found herself anew; she had found a way to sing all *her* cares away and the more her audiences chanted what would become an obligatory refrain, 'Judy, we love you!', the less she would be able to resist it. It took her ten years to reach the peak of her form with her celebrated concert at Carnegie Hall in April 1961, but even at a middling level her form never failed to mark her out as the most potent female entertainer of this century.

Her entrance was always preceded by an orchestral medley of her famous songs, in which a tantalisingly loud *legato* seemed continually to promise an appearance that was never going to happen. This protracted absence charged the air with mounting expectation, so that when she did—now 'unexpectedly'—sidle on from the wings, it was like tossing a match into a box of fireworks. Bowing meekly, she snatched the microphone from its stand and flung the wire disdainfully over her shoulder, all in one decisive gesture into which could be read both triumph and fear. The prickly, restless mobility with which she would course the stage spoke for the latter, somehow at odds with the instinctive knack she had for constantly milking the audience for affection. However, whether youthfully sheathed in long black stockings framed by top hat, tuxedo and black stiletto shoes, or in later years lavishly silhouetted in a gold trouser suit, as soon as her tiny, increasingly matronly body did settle into its famous arched-back, legs-enticingly-apart stance, she transmitted an almost timeless authority. Blinking those enormous, soft chocolate eyes, screwing up her urchin face to launch into song, she reassured you subliminally that there had been no spiritual detour from the Yellow Brick Road, that she still retained a basic innocence and vulnerability. Not least she still retained Dorothy's spirit against inconceivable odds. When she sang, her assurance, her elation knew no bounds.

There is a danger of allowing the sheer thrill generated by a Garland performance to obscure the fact that she *did sing*. In the final years the quality of her voice would become more of an irrelevancy to the overall effect, but on that special Carnegie night, as so often before, it revealed itself as a complex instrument of striking virtuosity. The compelling, bell-like clarity of her tone and the winsome phrasing of her intuitively trembling *vibrato* were in their mutual reliance the only proof needed that the borderline between childish innocence and adult pathos was here very hazy indeed. It has often been stated that Garland belonged to that small breed of singers which should be susceptible to dramatic rather than musical criticism. But while no one would dispute her ability as an actress, it was not merely this that allowed her to get away with a lack of complete technical flawlessness. There wasn't a song she sang into which she didn't instil the very essence of her own sadness or joy, the sheer soul of her own being. And in this sense she had no need to act at all. Whole numbers, single syllables even, could only be construed as comment upon her own dazzlingly explicit personal life. Beneath the words and the technical treatment of tone and phrasing she laid a heart-rending emotional charge. It is not enough to say that she meant every word she sang, more important to stress that she really *knew* what she was supposed to mean.

The magic and excitement at Carnegie Hall on the night of 23 April 1961 are fortunately preserved for ever on record and enable, even challenge, someone who was not there to detail her definitive performance. On that occasion she immediately made vocal amends for the teasing overture that had preceded her entrance, singing 'When You're Smiling' with beckoning sunrise inflections, and carrying over the mood of 'never-look-back' optimism into 'Almost Like Being in Love' and 'This Can't Be Love'. The strenuous vigour behind this denial was in marked contrast with the muted lingering caress of 'Do It Again' which followed. Here her seductive, breathtakingly soft approach could have lulled one to sleep with a head-on-shoulder inevitability, were it not for the rousing reveille provided by way of her hot-cha-cha effervescence in 'You Go to My Head'. The enchanting 'Alone Together' and an apt throw-it-away treatment of 'Who Cares?' made way for a snarly vocal leap into 'Puttin' on the Ritz'; the poignant ambivalence of 'How Long Has This Been Going On?' with its tell-tale piano accompaniment; and her upbeat celebration of Lovers' Knot and amatory imagination in 'Just You, Just Me'. Then she sang 'The Man That Got Away'; her vocal reputation could alone stand on that performance. Nowhere did she display to greater effect her miraculous capacity for making the sudden transition from a *crescendo* of soaring, strident emotion—'The dreams you dream have all gone a*stray*'—to the comparative dying fall of poised, subdued recollection—'The man that won you *has* run off and undone you'. On that sixth word her voice would vibrate tellingly with a special knowingness; but she was not interested in merely low-register effects. As she came into the second crescendo—'It's all a crazy game!'—her right arm was flung out extravagantly, for one moment a gesture of angry defiance, then the next a means of quieting the orchestra as she painfully choked, 'Good riddance—*good-bye*'. After the contrasting skirt-ruffling shuffle of 'San Francisco', she proceeded to transform 'I Can't Give You Anything But Love' into both lilting lullaby and the most memorable showcase for her ability to impart stress in song through speech: 'Dream awhile, scheme awhile, you're sure to find—Happiness, and I guess . . .' And then stunningly she dealt the next eight syllables off the top of the lyric casually, one at a time, in regular momentum: 'all-those-things-you've-al-ways-pined-for.' She could and did take all the time in the world and the audience still clung to every word. As she climbed down the scale of the sentence, many must have imagined a younger Judy climbing down the colours of a rainbow in counterpoint.

As if there was need to emphasise that this was a one-woman show, she then engagingly ploughed straight into the relative turmoil of 'That's Entertainment'. Her stentorian blues treatment of 'Come Rain or Come Shine', and the sedate 'You're Nearer' brought her to 'A Foggy Day', and if she was less at home singing of London than of her adopted 'Frisco, she rapidly made amends to Londoners everywhere with her own bitter-sweet rendition of Coward's 'If Love Were All'. 'Zing! Went the Strings of My Heart', the song with which she first auditioned for Louis B. Mayer, was gaily submitted to her 'C'mon, Get Happy', drum-majorette approach, and then followed the tour-de-force of 'Stormy Weather'. Her skilled *vibrato*, battling with the emotional elements which welled up within her, veered between strength gained and poignant let-down, between her defiant prayer to walk in the sun once more and the simple 'can't go on' in this absence of yet another man, until finally the voice succumbed to the quivering depths of her own despair. She entered the closing straits with a nostalgic medley, evoking the touching precocity with which at fifteen she confided 'Dear Mr Gable . . . You Made Me Love You'; the soft-shoe panache with which she tackled 'For Me and My Gal' with Gene Kelly four years later; the exhilaration that subsequently clanged through 'The Trolley Song' in *Meet Me in St Louis*. She dared to sing 'Rock-A-Bye Your Baby', for all its Jolsonian associations, but sent it soaring to the rafters with a pulsating richness, her sheer lung power and ferris-wheel personality confirming a right to do so which Jolson himself could not have disputed. Later the same applied to her treatment of 'Swanee', even more an anthem to the drive and professional vigour of the central vaudeville tradition, to which she belonged as inextricably as Jolson ever did. This was the moment when all emotion would have been spent in a lesser artist, yet the sustained effort with which head poised high, eyes glinting, she held the high notes on those last two words, 'When I get to that *Swa-nee-shore*', was full of hope and determination, and the encores that still came—the brisk and penultimate 'After You've Gone' and the tongue-in-cheek humour of 'Chicago'—their affirmation. By now there could be not the slightest doubt that that Swanee shore was actually within her grasp.

Still left to record is what remained for her contemporary audience the only possible climax, however many encores might ensue. Enveloped rather protectively between the razzamatazz guarantee of the two Jolson numbers came the moment when Judy, a child again, her legs dangling over the edge of the orchestra pit or crossed Miss Muffet-fashion on the boards, fragile beneath a stunning monolith of light, again held all hearts in her hand as she quietly, knowingly, with a youthful timbre restored to her voice, held out hope for all those dreams her audience really did dare to dream. Each intent listener, then as during the shared childhood which allowed so many to identify with her as they grew together out of the Depression and into a world war, had his or her own idea of the substance of such dreams, whether sentimental or realistic, whether of bluebirds, lemon drops, or adolescent sex. Through all her own troubles, Judy never abnegated the responsibility entailed in representing the synthesis of all such aspirations. When Mel Tormé suggested that she use this song as the basis for a comedy routine on her television show, she was adamant, 'There will be no jokes of any kind about "Over the Rainbow"! It's kind of . . . sacred. I don't want anybody anywhere to lose the thing they have about Dorothy or that song.' On another occasion she likened it to a prayer, 'especially the bit about the clouds being behind me'. But if the prayer, except for that brief lifetime of suspended disbelief while she sang it on stage, never came true, she could always console herself that through it she preserved her own special way of keeping faith with her audience, an audience which came to have her entire basic repertoire engrained in its memory. No mere inventory of the songs she sang—not even at her finest hour—can do justice to her talent, but the deftness with which any of her fans could have recited that inventory by rote is indicative of the power of that talent. If she skipped a number, she did so at her peril.

The personal commitment that came to underline her audience's relationship with Garland was alluded to by Spencer Tracy when he said, 'A Garland audience doesn't just listen; they feel. They have their arms around her when she works.' It is hard to believe that those arms were not clasped into position from their very first embrace of the story-book child along the Yellow Brick Road. In time, however, the rapport soared to an emotional pitch which few other entertainers have ever achieved. The abandoned hysteria which her presence invoked was the manifestation of a protective instinct towards herself which her needs came to prompt intuitively across the footlights. The basic empathy revealed itself in the way she could break informally out of her song schedule and with that hesitant catch in her voice request permission to light a cigarette or beseech the crowd, 'I don't ever want to go home, do you?'; in the worshipping human avalanche that rushed towards the stage at the close of her performance, when she could reach out

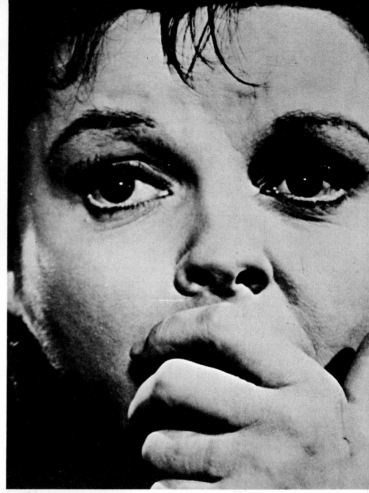

with those taut arms and actually touch what she knew represented the prime sustaining factor amid a life of instability and unease. During her last nightmarish season in London, a few weeks before her death, she could still confide to her audience in response to the now strained 'We love you, Judy' chant: 'I love you, too. I've been through a lot. People ask, "Is she going to appear? Is she dead?" Well, I'm here and you couldn't keep me away.' Beneath the self-mockery, she knew that there had never been a time when she did not need an audience's reassurance, whatever obstacles had to be surpassed in achieving it.

No performer ever demanded more of her public that it take her seriously as a star, because no performer ever stood in greater fear of not bridging that gap between the tinsel idea of the star and the sterner reality of living up to it. Sadly, as adverse publicity tarnished her image, so the gap widened, the prospect of reassurance receding as the hitherto foreign quality of cynicism came increasingly to erode the bedrock the audience had once proved. In relentless pursuit of that early ghost train had come an emotional switchback ride, fuelled by alcohol and despair, coasting over lawsuit upon lawsuit, whether brought by or against herself, not to mention a series of four divorces, each re-marriage to a man younger than his predecessor, and a myriad of minor quarrels and occasional reconciliations. In time the temperament inevitable in such a performer, a temperament welcomed by the public when viewed at a safe but teasing remove from the sidelines of publicity, became her own undoing, as actual performances were jeopardised, postponed, cancelled, delayed as a result.

And then, during her final London season in January 1969, the unimaginable, or what had once seemed unimaginable in the dazzle of her former triumphs, happened. After keeping the audience waiting for eighty minutes, she was booed, jeered, pelted with cigarette packets and left-overs. She seemed a parody of herself, looking, as one critic put it, like a 'walking casualty', her face no longer conveying the slightest nuance of feeling but a mascara mess, the throb in her voice now a haunting slur. When one woman actually seized the microphone from her and volunteered 'Over the Rainbow' herself, the audience voiced their encouragement of the tiro intruder, rather than their sympathy for the one-time heroine. From the time of her Palladium début her theatre audience had always included a distinctive, if sometimes exaggerated, sado-masochistic element which, feeding on her agonised past, treated her every performance as a vicarious opportunity for sharing her sufferings or, even more morbidly, as a peep-show for the possibility that one day she might just falter in the spotlight. That early fall on stage was both omen and guarantee that this would always be the case. Ironically, however, their parasitic satisfaction now *was* more justifiable, however callous, than that of those critics who, anxious to preserve some sort of sheen on her sadly tarnished legend, interpreted her haggard performance as a skilful, tension-packed act of equilibrium. Certainly each appearance was now the adventure of a desperate soul poised on a rope bridge in a raging gale. But if there was a catchpenny excitement as for most of the time she improbably maintained a hair-trigger balance, the happier side of success and failure, composure and tears, sweetness and diablerie, the indefinable quality which transmutes insecurity into thrill was missing. There had always been that certain edge in her performance, the unconscious theatrical manifestation of the reply given by Ethel Barrymore when a guest at Judy's home with George Cukor, Fanny Brice and Katharine Hepburn, to their hostess's question, 'What on earth do you suppose we all have in common?'. 'That's easy, my dear,' volunteered Miss Barrymore, 'We've all been on the brink of disaster all our lives!'

As Judy now wrestled with songs no longer assured of completion, unintentionally caught her stiletto heel in her feather boa, tripped over the microphone lead, she had never before been poised more perilously on that precipice. Above all else, however, she could no longer sustain the quality depicted in negative by John Osborne in his play *The Entertainer*, when he made his anti-hero, the jaded music-hall comedian Archie Rice, self-searchingly admit to the drab dead end of his career: 'It doesn't matter because—look at my eyes. I'm dead behind these eyes.' The difference between him and Judy is that *her* eyes *had* once been vibrantly alive. During that final season, however, at London's Talk of the Town, she at last allowed a chink of comprehension for those who previously had not been able to reconcile the magical star and the off-stage temperament that led a writer on her television show to christen her 'the concrete canary' and the studio itself to devise a deafening tape-recorded deterrent of massed bomb blasts, cannon fire, whistles, sirens and machine gun bursts to be relayed over the public address system should extreme measures be required to quell her emotional outbursts.

Her death, tragically bereft of surprise, took place in London on 22 June 1969, at the age of forty-seven, in the infancy of her fifth marriage, from a reported accidental overdose of sleeping pills. It was the final confirmation that the end of the rainbow had proved a morbid, cosmic black hole, voracious as it sucked into its expansive maw the legend it had helped to create and yet never allowed its owner to master. More down to earth, as befits a scarecrow, Ray Bolger patiently explained: 'Judy didn't die of anything, except wearing out. She just plain wore out.' That her reputation has so swiftly risen phoenix-like from the ashes of those final days testifies to the talent she once displayed. But all talent has to feed upon a basic guarantee of assurance and it was this which in Judy's case eventually became threadbare to a beggarly extreme. That she did bring herself again and again to go out on stage became her own way of asking for one more chance to prove herself. As long as audiences rushed to see her, she would never suspect that she herself was set head first on a perilous run to disaster, that each overture, each increasingly cracked-porcelain rendition of 'Over the Rainbow' was set on a brick road of diminishing returns.

At the last count she provided little more than a focal point of fascination for the homosexuals who predominated in that expanding audience of sado-masochists mentioned above. As these fans, who had come to respond to the heightened theatricality of her 'Madame Crematon' number from *Ziegfeld Follies* like Légionnaires d'Honneur to 'La Marseillaise', identified increasingly with this other creature to whom love—as one knew from those searching eyes—had also proved difficult both to recognise and to acquire, so the increasing seediness of her concert audiences made her death appear even more inevitable. She came to serve a dual purpose to them; there was a malicious side to their seal of approval. Her intrinsic femininity could never elude them, and here self-identification gave way to the obverse. As her powers waned, so they would find despicable and vengeful delight in her performance, now symbolic of a ritual sacrifice of the superfluous sex. By the end their applause had become a more stunning mockery than the performance itself. There was no sense of values; nothing was certain. Her knees were bound to give way. The morbid fascination was carried over to her funeral. No one has chronicled the grotesquerie of that event more effectively than John Lahr, the son of Bert Lahr, Judy's cowardly Lion, in his novel *The Autograph Hound*. As 21,000 fans filed past the glass-topped coffin in which she lay wearing the grey chiffon dress of her fifth wedding, outside Manhattan's Upper East Side echoed to the sound of Judy's sinewy soprano on battery-powered gramophones. As Lahr's characters tattoo the slippers she wore in *The Wizard of Oz* on their arms, or recall precious moments illegally spent riding the running-board of her Silver Cloud, the author, whether fictionalising or not, never ceases to be credible, capturing posthumously the exact tone of the camp clamour of her final days.

No memory of Garland, however, need forever be shackled to gloom. Whatever the pressures, the disappointments of her life, the essential frailty of her stage image, she was able defiantly to sustain for much of the time a capacity for making fun in the true Fanny Brice tradition. She could send herself up like no one could, and if her fans looked to this trait in their search for a figure-head in their own mockery of the world, they themselves were by no means exempt from her sting. In the opinion of Liza, the funniest remark ever made by mother to daughter recounted her own picture of adulation after death: 'When I die, my darling, they will lower the flag to half-mast at Cherry Grove. I can see 'em now, standing erect at the meat rack, singing: "Somewhere, over the rainbow".'

Today, Liza Minnelli herself robustly champions the tradition of live performance upheld for so long by her mother. At no point does she refer to her mother by name, sing any of her songs. She makes one concession, a rousing, Jolsonian 'Mammy' in implicit tribute. And yet there is not a moment in her act when she is not defying you to think the obvious thoughts. But they are ill-founded—Liza on stage is nothing like Judy on stage. Her reckless *joie de vivre* cuts right across the basic fear of failure and need for assurance which Judy always conveyed beneath the surface. But just as it is wrong to dismiss Liza as a mere carbon copy of her mother in performance, so it is unforgiveable not to recognise at the core of her own performance those qualities of her mother which Liza rates most highly and which her abiding image tended to keep in reserve. Liza's fondest memories are of Judy's humour, gaiety and irreverence, all at the total expense of a tragic image. In a recent *Rolling Stone* interview she announced:

> She was *truly* one of the *funniest* people I've ever known! A lot of times we had to sneak out of hotels because she was out of bread, and she would make an incredibly funny game of it. We would put on all the clothes we could, about five layers and just walk out leaving the rest, laughing. Mama'd say, 'Oh, hell, I needed a new wardrobe anyway.' . . . My mother was the ultimate comic! . . . Life with her was theatre of the absurd.

181   It was this side to Judy's character that had taken a hilarious delight in running up and down a chorus line of men singing 'Who Stole My Heart Away?' as from day to day she became more noticeably pregnant (with Liza) during the filming of *Till the Clouds Roll By*; that had the effrontery at the contract stage of her television series for CBS to sing to the assembled network executives a parody of Sammy Cahn's 'Call Me Irresponsible': '... but it's undeniably true, I'm irrevocably signed with you'; that once, while she was not merely hospital-bound but on the critical list, seemingly brought her out of a coma to pass comment on the concerned rank and file at her bedside: 'Spyros Skouras choreographs the Rockettes', before she flopped back down into a deep sleep; that in time never let a stage show go by without mocking her songs, her audience, herself, with that teasing smile around her lips: 'I'm going to do something extraordinary. Not only am I going to appear, but I'm going to sing a new song.' But in spite of her claim at countless press conferences—'Dammit, why am I so maligned? Why do people insist on seeing an aura of tragedy around me always? My life isn't tragic at all. In fact, it's all rather funny!'—she knew only too well that life could only ever be intermittently funny, and that whatever laughs came her way, she had been consciously paying for them for most of her life. The crunch of uncertainty came long ago, when during the shooting of *Summer Stock* she arrived early at the studio and instead of reading 'M–G–M' on the facia above the gate supposedly saw 'The time has come'. But, as we have seen, long before that moment in 1950, the seed of insecurity had been sown, the fear of self-doubt locked into the happiest of all her smiles.

On stage at the end of her life, she would dazedly, self-mockingly quip: 'They tell me I'm a legend.' It is doubtful if she ever knew how complicated it was. In retrospect there is not one aspect of her life, her talent, her temperament, that one could hope to extricate from that legend and in so doing leave the rest intact, more wholesome, more appealing. One can only console oneself that there *do* remain intact on celluloid those performances in which the sheer essence of her being burst upon the screen like juice squeezed straight from fruit onto tastebuds, a being as yet untarnished by the sordid, shabby dregs at its end. When she failed to win a second Academy Award for her soul-searing performance in *A Star is Born* (the road to Oz had already led her to a special Oscar for 'outstanding performance as a screen juvenile'), Groucho Marx described it as 'the biggest robbery since Brink's'. It must still remain Hollywood's greatest failure of omission, all the more so when one considers that Judy Garland was the first and may well be the only star ever to maintain the continuing interest of her public at a seeming level of no less than garden-fence intimacy through a *total* life span, from bobby-soxer childhood to premature, disillusioned old age. That is why *A Star is Born* is even more important now, plotting as it does more honestly than any other backstage musical the transition from utter innocence through emotional enlightenment to the brink of breakdown. In the film the character Judy plays is allowed to fight her way back, and it would be voyeuristic to imagine a life for Mrs Norman Maine beyond the end titles. It is sufficient to say that no true admirer of Judy herself would not wish to fade out a film of her own life with that defiant display of magisterial assertion in her final film when she sang, in step with the title: 'I Could Go On

Singing Till . . .'; but each song told its own life-story on her behalf. No one in fact caught the gist of Judy's tortured psychology more perceptively than the young Frank Sinatra who after recording an early radio show with her confided to an inquisitive Sammy Cahn, 'Every time she sings, she dies a little'.

Danny Kaye

Git-gat-gittle . . .

DANNY KAYE RAISED the idea of an entertainer's versatility to a higher and more fanciful plane than the twentieth century, with its almost authoritarian insistence on assigning individual talents to watertight compartments, had ever reckoned with before. The key was not in the sheer number of his gifts, but in their moonstruck fusion. Whereas with Jolson or Crosby there had been no obstacle in deciding where the singer ended and the comedian began, any attempt to subdivide Kaye's talents was as futile as consulting his shadow to detect the colour of his eyes. On stage his forte resided in the impression he gave of being besieged by his own capabilities, of a continual state of alert distraction. Whereas other versatiles laid out their gifts before an audience in a captivating mosaic, with Kaye this metaphor ran backwards, all his talents assailing him at once for the right of proper display. To understand this essential nature is to illuminate any debate that strives to categorise the total performer, whether as comedian or clown, mimic or virtuoso, as so much semantic self-indulgence. At his best Kaye is inimitable and as such inhabits a vacuum which would prove as uncongenial to a Groucho or a Chaplin as looking-glass milk would have proved to Alice's cat. It took time for Kaye to find his rare style, a melting-pot for pantomime, scat, and swing, double-talk, mimicry and balladeer ease. What is most striking now is the discrepancy one can see between the indecision and uncertainty bred by that style in embryo and the wild, untamed exuberance with which he would drive it along on birth.

When asked at a Broadway audition early in his career whether he was a singer, a dancer or a comedian, Kaye felt morally bound to reply in an embarrassingly self-perpetuating chain of negatives. He had been born David Daniel Kominsky on 18 January 1913, in that part of Brooklyn that would become disreputable as the breeding ground of Murder Inc. The youngest and only American-born son of Jacob, previously a horse trader in the Russian town of Ekaterinoslav in the Ukraine, now re-established as a tailor, he would find his early life drenched in that same appreciation of music and rhythm that permeated in a more religious context the family background of the young Jolson. Fortunately Kaye's father was more leniently disposed to allowing his son to work out his own destiny than the father of the older entertainer and when financial circumstances deprived the young Kominsky of the opportunity to acquire the formal education essential to realise his first ambition, to be a doctor, he drifted into the world of vaudeville. There was nothing about his immediate progress to undermine the validity of the three 'No's' he would give that potential Broadway employer. His attempts at emulating his singing idol, Bing Crosby, would fall on the stoniest ground as far as talent scouts were concerned, and besides he could not read a note of music; his early success as one of 'The Three Terpsichoreans', however much acknowledged by audiences, was not at first reciprocated by the impresario who hired the act wanting to leave Kaye out; he had found after one evening as a nightclub master of ceremonies that he was incapable of telling jokes *per se*. Had Broadway, however, been prepared to study the reasons behind Kaye's answers carefully, it might have deduced earlier that this entertainer's potential was far greater than the total face value of all three crafts together. With a lack of flexibility that belied his later style, Kaye himself hadn't seen then that the three rôles could overlap, that the flair with which he embroidered upon his first accidental fall with the dancing trio indicated as valid a comic instinct as that possessed by the most skilled deliverer of a joke, that the easy-going Crosby panache would gain a new lease of life not through Kaye's singing, but in the casual conversational rapport he would strike up with an audience, making jokes obsolete in the process.

His efforts at specialisation became all the more irrelevant when he took what amounted to his first regular employment in show business, as a tummler (pronounced 'toomler') on the Borscht summer camp and hotel circuit in the Catskills, a rôle which drew upon an entertainer's total resources as he improvised round-the-clock merrymaking as a decoy to keep customers from becoming disgruntled and anxious for home when the weather failed or the attractions of local geography palled. As Kaye once described it: 'If the skies clouded over, we would go into a dance in the lobby, fall off the roof, or put on an act of me chasing the chef with a cleaver. Anything, to keep those people from going home!' Under such conditions he first performed what became his special rallying call, 'Minnie the Moocher', in, of all places, an orchard. Another distinctive workshop for Kaye's special style was the Orient, where Kaye toured under the aegis of A. B. Marcus in the revue *La Vie Paree* in 1934. Marcus had by now revised his earlier judgement of the dancer he had tried to exclude from 'The Three Terpsichoreans' and had promoted Kaye to a solo spot, sharing the enthusiasm displayed by his two colleagues when in 1933 they allowed Kominsky, whose comedy had given their own act a boost, his first billing under his chosen professional name, Danny Kaye. His efforts to pierce the deadpan inscrutability of audiences that knew no English in Tokyo, Shanghai, Canton, Singapore and Bangkok, led to the birth of his nonsense songs, the scat delivery of arbitrary syllables with the interpolation of the odd recognisable native word as a point of comic reference. He began to improvise business on stage, as when a typhoon in Osaka plunged the theatre into darkness: sitting on the edge of the apron he went through his entire vocal repertoire, spotlighting himself with two hand-held flashlights. He observed the meaningful precision of Siamese hand gestures, so that with only a smattering of local vocabulary his own sensitive tapering fingers were able to enhance the simplest of stories.

The turning point, however, at which Kaye came to accept that any form of specialisation was destructive to his prospects of success did not come until, some time after his return to the United States, he met the young pianist-composer Sylvia Fine during a season at Max Liebman's Cape Tamiment Summer Playhouse. Kaye soon discovered that as children they had lived in the same neighbourhood and attended the same schools, without ever meeting. Within time they would marry. Far more important, however, was that his unique schizoid talent should now have found its ideal creative complement at such an auspiciously early stage in his career. The sophisticated satire of Fine, often working in collaboration with Liebman, was as meringue to the whisk of Danny's wholly idiosyncratic delivery. The season produced 'Anatole of Paris' and 'Stanislavsky', like all Fine's material at once songs and comic props. At its close Fine and Liebman pooled their best numbers into *The Straw Hat Revue*, which opened on Broadway in September 1939. The production starred Imogene Coca, but, in spite of a mere ten-week run, would mean most by way of recognition to Kaye and Fine. There followed an engagement at La Martinique, a venue which would mean to Kaye what the Copacabana came to mean to the rejuvenated Durante. At the nightclub his act was seen by Moss Hart who immediately wrote a part for him in *Lady in the Dark*. He now had no less than Kurt Weill and Ira Gershwin to provide tongue-twistable song material for him, most notably in that loony litany of Russian composers. On opening night this stopped the show immediately before the entrance of its star, Gertrude Lawrence, for 'Jenny', her own show-stopping prospect. Appropriately he was promoted to billing immediately below hers, and then to lead in the Cole Porter musical *Let's Face It*. But Sylvia had not been forgotten. At the insistence of Porter himself, she was commissioned with Liebman to write special material for the new show. The Kayes had an indisputable domestic monopoly when it came to upstaging; her 'Malady in Four F' received praise as the show's most striking number.

In the immediate future Kaye would consolidate his reputation as a live stage performer with a personal appearance at New York's Paramount Theatre, where he was held over for five weeks performing no less than five shows a day. Ironically, however, it would require leaving America to make an appearance at the London Palladium, where in 1948 he scored the biggest individual success in that legendary theatre's history, before he could qualify as the supreme live entertainer of the immediate post-war years. He did more than mesmerise his audiences. To the staid British, he professed an exotic quality substantiating J. B. Priestley's claim that all great clowns have a transient look which makes them appear not men of this world, but creatures from another planet, befuddled by the problems of our own. He had appeared in London ten years previously when he flopped in cabaret at the Dorchester Hotel. His own later comment on his failure was concise: 'I was too loud for the joint.' He omitted to mention that his opening had coincided with the night of the Munich crisis. Now success was scored at such a pitch that he was accorded that continuous accolade reserved only for visiting heads of state. Fêted by the royal family, entertained by George Bernard Shaw, praised by Churchill, presented with a cane by Lauder, Kaye could have been forgiven for not realising that probably his greatest compliment was paid by Hannen Swaffer, most intimidating and hardest to please of London drama critics: 'My boy, I have been going to the music halls for fifty-odd years, and I have never seen a greater personal triumph.' Then abruptly he caught himself in his own stentorian tracks, appalled that he had conceded praise, and added quickly: 'Of course, you didn't make *me* laugh!'

On the night of his Palladium début there was no disguising his nerves. That high-pitched giggle topped by his opening words, 'I'm shaking like a leaf, honestly'; the fact that he had literally to be pushed on to the boards in a state of stage-fright verging upon paralysis before he could deliver them, have passed into a mythology of their own. There were few nights when his performance on stage was not fired by a nervous energy, the adrenalin born of fear. Kaye has described his mood before a performance:

> I often have a sort of manic-depressive mood. I snap at my friends. To get out from under these malevolent influences, I sing, or dance, or stir up horseplay—anything to keep occupied. I find myself whistling like mad, and the more nervous I get, the more I whistle. It is more fun to shout 'all aboard' than to whistle all the time.

His last sentence refers to an incident that recurred during the run of *Let's Face It*. As part of his tension-reducing plan, he risked missing his own entrance at the beginning of the second act by rushing across the alley to the neighbouring theatre presenting *Beat the Band*. There he would bellow those two words on cue from the wings in a voluntary, unpaid capacity in a scene where Don Juan bade '*au revoir*' to a bevy of chorus girls from a train window. The practice became the despair of producer and callboy alike, but never did Kaye miss his own entrance.

And yet, if his nerves were frayed, his appearance suggested a refined, casual elegance. At a glance no one would have thought that his slim frame, attired on that Palladium occasion in light oat-meal sports jacket, chocolate brown slacks and brown suede brogues, could have harboured such a frenetic force. That is, until one peered further. If the face was handsome, it was also infinitely malleable, with a rubber mask propensity for the twitching grimace, the braying glare, every muscle expecting to work overtime should it be summoned. No eyes rolled and flickered, blinked and popped more energetically than those beneath that unruly slipshod patch of hayseed hair, described variously over the years as marmalade, orange, and corn-silk. When he moved, the long limbs beneath appeared spring-loaded, doing more than a little to bear out e. e. cummings' conviction that 'the expression of a clown is mostly in his knees'. And while Kaye's knees suggested a gadfly skipping, his arms, saved from indignity by the grace of his hands, went about a never-ending semaphoric spree of their own, whether gyrating or caressing, waving or simply leading the band. Not one pulse of rhythm was wasted as an excuse to deploy every molecule of excess energy. This is not to say that Kaye was incapable of calm. If he behaved with the momentum of a whirling dervish one minute, he could appear placid at the centre of his own chaos the next. He could change moods instantly, establishing a bridge between dream and a mayhem that never came near to nightmare. Kaye's particular frenzy was just the spontaneous reassertion of that primal vigour of the American character that had become increasingly eroded through the lack of confidence of all those duller than himself.

His approach to his so-distinctive songs reveals both his methods and effects. He had an outrageous knack of sliding down the banister of his audience's tolerance, for their own thrill as much as his own, decorously descending the initial steps, then abandoning all caution on the slippery rail. In 'The Little Fiddle', he recites the name of a German composer. He begins ordinarily enough—'Jakob'—but then plunges into his perilous slide: 'Herzheimderbofhausvonkleinstorpdaswetteristgemütlichderpfeifeldiekehk-ehvonausterlitzeindadaeindada', before pausing to leave one in no doubt that he has returned both to the normality of ground level with 'Junior'. Here in three words is his method in microcosm. All his comedy songs are zany landscapes in which the listener can pinpoint himself with no more geographical certainty than Buster Keaton knew whether he was amid traffic, amongst lions, at sea, or snow-bound, having walked into the film within a film of *Sherlock Junior*. Even the more familiar songs which others had sung before him were not safe from Kaye's dazzlingly unpredictable wiles, his wide, wild transitions from soft to loud, from slow to fast. His own treatment of 'Dinah', after whom he named his daughter by Sylvia Fine, demanded in Kaye's eyes a manic Slav accent, whereby the lady immortalised in the title became 'Deenah' to rhyme with 'ocean liner' now 'ocean leenah', 'China' now 'Cheenah'. By way of introduction Kaye lulls one along a vocal recreation of that nomadic trail through 'small willages and pretty cities' which, on his father's advice, led to his meeting his 'ferst womans. She was gowerjeous and sensach-ionally beautiful; when she walked, she was like a leetle gazelle strolling in the pastures, and when she spoke, her voice, her voice was like the sound of angels.' He stops, and then, no sooner having pierced the atmosphere with an earth-shattering delivery of 'Soft and mellow!', is back in a land of pastoral contentment. Neither is the ensuing chorus immune to his casual interpolation of a gay jumpy syncopation behind the authentic lyric or the 'rip-bit-biddle' stream of nonsense talk that cascades from his lips at the end. In a lesser known song entitled 'The Peony Bush', his easy-going baritone switched unpredictably with camera-shutter speed from coaxing coy to resonant r-r-r-rolling contortion in accepted operatic tradition, with a soupçon of mock-Satchmo for good measure, to differentiate between the description of the peony with its personal romantic associations and the 'zinnias and gardinnias' which were as weeds to his own intimate design.

His teasing way with an audience assumed a new dimension when the audience itself was expected to participate at the same time, a chore into which it would be shanghaied at every possible opportunity. He lured them with Red Indian war songs through African drum chants to his endless permutations of 'Frère Jacques', but no song served the purpose better than Cab Calloway's ragtime remnant, 'Minnie the Moocher'. As his beaming eye scanned the auditorium to find out who was not singing, Kaye subtly transferred the onus of the entertainment on to the paying customers. The story of the 'low-down hoochy coocher' who in Danny's version messed around with the King of Sweden and ended up regretting it, now took a back seat to the song's sub-title, 'The Ho-de-Ho Song'; that phrase now served as a base to the pinnacle of his own wildest imagination. Whatever he sings, they repeat, the tempo increasing all the time: 'Eh-loo-seh'; 'Eh-loo-seh'; 'Oolay-a-suppur', 'Oolay-a-suppur'; *'Ouvrez la fenêtre, Jean ou Sacque'*, *'Ouvrez la fenêtre, Jean ou Sacque'*; 'Heee-heee', 'Heee-heee', until, by way of intranscribable mock-Russian and Chinese and a sterling yodel, his speech pattern has taken on the sound of what one would imagine the pages of an obscure foreign-language phrase book to sound like when riffled fast, given that the pages could talk. What began as a game ends as a race, with Kaye pacing deliriously towards the winning tape with no contender anywhere near.

When Sylvia Fine began to write for him, he at last found material at manuscript stage with an imaginative quality on a par with his inspired interpretation of more conventional songs. The combination of their talents proved irresistible. In *Anatole of Paris* he became a hat-designer whose 'twisted eugenics' were the result of a 'family of inbred schizophrenics'. He tells with a tongue-tip precision, which seems only to emphasise its inconsequentiality, how, when he was born a month premature, his mother was frightened by a 'runaway sahahahalooon', while his father was forced to be a hobo because he played the oboe, 'an illwind that no one blows gooood'. The connection between family background and millinery career remains obscure, aside from the rhyme that links his position at the end of a long, long, line of 'bats' with 'hats'. There follows a zany celebration of his trade, launched with ghoulish glee as he recalls the six divorces and three runaway horses prompted by his 'hat of the week'. It becomes, in fact, increasingly difficult for him to say where profession ends and addiction begins. Let him get his paw on a little piece of straw and his enthusiasm knows no cosmic bounds. Then he becomes more intimate, anxious one should be in no doubt that it is 'the leetle theengs I do on it' that set the seal on his satisfaction, like 'placing yards of lacing or a bicycle built for two on it'. 'Give me *threeeaaad* and needle', he shrieks, no craftsman having ever offered a paean more exultant to the tools of his trade, the command a fanfare for him to go berserk as he proceeds to immerse one in the minutiae of his obsession: 'I itch and twitch to stitch; I'm a glutton for cuttin', for puttin' with the button, to snip and pluck, nip and tuck, fix and trim, round that brim . . .' Then in an instant, when no one is expecting it, one is whisked from the banks of the Seine to the vocal depths of 'Ol' Man River'—'tota thatta barge and lifta thatta bale'—but for no reason other than the mad intricacies of his unique comic instinct. A subliminal pause and he then proceeds, 'I'm Anatole of Paris . . .', as if nothing had happened, surprisingly relaxed and obviously expecting his audience to be the same, as he first admits to, then proffers the reason for his deliberately preposterous handiwork: 'I hate wimmin!'

No Fine routine proved a more successful vehicle for his tricksy vocal style than 'Malady in Four F'. This combined, through Danny's performance, a white man's revolutionary approach to the 'scat' technique as already practised by Louis Armstrong, Fats Waller, and Billy Banks, and, through Sylvia's material, a literary tradition that had roots in the Jumblies of Lear, the Jabberwocky of Carroll, and bore full fruition in the language of James Joyce, with no less than Humpty Dumpty cementing their link in the seventh thunderclap to symbolise the mighty fall of Finnegan in *Finnegans Wake*: 'Bothallchoractorschumminaroundgansumuminarumdrumstrumtruminahumptadumpwaultopoofoolooderamaunsturnup!' It is a far remove from the world of Irish hod-carrier to that of hypochondriac military recruit passing from preliminary medical examination through training to final honours in manoeuvres. But, with the exception of odd semi-recognisable phrases like 'Sar-gunt!' or 'Dock-tor!', 'shad-ap' or 'hut tut t'ree fo', used like Kaye's personal pantomimic whirlwind of grimace and gesture to point the action, that distance is diminished linguistically when one attempts transcription of what Kaye actually sang: 'Tardegitgatgaddlywadadadoozaygitgatgaddly-wikasatsoosayreeeetababoozay.' There were on average less than two actual words provided to each eight bars of music, and it is difficult to trace the exact demarcation between Fine's guidelines and Kaye's urge for improvisation. As Fine has herself remarked, Danny 'has to take the words in his mouth, eyes and hands. He must play with them, bend them, stretch them and cajole them, and—most important—bounce them against an audience before he can truly evaluate them.' Momentous words like Joyce's hundred-letter portmanteaus, however, provide the indisputable hard rock of challenge against which his slippery vocal talent can be tested, where making it up as you go along is strictly taboo. His ability to twist his tongue around such words at cyclone speed, while still endowing each precious syllable with perfect articulation, is one of his most impressive assets, not least because inimitable. While Joyce might be out of place on a vaudeville stage, the Gershwin montage of Russian composers assembled for *Lady in the Dark* had the advantage of semi-familiarity whereby audiences could become their own adjudicators. Starting with Malichevsky, Rubinstein, Arensky and Tchaikovsky he took no less than thirty-eight seconds to reach his ultimate destination of César Cui, Kalinikoff and Rachmaninov. No critic could fault him on the enunciation of any name, an achievement to which recordings still bear witness. One is reminded of Ogden Nash's assessment of Milton Cross, the dean of American radio opera commentators, as 'a man who can can get two "r"'s and three "t"'s into his pronunciation of "Rigoletto",' if not as a man who 'savours each name like a vintage rare and mellow'. In contrast, Kaye's beverage is one that demands swift quaffing, and yet with each taste-bud activated still.

It would be wrong to make out Kaye's voice to be no more than a medium of prodigious technical versatility. It is capable of easing its way into tender naïve ballads like 'Molly Malone' and the hip-swerving sway of Hawaiian numbers like 'Hula Lou' with a modest determination to please which wins through as much on vocal ability as on lazy charm. Apart from allowing him to sing with a cream-in-your-coffee ease, his baritone encompasses a range which enables him to imitate a German lieder singer, a Russian bass with hay fever, *and a coloratura* soprano in search of those elusive top notes. The flair for impersonation, however, is not hidebound by vocal technique. From his earliest days in the polyglot environment of the Brooklyn he knew as home, he has been blessed with an ultra-sensitive perception which would absorb a complete gazeteer of national traits and idiosyncrasies. These gifts, when wedded to his instinct for parody, found their perfect expression in the 'Lobby Song' or 'Manic-Depressive Presents', written originally by Fine for the film *Up in Arms*. The routine drove home all one's most dubious suspicions about the substandard American musical film in particular and much

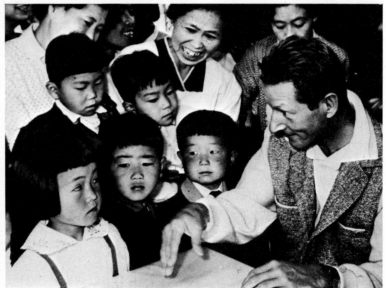

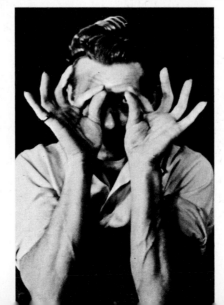

more of marshmallow Hollywood besides. Setting the scene with a growl more by courtesy of Bert Lahr than the M–G–M prototype that heralded that clown's entrance in *The Wizard of Oz*, Kaye slyly teases the audience about the tedium it has to endure before the film actually begins. At last he cuts from this verbal cat-and-mouse, whereby at the end of each block of sung credits one is still uncertain whether there are more to come, to a sneering introduction of those 'same old beautiful chorus girls', evoking spry memories of 'Cherry-Blossom Time' on a ranch somewhere in Fresno, California. In the ensuing scenes Kaye rides a rollercoaster of illogicality, as he mimics the hero Cowboy Dan, a 'galloping buckaroo' with a jaded yodel provided by that old cactus in the hide of him; Mary Sue Ann, the twittering heroine given to Stan Laurel outbursts of emotion, as well as the tap-dancing daughter of an old vaudevillian who abandoned her on the doorstep of an English castle as a baby; her step-father, Sir Basil Metabolism, who thwarts their romance and is exposed as a lethal German spy long pursued by the F.B.I., whose password happens to be none other than the name of Dan's ranch, 'Bar None'. Betraying the father who isn't her father to her fiancé, the heroine looks set to enjoy a happy-ever-after ending, until we, the audience, are saved by the *deus ex machina* of the husky Carrrmelita Pepita, the Brazilian Bombshell, and 'Whoever heard of a musical picture without Carrrmelita . . .?' But before one knows whether she succeeds in enticing the hero away from the prospect of cosy domesticity, one is back where teasingly one was brought in: 'This is a picture that ends in the middle for the benefit of the people that came in in the middle.' He certainly had no need to continue in order to convince that he could become anyone, or even anything, which his comic imagination desired. In another Fine routine, 'Stanislavsky', his mock-Russian tones guyed the whole concept of Method acting, while his physical doodling, if not what Stanislavsky had in mind, whimsically suggested that it was not impossible to imitate an inanimate object, whether a tree, a sled, or a purple spool of thread, a stone, a piece of lace, a subway train, or an empty place.

The British drama critic Alan Dent, in an attempt to sum up Kaye's special magic before an audience, quoted from *The Merry Wives of Windsor*: 'He capers, he dances, he has eyes of youth, he writes verses, he speaks holiday, he smells April and May.' 'No Music Hall artist', Dent added on his own account, ' "speaks holiday" as irresistibly as Danny Kaye'. This sustained mood of a Kaye performance is a far more accurate barometer of its effect on the public than a tally of laughs gained, the total volume of laughter achieved. Holidays are fun, rather than intrinsically funny. Deploying a winsome blend of aggressive charm and delicacy, he can take an entire audience into his confidence, stir it into revelry without seeming to try. Kenneth Tynan borrowed a metaphor for the process from Kaye's own account of 'the first git-gat-gittle number I did', the scat description for a gathering of jazz musicians of an operation performed by a surgeon friend. In Tynan's words, 'surgeon-like, he anaesthetises you, delicately makes the incision and removes your rational faculty, turns it upside down, pops it back, sews up the wound with practised fingers, and brings you back to reality. Except that, though you are not aware of it, you are not exactly the same as when you went under.'

With that persistent, disarming ingenuousness that characterises the entire tradition of great Jewish performers, Kaye went to greater extremes than any of his contemporaries to test his command of an audience. His act developed into a game of brinkmanship with his public, whereby at the Palladium he would sit dangling his feet over the edge of the stage, coax a cigarette out of the audience, and then proceed to chat nonchalantly, making the weariest platitudes sound acceptable and revealing himself to the extent where speculation about his private personality was unnecessary. His worship of the veteran Scottish entertainer, Sir Harry Lauder, of whom Kaye attempted a canny impersonation, was not kept a secret, nor was Lauder's own philosophy, 'Be content with yourself, and don't try to be anyone else'. He even theorised about the nature of his own rôle, how overjoyed he was to have broken down the iron curtain between performer and spectators and to have turned the theatre into one large drawing-room. It is a measure of his magnetism that never for one moment did an audience then feel disenchanted at having spent money to come into a drawing-room when it was their own drawing-room they were for that night escaping. And yet 'parlour' would have been an apter word. There were few who didn't become fly to his spider in this way. Significantly, the highlights of his distinguished television series in the mid-'sixties were the 'sit-down' sessions developed from such Palladium forays upon an English audience's reactions. One recalls the prediction of the great radio wit Fred Allen that the future big name of television comedy would be the performer who could simply converse through the screen in an amusing, intimate way, as if he were talking to an audience of one or two or three in their actual homes. Kaye had curiously mastered the technique long before he ever sat before a video camera.

Many of the gambits which Kaye, having established the sense of *famille en vacances* with his audience, has played are legendary. During one London season he missed his between-shows routine of tea and biscuits and, not realising this until well into his act, jokingly asked for refreshment to be served on stage. When it *was* served, he was as surprised as the audience. For two minutes he sat there sipping tea with splayed finger finesse, doing nothing else. From that moment Kaye always asked for tea on stage. There was the night in Philadelphia when he called for a screwdriver to mend an obviously unsteady microphone and then spent the first five minutes of his performance repairing it in full view of the audience, before asking for a second introduction to his act proper. Only Kaye could transform a song 'lyric', consisting of no more than the names of the twelve months, into something as witty as Cole Porter; could in a moment of depression, when he thought something had gone wrong with his act, skulk around the stage, hands weighted in pockets, kicking imaginary obstacles out of his path, excusing himself with a beguiling 'I'll be all right in a minute'; could say 'goodnight' to an enraptured audience with a line as parochial, as twee as 'Please drive carefully on your way home and, oh yes, don't take sugar in your tea. Not only will the tea taste better, but it's better for your inside too . . .'

Kaye's need to beard the approval of his audience in its lair became compulsive. He was well aware that he was performing impossible feats of audience control, outrageously courting all the dangers imaginable, like a juggler piling crocks into their own unsteady Tower of Pisa. And Kaye often came perilously close to placing the decisive plate that would transform tower into rubble. Once in Chicago when an audience was snapping its fingers in unison, he suddenly stopped and thoughtlessly cried, 'Somebody isn't snapping! Turn on the house lights. I want to see the culprit'. The lights went on and the audience immediately lost that anonymity which was as conducive to his own spell-binding effect as it had proved claustrophobic to Jolson. Fortunately mutual embarrassment was staunched with a life-saving ad-lib, 'So this is whom I've been dealing with!' Once, however, during his third London season, the essential give-and-take between audience and performer did give way. It was not enough for him to keep to the well-defined limits of his graceful, airy presentation of 'Ballin' the Jack', transformed by Kaye from routine description of a new dance step into a seeming catalogue of magical spells, a soothing anthem for released tensions. He purred his way through the lyric like a kitten teasing a ball of wool, interpolating phrases like 'Oh, you're delicious', and 'Listen to that man go; he's crazy; I swear he's crazy', skilfully calculated to add to the hypnotic effect. The audience might be pinioned to their seats, but his instruction 'Now follow me closely —reeeall close—and do me, after me' was still valid in its imagination. On the occasion in question, however, the resources of the imagination were not enough for Kaye. Convinced that they would become even more compliant, he sat on the apron's edge and asked the spectators to follow his modified actions, clapping their hands, touching their elbows in unison. In retrospect it seems a fair enough request to make. But Kaye had miscalculated, the ultimate orgasm had already been achieved. Like the juggler, the great entertainer will determinedly build his tower until the last possible moment and then stop, his teetering monument left standing sensationally, however precariously. No entertainer has driven himself to more dangerous extremes in this respect than Kaye. It is a mark of his brilliance that he has had to reckon with the pitfalls so seldom.

From the point of view of his film career, Kaye, while playing safer, has ironically met with greater disaster. After the inspired arabesques of lunacy woven into the early *Up in Arms*, *Wonder Man*, and Thurber's *The Secret Life of Walter Mitty*, which happily lived up to its author's own claim that 'presenting a humdrum "Walter Mitty" in Technicolor with Danny Kaye would be as difficult as presenting the witch scene from Macbeth on the centre court at Wimbledon at high noon on a summer day', he appeared, like Jerry Lewis after him, to opt for a milky geniality which lacked the *ouzo* bite of his stage charm and, but for isolated sequences, stifled his comic attack. On one occasion his conscious cultivation of sentiment and goodwill, at the deliberate cost of comic effect, did win through in its own right, in his portrayal of the Danish writer of children's fantasy, Hans Christian Andersen. As he talked to an inchworm, flew a kite, transformed his thumb into a tiny girl called Thumbelina, with a group of entranced children never far away, he won over a new audience as well as reminding those that remained from the old of that quality of Pied Piper innocence that permeated his stage act. This same quality enabled him to conquer an audience of adults with his version of 'The Three Bears' delivered in a gurgling baby voice, to cut into a serious speech with an impersonation of a child of five just back from the zoo. Part of his appeal had always been accountable for in one's unconscious

197

desire to return to things that made one laugh in childhood, the nonsense songs and verbal acrobatics, the marionette agility and impish hysteria. At ground level, however, the quality betokens a rapport with children themselves, a rapport consolidated by Kaye in his work for UNICEF, for which in 1954 he made the moving, fund-raising documentary *Assignment Children*. He has toured voluntarily as its Ambassador-at-Large ever since.

The secret of his success in this unusual area of diplomacy is a facility for jumping language barriers, once explained by Kaye himself:

> If an adult makes an idiot of himself with children, it establishes a basic communication between them. How many times have you stood over a baby in a crib and made unintelligible sounds? If you could stand off and see yourself, you'd think you were a lunatic. You can't say to an infant, 'How do you feel, old boy? Have you had your bottle? Did you sleep well?' The thing the baby enjoys is that you look and sound like a big pink rattle.

His unstinted devotion to the cause over a period of twenty years still raises the hackles of cynics who, refusing to accept it as an extension of a consuming interest in what makes not merely audiences, but people in general tick, dismiss it all as one colossal show-biz stunt. But even if, as the cynics insist, Kaye did choose his cause for the convenience of his image, the money raised, the time spent provide respectively both justification and rebuttal. Far more suspect is how Kaye can reconcile his involvement in an organisation like UNICEF, which functions on a human and not political level, with his openly passionate allegiance to a country like Israel, in whose conflict with the Arab world children of both sides have so often been revealed as mere pawns in a game far more sombre than that of Hans Christian Andersen picking petals off a marigold. His admirers, however, will be content to cling to those memories of Kaye far removed from any political arena, of the self-emptying live performer who played tricks with his talent that looked like miracles. With a mental somersault worthy of the entertainer himself, one is reminded of a performer from a different culture, the rock star Jimi Hendrix, who once, when approached mid-reverie by a reporter backstage: 'I'm from the *New York Times*,' replied, through half-shut eyes and the wryest of smiles, 'Pleased to meet you. I'm from Mars.' It is the poise Kaye himself maintains between the extra-terrestrial and the approachable, either of which could prove corrosive to the other, which must inform any lingering impression of this great stage performer in his one certain milieu.

Frank Sinatra

All the way

THE NAME STARES at you from the page defying you not to play games with it, the type of games which ensnared the insomniac Thurber; allowed Piet Hanema, the central male character in Updike's *Couples*, to see his entire fate constellated in his name, 'me, a man, amen ah'; and led a hopeful Norman Mailer to claim shaky anagrammatic kinship with Marilyn Monroe, whereby the letters in her name ('if the "a" were used twice and the "o" but once') would spell his own, leaving only the 'y' by the wayside, 'a trifling discrepancy'. Shatter the alphabetic prism of 'Sinatra' and those letters too make a revealing claim upon the cabalistic turn of mind. Not only do they yield the excitement of *sin* and those *rats* who would comprise his Pack, the excellence of *art* and the craftsmanship of the *artisan*, the sheen of *satin* and the shining status of the true *star*, but, by Mailerian default, even that re*straint* which is the single most impressive aspect of his total vocal performance. The name, which is arguably the most legendary single name in entertainment history, has proved apt in so many ways that it is hard now to believe that in his early years with the Harry James Band the young singer was urged by James himself to change it. He stubbornly refused, instancing the moderate success at that time of his cousin Ray, a musical director in radio, 'in spite of' the family name. By the time he came to make his first major film, *Higher and Higher* in 1943, not even James could dispute its effectiveness. And there, as proof, was his entrance. How many stars could boast that their opening dramatic line in the movies encapsulated their own name? No sooner had the maid opened the door than the then vulnerable young actor announced, 'Good morning. My name is Frank Sinatra.' Already he was seeing to it that things went *his* way.

Whether, at that early stage, he interpreted the mystical verbal undercurrent in his name as a portent or not, his overall achievement would in time more than live up to such symbolism. What is that achievement? He could be said to have succeeded in no less than bending the horns of a new moon until they touched. He at once stands for timelessness and tradition. The sometime teenage idol, in whose profile that doyen of American film critics, James Agee, once detected a fleeting likeness to the younger Abraham Lincoln, historically and decisively dominates the recent history of popular music. He represents the culmination of that cross-fertilization between vaudeville know-how, meaningful phrasing, and jazz technique already seen in the careers of Jolson and Crosby, the vocal hallmark of the touring big band era. In addition, he is the precursor to Presley as the first real leader of the movement which would identify popular music with teenage independence and social involvement. His talent, however, prevents any likelihood of his historical importance acting as a millstone around his professional neck. He is above fashion, if only for his seeming ability to take any song of his lifetime that meets the demands of his style and innate good taste, a unique blend of intelligence and instinct, and, however many times he has sung it before, sing it as if he were discovering its true meaning, its special charm for the first time. With Sinatra, nostalgia and immediacy would prove to be interchangeable; with Presley, the Beatles and Dylan, the former would always come as a corollary to the latter, an obstacle to vibrant new growth.

To whatever extent, however, the artist transcends his material, his myth transcends the artist, the analysis must always revert to the study of the voice which, smooth yet savage, alone would have guaranteed Sinatra's staying power as the most richly equipped popular singer of recent years. If its ability to flow effortlessly from note to note without ever seeming to allow its owner time to breathe seems reminiscent of the Dorsey trombone, that should come as no surprise. Many hours spent listening to the jazz expert's individual technique during his early days with that band led Sinatra to model his singing style on Dorsey's smooth *legato* approach to phrasing. Sinatra got it right down to the minutest physiological detail, even discovering what he has described as 'a sneak pinhole in the corner of Tommy's mouth—not an actual pinhole but a tiny place . . . In the middle of a phrase, while the tone was still being carried through the trombone, he'd take a quick breath and play another four bars with that breath.' To master his own breath control Sinatra even resorted to reciting lyrics while swimming underwater. Within time he, like Dorsey, could tackle six- to eight-bar phrases at a go, double the rate of most other singers in his field. Not all his inspiration was jazz-oriented. He has also explained how he would listen to Jascha Heifetz and 'found that sustaining the voice in song can be likened to the way Heifetz uses the bow, the way he draws it across the strings'. Symptomatic of such meticulous attention to vocal detail is his rumoured preference for a black microphone that will be lost in the camouflage of his tuxedo as he moves it shrewdly back and forth to prevent your hearing what intake of breath *is* inevitable, incidentally heightening the continuous purring tone that renders the voice instantly identifiable.

Such scrupulous technical concern could not but affect the way he interprets a song, always in Sinatra's eyes—if worth singing—a narrative to be advanced as meaningfully as possible, rather than an anonymous pattern of notes and bars and words. His breath control allows for sustained stretches of vocal understatement, planes upon which key words can the more effectively be thrown into relief. The impact with which he will invest a single syllable is legendary, his voice endowing words with an extra onomatopoeic quality as, say, it places the kick in 'I Get a *Kick* Out of You', or turns on the heat when it becomes 'too *hot* not to cool down'. His exquisite phrasing never reveals less than the edge and clarity of cut glass, each word assuming a crystalline shape in the mind until its successor likewise claims one's attention. And it is never less than unpredictable, single vowel sounds being stretched and rephrased to sound like two syllables instead of one, a word like 'again' to sound like three, one for each vowel. In a lesser performer such quirks might appear contrived, but Sinatra's good taste never allows them to spill over into that dubious area where refreshing originality becomes pretentious gimmickry. More likely it will be a rescue operation to lance the banality of a mawkish line, the only possible antidote being a change of emphasis, or even of words. Cole Porter once addressed a telegram to Sinatra asking why he sang his songs if he didn't like the way they were written. But if Sinatra's judgment had lapsed when he found himself murmuring 'this has too many words' half way through an early radio broadcast of Porter's 'Don't Fence Me In', the composer himself would eventually have had to concede that there are few songs which cannot hold their heads up higher when Sinatra has applied to them his unique stylistic flexibility, shuffling the words here, adding a twirl to the melody there.

His ability to invest the emotional shorthand of a hollow lyric line with the effortless ring of profound meaning would suggest a carefully considered attitude in the reading of a song. With specific reference to a ballad like 'Fools Rush In', Sinatra once attempted to put that attitude into words: 'It's just like reading poetry. And that's odd because poetry bores me. It always has. I'm one of the worst readers of poetry in the world. But when I do it in a song, I find that I enjoy it and I find that I understand the distance necessary per phrase.' Kenneth Tynan once quoted T. S. Eliot's views on the way verse should be written in an effort to describe how Dame Edith Evans spoke it:

(The common word exact without vulgarity,
The formal word precise but not pedantic,
The complete consort dancing together)
Every phrase and every sentence is an end and a beginning,
Every poem an epitaph.

Likewise, when Sinatra sings, he weaves the words of a lyric into a pattern that suggests simultaneously experience, understanding, discrimination, intensity, and that total personal commitment that binds the poet to his work. Not that Sinatra's commitment ends at this material. His involvement in a song would approach no more than cipher status if it did not prompt a reciprocal involvement from his listeners. He can render almost any type of song with such keen sensitivity that its ability to prick the shared memory of either sadness or elation, both yours and his, with the accuracy of a malkin's pin has become a foregone conclusion. So potent is the drive to communicate his own feelings that he can transform a slow ballad like 'A Very Good Year' from yet another trite catalogue of so many girls known to a point where it actually becomes credible as autobiography, and, if not, at least a poignant expression of the 'might-have-been'. More up-tempo, he subtly registers the romantic cynicism of Cole Porter's 'Just One of Those Things' as in fact the obverse of all our secret dreams, where trips to the moon on gossamer wings may well amount to the main form of transport. Here he makes a statement far removed from the flippancy of those throwaway versions by lesser performers, ironically excusable only for the way they mistakenly live up to the song's title. There can be no mistake, however, about the way Sinatra lives up to his own word: 'Whatever else has been said about me personally is unimportant. When I sing, I believe. I'm honest . . . You can be the most artistically perfect performer in the world, but an audience is like a broad—if you're indifferent, endsville.'

Complementing the informed persuasiveness of his vocal technique is an economy of movement and gesture in live performance which only in the more swinging numbers gives way to any surge of exuberance. And so, to emphasise the kick he gets out of you, he patrols the stage with a brisk urgency which matches the zing of his delivery, manipulating the microphone lead ahead of him to provide a snaky advance guard. Nothing can more effectively express the joy he derives from 'You Make Me Feel So Young' than his 'Silly Symphony' trick of seemingly conducting the orchestra with his vertebrae, not that any conductor's baton was ever as supple as Sinatra's backbone. But for every number where he does appear to have the world on a string, there is another where one will more likely find it on his shoulders. Then, huddled self-protectively, maybe on a stool, in the refuge of a seductive spotlight, he becomes caught up in a web of loneliness, introspection and anguish which, even in a world deprived of sound, would make itself known by the incisive dig of the elbows into his ribs, the physical quiver at the delivery of a key word. The oblique hold of the head which before, leaning first to one side, then to the other on the beat, suggested the easy-going regularity of a metronome, now tells us that emotionally time *is* out of joint. The hands which before danced through the air in arcs of contrapuntal emphasis now finger the microphone with reverential delicacy.

In any appraisal of Sinatra's performance there is always a danger that one will do him less than justice merely by concentrating upon the obvious high-points of his act. No one should underestimate the sheer effect, like a pellet of sodium upon water, his first appearance has upon an audience before even a note has been sung, nor his staying power before that audience who would cling to his presence until there is not a song left to be sung. In an extended routine the songs themselves give the impression of queuing for the honour of interpretation by that unique voice, until the point where, forty numbers on, Sinatra could sing 'I Belong to Glasgow' and make even that sound credible. Indeed, he can bring an audience to its feet with his version of Kern's 'Ol' Man River', banishing from its thoughts any hint of the unintentional humour the song has acquired through the years and for which he may well have been in small part responsible, through the parody he used to sing at the beginning of his career entitled 'Ol' Man Crosby' and his less-than-convincing appearance singing the same number in a pink suit on top of what resembled a giant wedding-cake in the 1946 film, *Till the Clouds Roll By*.

If there is one criticism of his accustomed act it must fall upon his apparent determination to be accepted at all costs as a monologue comedian. The credentials are in order: a raspy, self-mocking, devil-may-care style of delivery which suggests a hybrid between Durante and Bogart; a sense of repartee sharpened on the whetstone of his formative years in the jazz environment of the James and Dorsey bands with its traditional practical jokes and stag horseplay; an instinctive personalised feel for language, not unlike Crosby's, also dating back to those days of exposure to song-pluggers and soul-destroying one-night-stands. (Sinatra once translated the phrases 'a man can raise a thirst' and 'a Burma girl' from Kipling's 'On the Road to Mandalay', another of the unlikely but successful candidates for his attention, into 'a cat can raise a thirst' and 'a Burma broad', as such more in keeping with his jazz rendition.) And yet his efforts at spoken comedy pall, not merely beside his singing, but beside his flair (as revealed in the Kipling example) for injecting wit where appropriate into that singing, and for pinpointing the existing humour in a lyric. This aspect of his vocal talent should more than fulfil any need for identification with the clown image, once his favourite subject as an amateur painter, on Sinatra's part, and without the embarrassing sag in tension inevitable when song fails to follow song with the speed his status leads an audience to demand. His sardonic slang introduction—'This song is about a fellow who's got a problem—like his broad flew the coop—with another cat and all the bread, so he decides to take in a little sauce. Now he's in a bar after three days . . .'—invests the song 'One For My Baby' with its own tragi-comic mask, neither actually grinning nor actually groaning, which Sinatra sustains for as long as stool-perched he acts out that problem, his precarious tottering position its own symbol of the special knife-edge quality of his interpretation. It is an achievement of which most comedians would be proud and to emulate which many would give up monologues overnight.

Francis Albert Sinatra was born the only child of his Sicilian immigrant father and Genoese mother on 12 December 1915 in the hoodlum-infested dock area of Hoboken, New Jersey, which provided the background to the Elia Kazan film *On the Waterfront*. He is one entertainer the accounts of whose early life come closer to accuracy the more they veer away from the predictable. Far from being an under-privileged child, he came from a comfortable middle-income home, the resources of which enabled him to boast a personal account at the local department store, a wardrobe dandy enough to earn him the nickname 'Slacksey', and a second-hand Chrysler by the time he was fifteen. Such accessories could well be considered adequate compensation for the scars on the left side of his neck inflicted for life by the forceps of a clumsy doctor at a difficult birth which threatened to be still-born, until an alert grandmother showed the initiative to immerse him beneath a cold water tap. More likely is that they were a sop to Cerberus in lieu of the attention his conscience-torn mother, a sturdy force in local politics as a Democratic ward leader, could not pay him. There can be little doubt that her interests did much to broaden his horizons as a child, while his father, a sometime fireman and saloon-keeper, as if to fill those gaps where words and reason would fail, made his own strongest impression on his offspring as a bantamweight boxer who fought in his spare time under the name of Marty O'Brien. A substantial portion of the singer's later publicity would suggest that he had taken close heed of the paternal advice proffered him at an early age: 'If you're an outsider, and a small one at that, you need your fists.' From his earliest years Sinatra had suffered the side-walk indignity of being jeered as a 'dago' or 'wop'. Not only would such incidents make him indelibly sensitive to the question of racial prejudice throughout his life, but also underline the abiding first principle of loyalty to his family. Such a bond, at whatever the cost, was vividly exteriorised in his immediate environment by the Mafia and its leading figures, the *uomini rispettati* or 'men of respect', under whose influence Sinatra, like hundreds of other young Italian-Americans, almost inevitably came. It was a menacing milieu where, as Sinatra would later claim, 'Everyone carried a twelve-inch pipe, and they weren't studying to be plumbers'.

So far his early years have revealed in embryo both roisterer and moderate. When it came to musical influences one looks again to his mother, who often sang at social functions, and to an uncle who gave him the now unlikely-sounding present of a ukulele. That gift set this member of Hoboken's Demarest High School on a ladder which would lead no higher than school band and glee club status. Then he slid away from music into the workaday world as a delivery and copy boy for the local *Jersey Observer*. Not until 1936 and a visit to a vaudeville theatre in Jersey City to see a personal appearance by Bing Crosby was Sinatra fired by the ambition to become a professional singer. Severing his connections with journalism almost overnight, he sought and found work with local dance bands. He later reminisced about the impact that single performance of Crosby exerted upon him: 'He performed on stage with a guitarist named Eddie Lang. And I watched him . . . he had such great ease that I thought, if he can do it that easily, I don't know why I can't. That was one of the big turning points of my life.' What eventually, however, singled out Sinatra from the myriad other aspirants to the Crosby throne was a subsequent level-headedness which more than atoned for the breakneck speed of his career decision. He recognised that the world didn't need another, let alone a lesser, version of Bing. The style he subsequently developed drew as much, he later claimed, upon the Italian *bel canto* school as upon Crosby's casual throaty wistfulness. But the intensity of emotional expression he achieved, foreign as it was to the basic operatic tradition with its emphasis upon technique and ornamentation, proved that if Crosby had been less of an influence in a direct carbon copy way, his debt at this level to the great Negro songstress, Billie Holiday, was more than valid. Sinatra, who used to listen enraptured to her 'in 52nd Street clubs in the early 'thirties', some time before that red-letter Crosby night, holds that she 'was and still remains the greatest single musical influence on me'.

Sinatra's first professional breakthrough came as the singing member of an otherwise instrumental quartet, 'The Hoboken Four', on Major Bowes' Original Amateur Hour. They were awarded first prize and, even more valuable, the prospect of twelve months' experience with one of his travelling companies. After three months, however, homesickness led Sinatra to return to Hoboken. He found work at 15 dollars a week singing at the Rustic Cabin, a small roadhouse in New Jersey. He stayed eighteen months, until Harry James, once trumpeter with the Benny Goodman Band, now putting the finishing touches to his own outfit, heard a stray local radio broadcast by Sinatra and, impressed by his 'way of talking a lyric', stopped by to offer him a year's contract. After a six-month gestation period with James (which included, on 13 July 1939, the historical event of Sinatra's first two recordings, 'From the Bottom of My Heart' and 'Melancholy Mood'), Tommy

Dorsey offered him a break into the even bigger time. Fortunately, the relationship with James was close and when Sinatra asked to be released from his contract, the troubadour was sent on his way with a firm handshake, a cheeky grin, and an old pal's 'Get out of here'. Sinatra stayed with Dorsey for two years and eight months, his celebrity eventually matching that of his bespectacled master and contributing in no small measure to the band's overall success. In return, in the company of musicians as exalted as drummer Buddy Rich, trumpeter Bunny Berigan, pianist Joe Bushkin, arrangers Sy Oliver and Alex Stordahl, not to mention Dorsey himself, he discovered, like Crosby before him with the Whiteman Band, a *conservatoire* without equal for a popular singer of the time. Indicative of the industry with which he put his musical education to good effect was the way he soon acquired a reputation as a singer's singer. In his last year with Dorsey, *Metronome*, a discerning trade paper, voted him their 'Best Singer of '42'. Gathering friction, however, between him and Dorsey, attendant upon his snowballing popularity, led to his departure from the protective husk of that band in the September of that year. This time he had to buy his release, but while then bitter about the expense involved he never allowed it in future years to detract from the musical debt he felt to Dorsey himself.

On the eve of New Year's Eve, 1942, came the event that stamped the certain seal upon his status as a solo artist. He was billed as a mere 'extra added attraction' on a bill at New York's Paramount Theatre headed by Benny Goodman, the King of Swing. Such was his success, he was retained for eight weeks, by which time Goodman himself had moved on. The best person to describe his reception that opening night is, of course, Sinatra himself: 'The sound that greeted me was absolutely deafening. It was a tremendous roar. I was scared stiff. I couldn't move a muscle. Benny froze too. He turned around, and looked at the audience and asked, "What the hell is that?" I burst out laughing and gave out with "For Me and My Gal".' Here was the first of many waves of mass hysteria that would sweep over Sinatra at least until the war's end, a frenzy of adulation that had been matched in recent years by that afforded Lindbergh and Valentino, but never a singer of popular songs. Mesmerised by the earnest shyness of this spare young minstrel with the Shirley Temple bow-tie, errant curl, prominent Adam's apple, and ever-so-slightly emaciated look, who still had a long way to go before he could live up to Sammy Davis' claim that there were only two boys left who were not the boy next door—'Sinatra and Cary Grant', girls in their hundreds and thousands, mostly between the ages of twelve and twenty, offered themselves up like so much candy in vicarious sexual sacrifice to the first singer to set fire to the passions of their generation. The outward innocence of the bobbysoxers, symbolised by the short white half-hose from which they took their name, took on a more wanton complexion in the theatre, now a sighing, screaming vacuum for masturbatory fantasy where inhibitions could be discarded like clothes at a beach, until it was time for those that hadn't fainted to go home, for the safety valve that enabled them to play virgin for yet another night to cool down.

In the light of the scroll for 'The Most Effective Promotion of a Single Personality' awarded to his press agent by *Billboard* in 1943, there will always exist an uneasy twilight zone, where contrivance and authenticity

overlap, in any account of this stage of Sinatra's career. But if scepticism is the only safe reaction to many specific details, like that of the girl who took off her dress in the crowd and asked him to autograph her bra, or of another who fainted no sooner than she had covered with an elastoplast the spot where he had accidentally touched her arm, there could be no doubt of his spectacular effect upon an actual crowd, certainly not after 'The Columbus Day Riot at the Paramount', as it was referred to in the newspaper headlines of October 1944. On that day, with a school holiday to act as catalyst, the bare facts proved more than a match for any hyperbole the press might have fabricated. An estimated 20,000 teenagers crowded into Times Square, halting both traffic and pedestrians. The queue from the theatre itself amounted to at least half that number, snaking its way, six deep, west along 43rd Street, along Eighth Avenue, then east up 44th Street. According to news reports the total police personnel involved amounted to 789, not including the twelve proud steeds of the mounted police. Outside the theatre passers-by were trampled, the ticket booth was smashed; inside, fifty extra ushers could barely cope with the frenzy. At the end of his first performance in the 3,600 seat auditorium only 250 vacated their seats. There ironically was the very reason why Sinatra was never allowed to break the house attendance record at the Paramount, in spite of the measures taken by the management to clear the house, like attempting to confiscate packed meals, and ensuring that the accompanying film would be box-office anathema to the captive audience, all to little avail.

Bruce Bliven writing in the *New Republic* likened the hysteria aroused by Sinatra to the Children's Crusade of the Middle Ages, while, appropriately, the less intellectual press revived the old mediaeval word for fainting. Soon the names 'Sinatra' and 'swoon' were as inseparable as Ogden Nash and his rhyming dictionary. The label that eventually stuck to Sinatra with fly-paper tenacity was 'The Voice', but there were many contenders. In a *New Yorker* article towards the end of 1946 E. J. Kahn catalogued just some of the outlandish titles the press had been fanciful enough to conjure up:

> the Lean Lark, the Croon Prince of Swing, Moonlight Sinatra, the Swoonlight Sinatra, the Boudoir Singer, the Swoon Kid, the Groovy Galahad, the Swing-Shift Caruso, the Sultan of Swoon, the Swami of Swoon, Loverboy, Dreamboat, The Larynx, Prince Charming of the Juke Boxes, the Mooer, Shoulders, Mr Swoon, the Bony Baritone, the Svengali of Swing, Frankie Youknowwho, Too-Frank Sinatra, and Angles.

If any of them appealed to Sinatra himself, it was the last one. He had to admit that there was nothing he was not constantly trying to figure out new 'angles' of.

As a barometer of how extreme and erratic reactions to the new phenomenon were, no one fulfilled the rôle more entertainingly than society hostess and self-appointed arbiter of public taste, Elsa Maxwell. In August 1943 she described the singer as 'the glorification of ignorance, musical illiteracy, and the power of fake, synthetic, raw publicity in its greatest arrogance—propaganda in its most cynical form'. When three months later a mixture of curiosity and self-promotion brought her actually to meet Sinatra, she changed her tune spectacularly—'I found a simple unspoiled singer of songs', but obviously not so simple, so unspoiled as to preclude her re-nominating him 'my *bête noire*' twelve months after her original stand. Then, thirteen months later again, the cuckoo had turned mother hen, Sinatra himself now 'my adopted son'.

His hypnotic effect upon audiences released an avalanche of psychological speculation. The image of the 'simpering, whimpering child' clinging to a microphone which he projected beneath a wafer-thin veneer of brash self-confidence certainly appealed to a basic maternal instinct. Routine faddism, rebellion against adult authority, Sinatra as father figure, as success symbol, were just some of the explanations advanced. One Detroit radio station ran a competition, 'Why I like Sinatra'. In the *New Yorker*, Kahn quoted one girl's entry:

> I think he is one of the greatest things that ever happened to teenage America. We were kids that never got much attention, but he's made us feel like we're something. He has given us understanding. Something we need. Most adults think we don't need any consideration. We're really human and Frank realises that. He has given us *sincerity* in return for our faithfulness.

It is hard not to believe, however, that when all the theorising was said and done it all came back to sex. Sinatra himself had volunteered for army service, but had been rejected on account of a perforated eardrum. Now he represented the surrogate figure for every boy who had been drafted away from corner drug-store to battle front, the focal point for the innermost desires of every girl he had left behind. And as they succumbed to the lingering try-a-little-tenderness thrill of his vocal fondling, one could be forgiven for supposing that they would never want it any other way.

The earliest Sinatra euphoria was a manifestation of what the film director Billy Wilder has since described as something in the entertainer 'beyond talent . . . some sort of magnetism that goes in higher revolutions'. In time the bobbysoxers would grow up and Sinatra would find himself supplanted in the affections of a new generation by a pistol-punching parade that included Frankie Laine, Guy Mitchell, and, with loudest report, Elvis Presley. But if a slide was inevitable, the magnetism would remain intact, first dormant, but then spiralling to the giddiest heights. To his associates he had always seemed less than surprised by the freakish level of his first success, regarded by himself as the proper reward for his special talent. Such conviction alone should have suggested that a comeback was on the cards; but with Sinatra half-measures are as foreign as pastoral imagery in a Chandler novel. His comeback might surpass that of any other entertainer in significance; but by the same token the initial decline would be far from a soft-cushioned let down.

It is not enough to say that the adulation of his public drooped, to make changing trends the whipping-boy for his fall from favour. His film career, in which he had never been stretched beyond a vapid stereotype rôle, crumpled around his feet like an oversize demob suit. At the turn of the decade, his vocal chords started haemorrhaging. As his first wife, the mother of his three children, obtained a divorce, he found himself, in the less tolerant climate of October 1951, the target for much unfavourable publicity. Public disapproval increased with his marriage eight days later to actress Ava Gardner. This event, which might have proved the harbinger of revived good fortune, instead raised the curtain on a new chain of disasters. As if a house of cards were collapsing around him, he was dropped by Universal, who had a non-exclusive option on him for a further two films; by CBS Television; by his agent MCA; and, because record sales had now slumped, by Columbia Records. Any one slight would have been wounding enough; but the discharge from MCA, its pretext a disagreement over the payment of back commissions, smarted in particular. For years afterwards he would sigh incredulously: 'Can you imagine being fired by an agency that never had to sell you?'

In retrospect it becomes hard not to see the nadir of Sinatra's career as part of an overall predestined plan. With the world prepared to cast him to oblivion, Sinatra in early December 1952 made one last desperate nail-tearing grab at survival. Inspired by the character of Private Maggio in James Jones' epic Second World War novel, *From Here to Eternity*, he pleaded with Columbia to allow him to play the part in the scheduled film version and to do so eventually sold himself for the humiliation of a screen test and 8,000 dollars, as distinct from the 150,000 dollars he had asked for his previous two films. Fortunately the first choice, Eli Wallach, had opted to do a Broadway play and so Sinatra, amid unproven rumours that the Mafia had exerted not a little influence, achieved not only his ambition, but an Oscar for Best Supporting Actor as an encore. His conviction that he was the only actor who could play the temperamental Italian-American G.I., killed by a sadistic sergeant, was unwavering: 'I knew Maggio. I went to High School with him in Hoboken. I was beaten up with him. I might have been Maggio.' Fortunately Harry Cohn, the Iron Duke of Columbia Pictures, didn't need persuading. As he pointed out to the reluctant producer, Buddy Adler, 'Did you ever see that guy without a shirt on? This is a thin, little guy with a caved-in chest, but with a great heart.' They both omitted, however, that at no other stage in his career, in remnants as it was around him, could he have identified so incontestably with Maggio. The timing with which actor met part was both as lucky and impressive as that practised by a crouched Keystone cop roller-skating beneath a passing pantechnicon. His immediate experience qualified him for the rôle and, for the first time, his acting assumed the depth and sensitivity that had already marked his singing style.

The Sinatra comeback, however, was more than a comeback, as much a professional change of life for the minstrel whose compelling hold on an essentially female following had been secured through a soothing vulnerability which in lesser hands would have become blurred with sentimentality. It is doubtful if even those fans who could detect the dash of delinquent ruthlessness in his earlier image had ever suspected that he would re-emerge so completely, as a wry, wiry, resilient leader of the pack. A snap of cynicism crept into the voice; an aura of precarious excitement hung around his physical presence. He began to project a truculence, a hint of menace which,

213

recalling *High Society*, made the prospect of collision with Mars next July sound credible. Moreover, if the recent roller-coaster side to his career had captured the imagination of the public, his increasingly publicised friendships told it that the amusement park was still open.

The phrase he favoured in any retrospective of the ups and downs of his career was 'the rise and fall and rise again' and at times one could be forgiven for mistaking in such stark oscillation a pattern for so many of his personal relationships. In a display of friendship to Phil Silvers in 1946, when he heard that burlesque comedian 'Rags' Ragland had died days before the two were to open at the Copacabana in a double act, Sinatra flew from Hollywood to New York as a self-appointed duty to offer himself on opening night as a surprise partner to his friend in Ragland's place. And yet when CBS placed Silvers' 'Sergeant Bilko' television show opposite a Sinatra series on ABC, he openly snubbed the comedian mid-performance in a Miami hotel: 'You had to go on Fridays, huh?', as if Silvers had personally scheduled his own transmission to challenge his old friend. That was in 1956. Silvers didn't hear from Sinatra again for sixteen years, until a stroke threatened to end his career and he received one special telegram: 'We're all praying for you . . . Positive you'll be fine in good time . . . Love, Frank Sinatra.' When Sammy Davis, along with Dean Martin and Peter Lawford a supposedly secure stalwart of Sinatra's much-publicised Clan, deigned to criticise his leader, he was excommunicated from favour for several months. Not even Brad Dexter, movie heavy and Sinatra bodyguard, who once saved Sinatra's life in a Pacific tidal race and has been heard to utter 'I'd kill for him', was sacrosanct. In Sinatra's eyes the loyalty of friendship—like that of the family—must be absolute, know no bounds; the smallest slight, whether real or imagined, is enough to topple a whole mountain of camaraderie and goodwill.

An outsider will find it hard to reconcile the openhandedness and the bigotry that chafe against each other in such an outlook. Those close to him will accept both as just one of the paradoxes which encase the performer like so many overlapping plates on an armadillo. His total image is a maze of provocative contradictions which generates a mystique matched by none of his contemporaries: the survivor who never appeared to compromise; the man of fastidious good taste and deep concern for his dignity who would sooner resort to fisticuffs than civilised argument; the successful aspirant to the social and cultural élite who still couldn't resist associating with allegedly dubious company; the champion of equality and the underdog whose mere presence relegated all around him to that very rôle; the ladies' man and last word in charm who, when he saw a female columnist who had been less than kind to him in the past wearing dark glasses at a nearby nightclub table, couldn't resist walking by to drop a dollar into her coffee cup by way of underlining the point he wished to make to his bewildered friends: 'I always figured she was blind.' In his eyes that probably went for most of her rivals too. Few performers have been given a more tempestuous passage by the press than Sinatra. His brawls with over-anxious reporters have become a byword; the extreme lengths to which they have gone to invade his privacy, and he has gone to protect it, are best summed up by the sign that warns callers to his Palm Springs home that their reason for pressing the buzzer 'had better be good', and by the words 'Go away' emblazoned on the doormat. He became incensed at the prominence they gave to the dishevelment of his three failed marriages, to Nancy Barbato, Ava Gardner and Mia Farrow, in preference to the Sicilian reverence he always maintained towards his first wife and family. He has dismissed as 'vicious' the way they combed every cranny for the chink that would throw realistic light upon the *padrone* fantasy he cultivated as the leader of his famous clan and a purveyor of excessive generosity, adding defiantly 'I don't investigate everyone I meet before I shake hands with him'. But while he might well recoil at the way the whiff of underworld scandal asphyxiated his stately friendship with the Kennedy family, led him to sell out his gambling interests in Nevada, and as recently as February 1970 found him labelled by the head of the New Jersey State Commission investigating crime as someone who 'holds himself above the law', he must also be shrewd enough to know that the resultant press coverage, far from endangering his public image, increased its excitement.

Sinatra proved at the time of his comeback that his appeal was valid on a level beyond actually being *liked*. He professed an inner resilience which, as he denied the allegations thrown at him, toughened itself on them. It made for a very special authority over an audience, inducing a pre-performance tension which Nelson Riddle, one of the most outstanding of his musical directors, unknowingly came close to describing in an account of working with him:

> . . . always a challenge . . . Never a relaxed man, he was a perfectionist who drove himself and everybody around him relentlessly. You always approached him with a feeling of uneasiness, not only because he was demanding and unpredictable, but because his reactions were so violent. But all of these tensions disappeared if you came through for him.

A Sinatra audience, pre-conditioned not to expect the extended easy-going lullaby of an Andy Williams, welcomes its star with a nervous respect bordering on the masochistic. The challenging eyes, the restless energy communicate to the audience what the press has intimated, what his mother observed, 'My son is like me. You cross him, he never forgets'. And not to applaud, to respond *would* be to cross him, not that there is ever a performance where Sinatra and audience do not both come through for each other. The highest pitch of the excitement he generates must be seen as the culmination of a process whereby every known facet of his off-stage personality, whether accurate or not, has become fused with the performance. One is reminded of the old Hollywood adage that one of the rôles of publicity is to create people. The ultimate paradox of the Sinatra legend is that while no entertainer has more vividly borne out the literal truthfulness of such a claim, no entertainer possessed such sheer intrinsic talent as to need that publicity less.

As this is being written, the man Marlene Dietrich once called 'the Mercedes-Benz of men' is making the second sensational comeback of his career at Caesar's Palace in Las Vegas. No one could reasonably have believed that his decision in March 1971 to retire from public entertaining would prove irrevocable; that the period of self-imposed retreat he intended 'for reflection, reading, self-examination, and that need every man has for a fallow period, a long phase in which to seek a better understanding of the vast transforming changes now taking place everywhere in the world', would dovetail neatly with the three 'Fruitful, busy, uptight, loose, sometimes boisterous, occasionally sad, always exciting' decades to which he was bidding farewell. One should not underestimate the serious streak of a man who spoke out on behalf of civil rights for Negroes long before it became the fashionable thing to do so, who throughout his career has pursued the cause of religious and racial harmony with the same high-voltage sense of purpose which achieved perfection in his professional field. But Sinatra must have sensed that even if the front pages had lost no interest in the hectic escapades of his swinging maverick figure, his achievements as an entertainer had long passed beyond criticism, floating on a cloud of theatrical inaccessibility. Professionally he had run out of challenges. Who can blame him if he did decide to stage-manage one of his own?

Now he can have nothing left to achieve. His executive power in all areas of the leisure industry, and in not a few beyond, is undisputed. That the ultimate source of that power is his unique voice will be to Sinatra his greatest compliment. As he vigorously approaches his sixtieth year, he can repeat an already oft-spoken wish, 'Hope I die before I get old', from a platform of indestructability that makes both seem unlikely. When he does die the whole world will clamour to provide an epitaph. None will be so apt, and maybe so welcome, as the one he unwittingly provided himself in an assessment of Pancho Gonzales, the tennis-player of Mexican immigrant origin, during a casual after-dinner conversation in London in 1962. The eminent British journalist Kenneth Allsop caught it for posterity, and it read: 'He was very much discriminated against . . . He got through because of sheer professionalism. He was a public playground boy. He learned to play on concrete.' As we have seen, there was more to it besides, but epitaphs, like lyrics and newspaper columns, dictate their own length.

An UNDERTOW OF pessimism is an occupational hazard when anything draws to a close. And yet here it is entirely unwarranted. In an age when so many standards, not least those of language and literacy, manners and morals, are supposedly set in irrevocable decline, it is reassuring that the engaging combination of style and star quality assessed in this book still remains a vibrant entertainment force in the person of the great performers of today, performers as likely to prove eligible for the all-time pantheon of greatness as their counterparts in the generations before them.

One has only to think of Presley jerking his shoulders, swivelling his hips, and yet through sheer presence denying that the 'fifties ever existed in a way that the likes of Bill Haley and the Everly Brothers could never do; of Sammy Davis Jr., the jagged verve of this 'one-eyed Jewish Negro' (his own description) etching itself on to one's consciousness as he proves himself the worthiest current contender to the decathlon for all-round performance in the mainstream vaudeville tradition; of Joel Grey, a cross between whirling dervish, George M. Cohan, and demonic sprite as he darts around the stage with the unpredictability of a firework, surely the answer to Gene Kelly's recent query, 'Where's that new song-and-dance man coming over the hill, showing us a new style, a fresh way of doing things?'; of Streisand letting her voice go like a flamingo in need of space to flaunt its mellifluous wings; of Bette Midler, shimmying swashbuckler of the mop and coffee-morning set, 'the last of the tacky ladies' purveying in her own words 'trash with flash . . . sleaze with ease' as she proves herself at once the princess of pastiche and self-parody, and the most approachable of modern stars. The latter is a superlative she shares with Liza Minnelli, who in keeping with an authority beyond her years transforms 'Yes', the frequent opening number of her own routine, from a basically trite inventory of humdrum experience into a hymn to that diamond-hard independence of spirit which characterises all these entertainers. It is as such an affirmation that this book is intended, and must be accepted, if it is to succeed.

'Call them irreplaceable' Special lyrics: Sammy Cahn

Chorus: (read with great warmth!)
Call them irreplaceable,
Legends un-eraseable,
Ladies, silk and laceable, too.

All the rest must seem penny ante
Next to Hope, Jack Benny and James Durante.

Mister Crosby, Danny Kaye
And Sinatra, all the way,
Dietrich and Astaire, pas de deux.

Jolson and the Great Maurice,
Noël, Judy, rest in peace:
Each in show-biz crown was a gem!

This verse and book is with love,
For them!!!

(Written in London for my good friend John Fisher, who had the time, talent, and taste to bring about this glowing book about glowing stars that we've all known and loved! *Sammy Cahn*)

Acknowledgements

My thanks are due to many people for the part they have played in the completion of this book. It is impossible to list every single individual, but I should like to place on record the help and/or encouragement received from Ken Barnes, Lou Barron, Maggie Chapman, Bill Cotton, Richard Evans, Irving A. Fein, Denis Goodwin, Vivien Green, Carolyn Hart, Tony Hawes, Richard Kuttner, Mike Parkinson, Maureen Ressler, Don Stone, Lynette Trotter, Alan Warner, Reg Williams, and Fred Zentner.

If one name should be singled out for special attention the spotlight falls almost inevitably on Sammy Cahn, indefatigable writer of award-winning lyrics as well as one of the funniest entertainers in the world. When in the autumn of 1974 during the London season of his one-man show I approached him tentatively for permission to use a parody of his famous song-title 'Call Me Irresponsible' as the title for this book, his reply was, 'Sure, go right ahead, and I'll pen a special lyric to go with it. Just let me have the names of everyone you've included in the book.' Within 24 hours this most generous of men had turned 'Call Them Irreplaceable' into a lyric of its own. Its inclusion in these pages, together with the unique Hirschfeld drawings, sets a very special seal on my own humble efforts.

Likewise worthy of special thanks and emphasis are the enthusiasm met behind the scenes at Elm Tree Books from Brian Stone; the insight, efficiency and flair of both my editor Colin Webb and his assistant Kate Dunning; the unflagging encouragement of my agent Richard Simon; and the untiring patience of my wife Sue.

Finally, I am indebted to the following for permission for copyright material reproduced in this volume. For photographs: Bettman Archives; Cinema Bookshop; Culver Pictures; Ian Dickson; Michael Freedland; Globe Photos; Ronald Grant; Keystone Press Agency; John Kobal Collection; Mander and Mitchenson Theatre Collection; Popperfoto; Warner Enterprises. For extracts from plays and songs: Irving Berlin (England) Music: from the film *Carefree*, 'Change Partners', lyrics copyright © 1938 by Irving Berlin, from the film *Top Hat*, 'Cheek to Cheek', lyrics copyright © 1935 by Irving Berlin, and 'Isn't This a Lovely Day?', lyrics copyright © 1935 by Irving Berlin, used by permission; Chappell & Co. Ltd: 'A Talent to Amuse' (Noël Coward), 'Anatole de Paris' (composer and author: Sylvia Fine), copyright by Chappell & Co., Inc., 'Fascinatin' Rhythm' (composer: George Gershwin; author: Ira Gershwin), copyright © 1924 by Harms Inc., 'The Lobby Song' (composer and author: Sylvia Fine), copyright © 1944 by Samuel Goldwyn Productions, and 'Marvellous Party' (Noël Coward), used by permission; the Noël Coward Estate: 'If Love Were All' (from *Bitter-Sweet*), *Design for Living*, introduction to Dietrich, 'Marvellous Party', and *Private Lives*, published by William Heinemann Ltd and Doubleday & Co., Inc. (USA) and reproduced by permission of the Estate; B. Feldman & Co. Ltd: 'Bright Eyes' (Motzam, Smith & Jerome), reproduced by permission; Francis, Day & Hunter Ltd: 'Get Happy' (Arlen & Koehler), reproduced by permission; Mills Music Inc. (USA): 'Bright Eyes' © 1920, renewed 1947; 'I Can't Give You Anything But Love' © 1928, renewed 1956, all rights reserved, used by permission; Edwin H. Morris & Co., Ltd (and Edwin H. Morris & Co., Inc., USA): 'The Man That Got Away' (composer: Harold Arlen; author: Ira Gershwin), copyright © 1954 by Harwin Music Corp., all rights reserved, used by permission; Warner Bros. Music (USA): 'Fascinatin' Rhythm' © 1924 by New World Music Corp. and 'Get Happy' © 1929 by Remick Music Corp., copyrights renewed and all rights reserved, used by permission; Warner Bros. Music Limited: 'Rosie, You Are My Posy' (John Stromberg & Edgar Smith), reproduced by permission; Lawrence Wright Music Co., Ltd: 'I Can't Give You Anything But Love' (J. McHugh & D. Fields) © 1928, and 'Minnie the Moocher' (C. Calloway & I. Mills), © 1931, used by permission.

Every effort has been made to trace the copyright holders of the photographs and quoted material used in this volume, and it is the belief of both myself and my publishers that the necessary permissions have been obtained. However, should there be any omissions in this respect, we apologise and shall be pleased to make the appropriate acknowledgements in future editions.

Bibliography

Agate, James. *Around Cinemas (i)* (Home & Van Thal, London, 1946)
   Around Cinemas (ii) (Home & Van Thal, London, 1948)
Agee, James. *Agee on Film* (McDowell, Obolensky, New York, 1958)
Allen, Steve. *The Funny Men* (Simon & Schuster, New York, 1956)
Allsop, Kenneth. *Scan* (Hodder & Stoughton, London, 1965)
Astaire, Fred. *Steps in Time* (Harper & Bros., New York, 1959)
Auden, W. H. *The Dyer's Hand* (Faber, London, 1963)
   Secondary Worlds (Faber, London, 1968)
   A Certain World (Faber, London, 1971)
Bankhead, Tallulah. *Tallulah* (Gollancz, London, 1952)
Barnes, Ken. *Sinatra and the Great Song Stylists* (Ian Allan, London, 1972)
Beaton, Cecil and Tynan, Kenneth. *Persona Grata* (Wingate, London, 1953)
Beaton, Cecil. *The Best of Beaton* (Weidenfeld & Nicolson, London, 1968)
Behrman, S. N. *Tribulations and Laughter* (Hamish Hamilton, London, 1972)
Bentley, Eric. *The Life of the Drama* (Methuen, London, 1966)
Berger, John. *Success and Failure of Picasso* (Penguin, London, 1965)
Blesh, Rudi and Janis, Harriet. *They All Played Ragtime* (Knopf, New York, 1950)
Brook, Peter. *The Empty Space* (MacGibbon & Kee, London, 1968)
Burns, George. *I Love Her, That's Why* (W. H. Allen, London, 1956)
Cahn, William. *A Pictorial History of the Great Comedians* (Grosset & Dunlap, New York, 1970)
Cantor, Eddie. *Take My Life* (Doubleday, New York, 1957)
Cerf, Bennett. *Try and Stop Me* (Simon & Schuster, New York, 1944)
Chevalier, Maurice. *The Man in the Straw Hat* (Odhams, London, 1950)
   With Love (Little, Brown & Co., Boston, 1960)
   I Remember It Well (W. H. Allen, London, 1971)
Clurman, Harold. *The Fervent Years* (Hill & Wang, New York, 1957)
   Lies Like Truth (Grove Press, New York, 1958)
Cohn, Nik. *Awopbopaloobop Alopbamboom* (Weidenfeld & Nicolson, London, 1969)
Cooke, Alistair, ed. *Garbo and The Night Watchmen* (Secker & Warburg, London, 1971)
Coward, Noël. *Collected Sketches and Lyrics* (Hutchinson, London, 1931)
   Present Indicative (Heinemann, London, 1937)
   Future Indefinite (Heinemann, London, 1954)
Croce, Arlene. *The Fred Astaire and Ginger Rogers Dance Book* (W. H. Allen, London, 1972)
Crosby, Bing. *Call Me Lucky* (Frederick Muller, London, 1953)
cummings, e. e. *A Miscellany* (Peter Owen, London, 1966)
Damase, Jacques. *Les Folies du Music-Hall* (Editions 'Spectacles', Paris, 1960)
Daubeny, Peter. *Stage by Stage* (Murray, London, 1952)
Dietrich, Marlene. *Marlene Dietrich's A.B.C.* (Doubleday, New York, 1962)
Douglas-Home, Robin. *Sinatra* (Michael Joseph, London, 1962)
Durgnat, Raymond. *The Crazy Mirror* (Faber, London, 1969)
Fowler, Gene. *Schnozzola* (Viking Press, New York, 1951)
Freedland, Michael. *Al Jolson* (W. H. Allen, London, 1972)
Frewin, Leslie. *Dietrich—The Story of a Star* (Frewin, London, 1967)
Gill, Brendan, intro. *Cole* (Michael Joseph, London, 1971)
Gill, Brendan. *Tallulah* (Michael Joseph, London, 1973)
Green, Benny. *Drums in my Ears* (Davis-Poynter, London, 1973)

220

Hadfield, John, ed. *Cowardy Custard* (Heinemann, London, 1973)
Hayman, Ronald. *Playback* (Davis-Poynter, London, 1973)
Hope, Bob. *So This is Peace?* (Simon & Schuster, New York, 1946)
    Have Tux, Will Travel (Simon & Schuster, New York, 1954)
    I Owe Russia Twelve Hundred Dollars (Robert Hale, London, 1963)
    Five Women I Love (Robert Hale, London, 1967)
Hyers, M. Conrad. *Zen and the Comic Spirit* (Rider, London, 1973)
Jackson, Arthur and Taylor, John Russell. *The Hollywood Musical* (Secker & Warburg, London, 1971)
Janis, Harriet and Blesh, Rudi. *They All Played Ragtime* (Knopf, New York, 1950)
Jessel, George. *Elegy in Manhattan* (Holt, Rinehart & Winston, New York, 1961)
Kahn, Jr., E. J. *The Voice* (Musicians Press, London, 1947)
Kanin, Garson. *Tracy and Hepburn* (Angus & Robertson, London, 1972)
Kerensky, Oleg. *Ballet Scene* (Hamish Hamilton, London, 1970)
Kimball, Robert, ed. *Cole* (Michael Joseph, London, 1971)
Kobal, John. *Marlene Dietrich* (Studio Vista, London, 1968)
    Gotta Sing, Gotta Dance (Hamlyn, London, 1970)
Lahr, John. *Notes on a Cowardly Lion* (Knopf, New York, 1969)
    The Autograph Hound (Jonathan Cape, London, 1973)
Lawrence, Gertrude. *A Star Danced* (Doubleday, Doran, New York, 1945)
Lejeune, C. A. *Chestnuts in her Lap* (Phoenix House, London, 1947)
Martin, Kingsley, ed. *New Statesman Profiles* (Phoenix House, London, 1957)
MacInnes, Colin. *England, Half English* (MacGibbon & Kee, London, 1961)
    Sweet Saturday Night (MacGibbon & Kee, London, 1967)
McCaffrey, Donald W. *The Golden Age of Sound Comedy* (Tantivy, London, 1973)
McCarthy, Albert. *The Dance Band Era* (Studio Vista, London, 1971)
McCrindle, Joseph F., ed. *Behind The Scenes* (Pitman, London, 1971)
McLean, Jr., Albert F. *American Vaudeville as Ritual* (University Press, Kentucky, 1965)
McVay, Douglas. *The Musical Film* (Zwemmer, London, 1967)
Melly, George. *Revolt into Style* (Allen Lane, London, 1970)
Morgan, Pete, ed. *C'Mon Everybody: Poetry of the Dance* (Corgi, London, 1971)
Morley, Sheridan. *A Talent to Amuse* (Heinemann, London, 1969)
Niven, David. *The Moon's a Balloon* (Hamish Hamilton, London, 1971)
Osborne, John. *The Entertainer* (Faber, London, 1957)
Seldes, Gilbert. *The Seven Lively Arts* (Sagamore Press, New York, 1957)
Shaw, Arnold. *Sinatra* (W. H. Allen, London, 1968)
Shipman, David. *The Great Movie Stars: The Golden Years* (Hamlyn, London, 1970)
    The Great Movie Stars: The International Years (Angus & Robertson, London, 1972)
Silvers, Phil. *This Laugh Is On Me* (Prentice-Hall, Englewood Cliffs, N.J., 1973)
Simon, George T. *The Big Bands* (Macmillan, New York, 1971)
Singer, Kurt. *The Danny Kaye Saga* (Robert Hale, London, 1957)
Talbot, Daniel, ed. *Film: An Anthology* (University of California Press, Los Angeles, 1966)
Taylor, John Russell and Jackson, Arthur. *The Hollywood Musical* (Secker & Warburg, London, 1971)
Tormé, Mel. *The Other Side of the Rainbow* (W. H. Allen, London, 1971)
Tyler, Parker. *Sex Psyche Etcetera in the Film* (Horizon Press, New York, 1969)
Tynan, Kenneth. *He That Plays the King* (Longmans, London, 1950)
    Curtains (Longmans, London, 1961)
    Tynan Right and Left (Longmans, London, 1967)
Tynan, Kenneth and Beaton, Cecil. *Persona Grata* (Wingate, London, 1953)
Vallance, Tom. *The American Musical* (Zwemmer, London, 1970)
Von Sternberg, Josef. *Fun in a Chinese Laundry* (Macmillan, New York, 1965)
Walker, Alexander. *Stardom* (Michael Joseph, London, 1970)
Whitcomb, Ian. *After the Ball* (Allen Lane, London, 1972)
Zolotow, Maurice. *No People like Show People* (Random House, New York, 1951)